Economic Growth

Rationale, Problems, Cases

*Proceedings of the Conference on Economic Development
Sponsored by the Department of Economics and the
Institute of Latin American Studies at the
University of Texas in 1958*

Economic Growth

Rationale, Problems, Cases

Edited by Eastin Nelson

Proceedings of the Conference on Economic Development
Sponsored by the Department of Economics and the
Institute of Latin American Studies at the
University of Texas in 1958

BOOKS FOR LIBRARIES PRESS
FREEPORT, NEW YORK

INTERNATIONAL STANDARD BOOK NUMBER:
0-8369-5811-X

LIBRARY OF CONGRESS CATALOG CARD NUMBER:
70-157350

PRINTED IN THE UNITED STATES OF AMERICA

CONTENTS

INTRODUCTION

The Department of Economics of The University of Texas was host to a conference on economic development April 21–23, 1958, as its contribution to the celebration of the seventy-fifth anniversary of The University of Texas. The decision to hold such a conference was taken in full cognizance that development has been the theme of an increasing volume of economic literature since 1945. It was taken in spite of the fact that similar conferences have been held frequently during recent years--in Chicago, Louvain, Tokyo, to mention only a few. The Department elected to sponsor a conference on economic development perhaps not in spite of, but rather because of, the fact that the area continues to be the subject of an immense amount of technical study by numerous and varied agencies: international organizations, the national governments of technologically developed countries such as our own, the great financial and industrial corporations with overseas interests, and such excellent, privately financed groups as the International Association for Research in Income and Wealth.

The choice of the theme, economic development, can be better appreciated in the historical frame of reference of this phrase, which has become the keystone of economic policy in at least half a hundred nation-states scattered around the world. Any observer must be impressed by the restless urgency, the aggressive optimism of three-quarters of the people of the world on the march to achieve in some degree the better economic life obviously enjoyed by perhaps one-quarter of the world's people living in industrial societies. This determined effort is the more impressive to the observer who remembers the cautious conservatism of the twenties and the desperation of the thirties in the industrial countries.

It has been known, and perhaps for a long time, that the English-speaking nations and a half-dozen North European nations enjoyed a great industrialization boom beginning somewhere around 1850, reaching a climax around the middle of the ninth decade and subsiding fairly steadily until the rate of growth actually became negative during the 1930's. Simon Kuznets, in his study "Long-term Changes in the National Income of the United States of America Since 1870,"[1] has established beyond a reasonable doubt this decline in the rate of

---

[1] The International Association for Research in Income and Wealth, Income and Wealth Series, Vol. II (London, 1942).

growth. Trends have not, perhaps, been so well measured in other
Western countries, but it is well established that real wages started
down in Great Britain by the end of the century, after almost a century
of rising trends. This secular slowing of the rate of growth is very
significant. It not only incited the industrial countries of the world to
begin measurement of aggregate income, but it spelled the end of an
era--the end of the era of laissez faire and free trade, the end of
foreign investment and foreign trade as the driving forces of expan-
sionist optimism. So clear by 1931 was the policy interregnum beginning about 1913 that the nations which had profited so greatly by
the boom began to examine their policies and circumstances carefully
and painfully. A new body of interventionist economic policy, con-
serving as many as possible of the virtues and values of the nineteenth-
century arrangements under which they had profited so greatly, began
to take shape among the English-speaking countries and their co-
beneficiaries of Northern Europe.

In the meantime, the countries that had come to depend on them for
markets for raw products and for investments in transportation and
communications were left in a state of inactive suspension. The revolution in economic policy in the underdeveloped countries, which was
to produce the conscious developmentalism nearly universalized since
1945, may be said to have begun by 1934 with the bold étatisme of
Ataturk, with the timid grain-price guaranteeing of Argentina, with the
"hundred days" of Marmaduke Grove in Chile. It is, of course, impossible to date so broad a movement with any precision. It was fully
matured in Uruguay by 1919 and presaged in the Mexican Constitution
of 1917.

In the beginning, the metropolitan countries embraced not much
more than 10 per cent of the population of the world. The benefits of
their rapidly evolving industrial system were passed on to non-
European peoples in such limited and halting fashion that the end of
the century found rapidly widening the gap in living levels between the
peoples of these few industrial countries and the peoples of the underdeveloped countries, with which they came to have increasingly important relations, political as well as economic. Colonialism came
to embrace large areas of the world. "Economic imperialism" is the
proper phrase with which to describe the relations between many
metropolitan countries and many independent underdeveloped countries during the last half of the nineteenth century and the early decades of the twentieth.

But the picture is not one of malevolent exploitation. Rather it is
a picture of a limited beachhead economy abroad and a self-limiting
economy at home. It was the self-limiting character of the metropolitan economies that caused their own loss of confidence and started
the revolution in economic policy which was, within the limitations of
private property and individual initiative, to reverse the laissez-faire
policies of the nineteenth century.

The shape of current economic-development policy in the Western world at mid-century is not easy to describe because it is in constant evolution. It retains, for the most part, the essential eighteenth-century belief in the importance and effectiveness of freedom of the individual, its strong belief in universal education and suffrage. The revolution in economic policy--away from laissez faire and free trade--has not, then, abolished either capitalism or democracy. In some respects it has broadened the participation base of these two aspects of the philosophy of individualism.

The most profound reversal from the nineteenth to the mid-twentieth century is the shift from laissez faire, under which development proceeds from the action of individuals, to development as a goal to be sought collectively. This difference in economic policy is a matter of degree, of course, because no purely laissez-faire system ever existed, and certainly the developmental channeling of a minor part of investment funds which takes place under Western democracy is no fixed system. However, the degree of difference is important. Though no doctrine guides the process, the exigencies of development have caused some eight or ten nations to erect steel mills, build oil refineries, promote automotive transport factories, and to perform a great number of industrial services formerly left to private initiative. Though no doctrinaire socialist government has long held power in Latin America, the basic public services tend increasingly to be nationalized, often by default. It may be said that there is a strong tendency for governments of underdeveloped countries to construct plants for basic industry--by default of other capital sources. These often remain government or mixed-corporation property. The general deficiency of banking resources in underdeveloped economies has caused large ventures in finance and banking to be developed under state ownership--and to exist side by side with private ventures of more limited and conventional scope. The underdeveloped nations are in a hurry--and they are unwilling to wait for the slow evolution of their systems, as most of the presently developed countries did.

The success of a number of the underdeveloped countries has tended to react on the European nations formerly thought overdeveloped. Italy faces its problems of unemployment with a development corporation for south Italy. France developed its Monnet and Schumann Plans.

Almost unbounded optimism for the future seems to possess the Western world. In the United States, with the highest per capita income levels in the history of the world, adjusted aggregate income increased some 30 per cent during the seven years ended with 1957--culminating a sixteen-year period of growth at a rate which had not been achieved since the middle eighties. Truly the mid-century saw the world involved in the most general and most rapid growth of all recorded history. It is small wonder that "development" should be

the key word now in economic policy, and it was almost inevitable
that economic development should be the theme of the economic conference commemorating the seventy-fifth year of The University of
Texas.

A committee of three, composed of the writer as chairman and
Professors E. E. Hale and Murray E. Polakoff, was set up to formulate the program. However, each member of the Department was frequently consulted, and both the selection of personnel and the choice
of topics, within the limits of available resources, represent the Department.

The Department of Economics held its own members to minor participation roles in the Conference. It was motivated by the challenge
which this opportunity offered, with the full and generous support
the administration, for bringing to the campus outstanding economists
of the world. No conference of manageable time limits could hope to
cover the entire ambit of the developmental literature during the last
ten years, even representatively. In general, the topics which were
included were determined by the positive interests and predilections
of the Department. Certain aspects of developmental literature were
omitted because of the necessity to make choices in the use of limited
resources. For example, no paper on population was provided. This
omission is not attributable to a non-neo-Malthusian bias of the pro-
gram-planners, but in part to the very wealth of literature on population in relation to development recently published by such men as
Moore of Princeton, Spengler of Duke, and Davis of California, to
mention only three.

The omission of the Soviet Union from the Conference stems from
two considerations. First, though it obviously is much concerned with
problems of economic development, it can no longer be considered an
underdeveloped economy. Second, the subject has been and is being
constantly studied by organizations with professional resources far in
excess of our own. The Conference would have liked to present a
paper on China but was unable to contact sufficiently early an American scholar with competence in the economy of that country.

The Conference endeavored to make a contribution to a general
rationale of economic development. With a view to achieving balance
between what might be formulated with respect to general theory, and
what might be brought out incidentally in progress and resource reports on particular countries, half the papers deal with general problems and theory, cutting across national lines, and the other half deal
with national states.

The decision of where to focus the Conference was determined in
no small part by factors outside the control of the Department. The
nature of the development movement at mid-twentieth century, involving primarily the three-quarters of the world's population as yet
untouched by industrialization, or recently and inadequately affected

by it, was the most important determining factor. The orientation of The University of Texas in a country central to the complex of Western democracy was another important factor shaping the program for the analysis of developmental action. Even more specifically, the position of the University on the borderland between Anglo and Latin-American cultures, coupled with its resources for the study of, and interest in, Latin-American development, dictated that considerable inquiry would be concentrated on Latin America.

Limitations of time, space, and funds dictated that no more than ten principal papers could be read, with twenty briefer discussions of them by other social scientists.

The papers of the conference fall into three main divisions. Part I: three papers working toward a rationale of economic development; Part II: three papers dealing with problems that have tended generally to arise from rapid economic development; Part III: four case studies in economic development.

The Department gave the participants considerable latitude in choosing the specific subjects of their papers. In the minds of the committee, the selection of the participants set up a strong probability that, in general, the paper would be written within a certain analytical area. It is not accidental, for example, that Professor Carter Goodrich, of Columbia University, should have been selected to keynote the Conference with a paper on economic history and economic development. Our invitation to him to deliver the opening address reflects the strong interest of the sponsoring organization in economic history as a method of investigating problems of policy and development. Professor Simon Kuznets, of The Johns Hopkins University, world authority on national-income measurement, is also an economic historian who has done much to quantify the economic history of the United States. His paper contrasting conditions of the presently developed countries in their pre-industrial phase with present conditions in currently underdeveloped countries tends to confirm the belief of many economic historians that the industrial revolution in northwestern Europe really began much earlier than is popularly supposed by men concentrating primarily on the changes following the spate of textile manufacturing innovations beginning about 1763.

Professor Benjamin Higgins, of the Massachusetts Institute of Technology, who has spent four years in charge of the research on Indonesia, has contributed an important paper called "Elements in a Theory of Underdevelopment." The paper has accomplished significant groundwork in preparation for a theory of economic development. The papers included under "problems" also seek to contribute to a general theoretical framework for economic development, with somewhat different emphasis. Professor Singer, many times a consultant in national economic programs, economic analyst for the United Nations, and holder of other important posts, has always shown an interest in working toward a rationale for economic policy, and his paper, "The Concept of Balanced Growth in Economic Development," is part of the general pattern. The Conference could not afford to bring participants from Europe, but was fortunate to discover Professor Geoffrey Maynard, of the University College of South Wales and Monmouthshire, in residence at The Johns Hopkins University, concentrating his year's work on inflation--a problem of very current interest all over the world.

In collaboration with the Institute of Latin American Studies, the Department of Economics invited Dr. Raúl Prebisch, Director of the Economic Commission for Latin America, to present a paper on his country, which he calls "The Structural Crisis in Argentina and Its Prospects of Solution," as the annual Hackett Memorial Lecture and as the last in the Conference series. Unfortunately an emergency made it impossible for Dr. Prebisch to attend, but he sent his paper and it was read to the Conference. Dr. Prebisch's paper might have been classified in Part III as a case study on Argentina. Since he has approached the problem from the standpoint of structure, however, it seems more appropriate to classify his paper in the "problems" section.

In the light of its interest in Latin America, it is not surprising that The University of Texas should elect to receive papers on two of the bright showplaces of rapid economic development under Western Hemisphere democracy: The Commonwealth of Puerto Rico and the Republic of Mexico. In Mexico one century was much like another until the fruits of the social revolution, codified in the Constitution of 1917, began to be gathered. Dr. Alfredo Navarrete, Director of the Department of Economic Studies of Mexico's federal investment bank, Nacional Financiera, has documented the dynamic period of his country's economic development--1939 to the present. Puerto Rico, with good luck, good judgment, indefatigable application, and a convenient population outlet, has lifted itself from the state of hopeless rural slum in 1934 to an annual real per capita income growth of 4 per cent. Mr. Alvin Mayne, Director of the Puerto Rico Planning Board, has left an excellent report of the Island's triumph, in his paper "Progress, Planning, and Policy in Puerto Rico."

The Conference committee was fortunate enough to discover Professor Rudolf Bičanić, of the University of Zagreb, Yugoslavia, serving as visiting professor in the Department of Government at The University of Texas. Because of his interest in contributing to a general rationale, his paper "Economic Growth, Development, and Planning in Socialist Countries" was substituted for the paper "Sector Analysis of Economic Growth in Yugoslavia," which the committee had expected would give the Conference a progress report on his country.

The topic of the paper by Professor Bert Hoselitz, of the University

of Chicago, was somewhat fortuitously determined. Long interested
in formulating a rationale for economic development, he would have
been invited to do a general paper but for the circumstance that the
Conference committee tracked him down at work on a project in New
Delhi. The fact that he was there on an evaluative mission and would
shortly return to the University of Chicago determined the subject of
the paper which he was invited to present, " The Prospects of Indian
Economic Growth."

Eastin Nelson

Austin, Texas
1960

Part I

Toward a Rationale of Economic Development

Papers: Goodrich

Kuznets

Higgins

ECONOMIC HISTORY AND ECONOMIC DEVELOPMENT

Carter Goodrich

Columbia University

The current widespread interest in economic development, of which your decision to organize this Conference is a significant illustration, offers to economic historians both a special opportunity and an important challenge. The opportunity arises from a kinship between the types of questions raised by the economic historian and by the student or practitioner of economic development. Both are concerned with economic change, primarily with changes that are long run, irreversible, and cumulative in character and that involve alterations in fundamental economic and social institutions. By contrast economic theory, at least in its more conventional and static aspects, is concerned with change, if at all, mainly as movement around an equilibrium. It attains its maximum precision by basing its analysis on the assumption that institutional arrangements, including the state of the industrial arts, remain unchanged. Again, analysis of the business cycle, by definition, is concerned primarily with fluctuations around a trend line rather than with long-run changes. If economic history is to be defined as the study of the elements, or factors, that remain equal for the purposes of short-run economic analysis but do not remain equal in the long run, then economic development may be said to have as its purpose the deliberate change of these elements.

This kinship is evident in the literature of the two fields. For example, the phrase Economic Development and Cultural Change, appearing as the title of both an institute and a journal, is wholly congenial to the economic historian. Though some of the studies of development have a strictly contemporary emphasis, and represent the application of an almost unvarying set of questions to varying institutional backgrounds, much of the work is concerned with the interpretation of the relevant institutional factors in the particular nation and the changes taking part in them. Economic development is therefore genuinely historical in spirit and methods, even though the time spans considered are often short. It may indeed be said that current research efforts, eagerly pursued and generously supported, are making notable progress toward the creation of a comparative economic history of the underdeveloped countries.

There is, however, much less current effort to promote and pursue the study of the comparative history of the more highly developed countries, and to ask, for example, how the obstacles to economic growth were overcome and how the "break-throughs" were accomplished in Great Britain or Germany or the United States. The situation is somewhat paradoxical. One might suppose that the planners and leaders of industrial development would have more to learn from the history of the countries that have succeeded in making the change than from the history of those that have not. It is, after all, the experience of the former that they wish to emulate.[1]

Without serious examination of this experience, advice freely offered to underdeveloped countries is sometimes based on hasty and oversimplified generalizations about the history of the United States or other countries. American aid officials, for example, sometimes oppose this or that governmental measure in an underdeveloped country on the sweeping argument that in the United States such development was accomplished by private enterprise. Their objection may often be sound in a particular case, but such an appeal to history disregards the robust uses of subsidy in the promotion of American development, of which the 32,000,000 acres of land given to the railroads by the state of Texas are a striking illustration. A few weeks ago I heard the argument presented that American businessmen should not be encouraged to enter into joint ventures with government capital in other countries because such a mixture of private and public enterprise is contrary to the American ethos. Perhaps that is true now, though the Atomic Energy Commission's contracts for industrial atomic power would seem to contradict the doctrine, but it was not true historically. The Pennsylvania and the Baltimore and Ohio railroads achieved the crossing of the Appalachians as private-public enterprises. Also applied to the underdeveloped countries is the argument that it is unwise to encourage a government to embark on any course of economic activity because such involvement, once started, is sure to spread. Yet the history of the railroads in America, as well as the experience of other countries such as Mexico and Japan,[2] shows that in a number of cases a field of activity where innovation came largely from government sources has been cheerfully relinquished to private enterprise as soon as it was ready to take over the burden. These particular misinterpretations, or half truths, I have taken from lay sources; but it would be possible to present also instances of what I would consider the misreading of American economic history even in the work of the academic theorists of economic development.

Today, however, I am much less interested in complaining of the relative neglect of certain parts of economic history or of its occasional misuse than in celebrating the increasing recognition of its importance that has resulted from the current emphasis on development.

"In our generation the most natural meeting place of theory and history," said Walt Rostow at the last meeting of the Economic History
Association, "is the study of comparative patterns of dynamic change
in different societies, focused around the problems of economic
growth." In approaching what he calls "the major common task . . .
of economists and historians,"[3] I would like to suggest some contributions that economic history has to make toward the understanding
of three of the major problems of economic development: technological progress, capital formation, and "balanced growth."

For the first--the creation and spread of improved technical meth-
ods--the relevance is obvious. Technology is an awkward subject for
the economic theorist. He does not treat it as one of the conventional
factors of production and cannot do so because it cannot be properly
priced. Only occasionally is it paid for separately, as in the purchase
of patent rights; in other cases, its price might be imputed as part of
the capital cost of a machine or of the salary of a technician; in still
others, it has long since become a free good. The subject therefore
tends to elude analysis in terms of the relation of price to the proportion of factors. Yet in comparing the productivity of one period with
that of another or of one country with that of another, differences in
technology are likely to be more decisive than any others that can be
stated in terms of the standard factors. It is therefore not surprising
that, in listing the factors on which economists need information in
order to understand economic growth, Rostow should have placed first
what he called the propensities "to develop fundamental science" and
"to apply science to economic ends."[4] Economic historians have always recognized the study of technological advance as one of their
main functions, and they will continue to do so, though I see little
chance of their providing numerical values for these "propensities"
that would permit their ready use in the theorists' equations.

The second problem, capital formation, stands in a very different
position. Here the concept falls squarely within the theorist's formulation, and every student of economic development owes a debt to
Ragnar Nurkse and the other theorists who have emphasized its crucial importance. No development planner can afford to disregard
Nurkse's warning that if all the gains from an increase in production
are spent on immediate consumption, the precious opportunities for
future increase will be lost.[5] Yet it remains for economic historians
and observers of current development to point out that in the actual
historic process, production and consumption are not quite so clearly
distinguishable and that increases in the one are sometimes inseparably connected with increases in the other. Let me take two recent
examples from Bolivia.

In 1953 a drastic land reform turned over most of the agricultural
land to the Indian <u>campesinos.</u> A year later the President of Bolivia
offered as proof that the reform was a success the assertion that the

Indians were now buying bicycles. Was this bad economics, to rejoice
in an increase in consumption when what a poor nation needed was
capital formation? Perhaps; but the greater danger--as later experience seems to have shown--was that for lack of incentive, for lack of
things they wished to buy, the Indians would fail to produce for the
market at all. The second example is a simpler one. The workmen
on the Cochabamba–Santa Cruz road bought from the commissaries
of the North American construction company better and more expensive food than they had been accustomed to. Was this also to be set
down as a deplorable "leakage" into consumption? Perhaps; but not
if the better food served as an incentive or if--as analogous to the
football training table--it provided the energy for harder and more
effective work on the job itself. This last point is familiar and obvious enough, yet it introduces a complication in the statement of development theory since, in the standard, or "Euclidean," language of
economics, expenditure on better bodies falls under the heading of
consumption, and expenditure on better tools is treated under the
headings of savings and investment.[6]

The third problem is that described as "balanced growth." On this,
one thing that can be said with certainty is that the phrase, now become so popular in the field, would never have been invented by an
economic historian. In 1830, about the time the United States began
what development theorists would call its "take-off into sustained
growth," 70 per cent of the working force made their living on farms.
In 1950, 88 per cent of the working force were engaged in nonfarm
occupations. The one hundred twenty years between were a period of
tremendous growth, but it would seem to me an odd use of words to
describe it as "balance"; the striking thing was the magnitude of the
change in the emphasis and direction of economic activity. Now it is
true that the theorists of balanced growth take account of differences
resulting from the elasticity of demand, particularly between demand
for foodstuffs and that for the products of manufacture, and therefore
recognize that all sectors of the economy "do not have to grow at the
same rate." Arthur Lewis, for example, uses the adjectives "proper,"
"appropriate," and "right" rather than "equal" or "even" in describing
the relationship between these rates of growth. Yet his insistence that
"in development programmes all sectors of the economy should grow
simultaneously," and even Nurkse's less sweeping reference to the
"more or less synchronized application of capital to a wide range of
different industries,"[7] raise serious questions in the mind of the economic historian. It is easy to see the theoretical advantages of the
simultaneous growth of a number of industries, each neatly supplying
the demand for the product of the others; but it is hard to believe that
this is the way the most vigorous economic growth has occurred in
the past. It may not be necessary to follow Schumpeter's theory of
economic development to the extent of erecting cyclically unbalanced

growth, with alternations of sudden advance and subsequent slackness, into a law of economic history. But when he describes development as proceeding "not . . . evenly as a tree grows but as it were jerkily," or when Forest Hill speaks of industrial advance in California as characterized by "frequent spurts of industrial growth, rapid exploitation of the potential gains, relative 'saturation,' and then further industrial break-throughs,"[8] the descriptions are recognizable to every economic historian. The most notable historic instances of rapid economic growth, whether originating as in Schumpeter's model from innovations "in one or a few branches of industry"[9] in the more developed countries or from the impact of international trade in those countries less highly developed industrially, have proceeded, as J. R. T. Hughes has put it, precisely by the creation of imbalances;[10] and the correction of these imbalances by growth in other parts of the economy has in practice been not only uneven in amount but highly irregular in timing.

Historically these imbalances have been created within individual industries, as in the familiar case of spinning and weaving in cotton textiles, between industries, or between industry and various branches of primary production. The record of their creation and of the responses to them is a large part of economic history. I would like to take one illustration of the process from the story of your own state. When toward the end of the 1860's the railroads were reaching out to the eastern border of the Great Plains in Kansas and Nebraska, I doubt if any of the railroad builders thought of this as implying or requiring synchronization with the economic development of the state of Texas. But a few Texans saw great economic opportunity in the expanding railways. The stockyards and the hungry industrial populations behind them were now accessible to Texas, with its vast stretches of grass-covered plains, its herds of stock, and its Spanish-Mexican techniques of handling cattle on horseback. The railroads had furnished the link between supply and demand. The results were the familiar saga of the Chisholm Trail, the Long Drive, and the rise of the cow country--the growth of a highly developed, even overdeveloped, industry, from almost nothing, and all within some fifteen years.

Perhaps you may prefer to consider this story as only one of a number of examples of the generalization that Alfred Marshall's favorite motto, "Natura non facit saltum," does not apply to the history of Texas! But I suggest that it is also an illustration, though no doubt an extreme one, of a familiar phenomenon in economic development. It was, to be sure, not a very orderly process and it led to speculative excesses; but those who have the very proper desire to attempt to make economic development more orderly have also the obligation to take care not at the same time to make it less vigorous.

When all this is said, the fact remains that the theorists of balanced growth have isolated and emphasized one of the most serious of the problems confronting the underdeveloped countries--the problem of the existence within their borders of isolated sectors of high productivity, typically oriented to export trade, surrounded by great areas of a more primitive economy with low productivity which receive little income and little stimulus from the more modernized sectors. One of many cases in point is that of Bolivia, in which a highly capitalistic tin industry flourished for half a century without bringing about a significant increase in domestic manufacturing and without causing any appreciable change in the primitive feudalistic system of agriculture that had come down from the early days of the Spanish Conquest. Under circumstances like these, successful development clearly requires the promotion of a type of growth that will spread from one area to another, that will be contagious and pervasive--I suggest these adjectives as substitutes for "balanced"--and that will therefore be mutually-supporting and cumulative in its effects. To stimulate this process, to secure sufficient mobility of the factors of production so that the impulses of growth are in fact transmitted from one sector of the economy to another, is indeed one of the greatest tasks of economic statesmanship in the developing countries.

A historical comparison may throw light on the nature of the problem. I would like to mention some of the contrasts between the responses to the opening of the Erie Canal in 1825 and to that of the Cochabamba–Santa Cruz road in 1954.[11] Each was a great public work, the one by the state of New York, the other by the Republic of Bolivia, and each drew heavily on foreign capital. Both were cases, in the parlance of modern development, of providing "public overhead capital" in relatively underdeveloped countries. Both improvements were designed to open up for settlement and trade a large area of good agricultural land previously cut off by lack of transportation. But the differences in the two stories are as conspicuous as the similarities. In the nineteenth-century North American case, no one thought that it was the business of government to direct settlers to northern Ohio or Michigan to take advantage of the new opportunity or to tell them that wheat would be a good crop to grow, to advise merchants to be ready to buy the wheat or to tell manufacturers to build mills to grind it into flour. No one doubted that these responses would be made, as in fact they were.

In the twentieth-century South American case, on the other hand, it was felt that the proper exploitation of the new opportunity required a number of organized measures in addition to the building of the road itself. The Bolivian government built a sugar mill in the new area; the mutual aid program of the United States government assisted the development by special allocations of agricultural machinery and by aid in agricultural research and guidance; and the Andean Highlands Mission of the international organizations created a model colony to facilitate the migration of the somewhat reluctant Indians from the

altiplano and the higher valleys to the lowlands. Progress in the development of the Bolivian Oriente, for which it is still rather too early
to assess the results, thus proceeds with a variety of special aids that
were not thought necessary in the development of our own Middle West.
If this comparison illustrates the importance of factor mobility in
economic development, it serves also to demonstrate the differences
in the degree to which its promotion, under varying circumstances,
is made a matter of deliberate development policy. It is a part of the
business of economic history to contribute to the understanding of
these controlling circumstances as they vary from nation to nation,
from culture to culture, and from period to period.[12]

I have suggested several questions concerning which the findings
of economic historians should be of value to students of economic development as they work on their common task. I should, however, be
making very bad use of the privileges of this occasion if I confined
myself to advertising the wares of economic history or to rejoicing
that economic historians are receiving somewhat greater recognition
as the result of the current interest in development. In this situation
the challenge to economic history is as obvious as its opportunity, and
there are pertinent and searching questions to be put to the workers
in the field: Why is it that economic history as it has been written
has not been of greater value to students of economic development?
And how can it be written in such a way that it will be of greater
service to them in the future?

Part of the answer to the first of these questions lies in the fact
that too much of economic history has been written without placing
questions of economic development in the forefront of the inquiry.
Some of it, indeed, seems to have been done without any explicit formulation of economic questions, and largely as chronology, or story-
telling, or even the collection of curiosa. Other works have been devoted to major questions that are quite different from those of the
modern enthusiasts for development, such as the relations between
technical and economic changes on the one hand and social structure
and political alignments on the other, or of the effect of economic
change on the distribution of income. Moreover, an important part of
the literature of economic history is devoted not to celebrating the
triumphs of development but to an examination of its costs and the
difficulties of adjustment which it has created. This emphasis is by
no means confined to Engels' Condition of the Working Class in England or its successors in the Marxist canon. Herbert Heaton has
called attention to the stress laid on the "evils of the industrial revolution" rather than on its advantages in conventional Anglo-American
treatments of economic history before the work of Clapham.[13] Nor
has the emphasis wholly changed in later writings. The author of
The Great Transformation[14] draws from his re-examination of the
industrial revolution the conclusion that the net human advantage

would have been greater if the process could have been slowed down
rather than accelerated.

Will you permit me to add a personal illustration which I find
relevant though perhaps a little embarrassing? A good many years
ago I made a study of a set of technical changes that were taking place
in the bituminous coal mines of the United States, notably the introduction of the mechanical loader. In doing this I paid no attention
whatever to the question of how these technological changes could be
introduced more rapidly or more effectively but instead confined myself entirely to the effect of their introduction on the working life of
the miners.[15] If anyone had then accused me of economic irresponsi-
bility, and of neglecting the overriding problem of development, I
should doubtless have replied that there were plenty of people in the
United States concerned with increasing industrial efficiency and too
few interested in the quality of the life lived within working hours.
But I can hardly imagine taking exactly the same position if I were
asked to make an investigation today of the tin mines of Bolivia.
There I should indeed consider it economically irresponsible not to
put the question of technical improvement in the forefront of the inquiry.

Economic history need not apologize for its tradition of social
criticism. It should continue to record the difficulties as well as the
advantages of economic development and to provide the materials for
criticism as well as for the celebration of its achievements. The
performance of this function is important not only for the older industrial nations but also for the developing countries, so that their
leaders may be forewarned of the problems they are likely to con-
front. Yet the emphasis may well be different. There are many parts
of the world in which a sustained pressure for technical advance certainly cannot be taken for granted. For their sake it seems to me entirely natural that theorists and planners should ask for an economic
history more fully and more explicitly dedicated to an examination of
the processes of economic growth. My own belief that economic historians should respond to such a demand was strengthened when, in a
city in which workmen staggered around the streets and up the stairs
of office buildings with two-hundred-pound loads on their backs, I
heard an aristocrat-turned-demagogue proclaiming as his platform
that the workers of his country would never become slaves to the
machine!

How, then, can economic historians organize their work in such a
way as to be of greater service to those concerned with the planning
of economic development? The first and most obvious answer is: by
paying a closer and more conscious attention to the questions and
concepts of development theory. In part this means a more systematic exploration of the themes which I have already referred to. With
respect to technological advance, for example, John Jewkes and his

associates explicitly describe their new historical and analytical work, The Sources of Invention, as their part in the current swing of the economics profession toward greater concern over development.[16] The recent work of John H. Dales on hydroelectricity and industrial development in Quebec,[17] together with Professor Usher's Introduction to it, serves to remind us that the old theme of the effect of power on economic development, and of the differing effects of one power source as against another, needs to be applied to the possibilities of atomic development in the less industrial countries. The subject of capital formation has always been the concern of economic historians; and the students of American manufacturing have particularly stressed one point of great importance for development theory--the vital part played by the "ploughing back" of earnings. A recent article has shown the possibility of bringing greater precision to its study.[18] With respect to the sources of original investment in the American factories, what we know of the shift of substantial funds from foreign trade in the case of the larger Massachusetts textile firms needs to be supplemented by studies of more obscure cases in which almost purely agricultural communities managed to scrape together from their own local resources the capital for manufacturing enterprise. With respect to the issues of "balanced" or spreading growth, it would be well for economic historians to give more explicit attention to the processes by which a stimulus spreads from one part of the economy to another, as well as to the circumstances under which the people of one sector within a highly developed economy--an English "depressed area," for example, or our own Southern Appalachians--may for a long period fail to respond either by migration or emulation to the growth of other sectors.

A second way in which economic history can contribute more effectively to the understanding of economic development is by giving greater and more expert attention to the scorekeeping of development in the quantitative study of economic growth. I need not speak at length of the significant pioneering in this field now being carried on by Simon Kuznets and others, since he himself will illustrate it during this Conference. There are of course great difficulties in making meaningful quantitative comparisons, particularly of income, between nations and periods of different social and economic organization, as Kuznets himself has reminded us.[19] These difficulties are particularly great at that significant point in economic change, so relevant to the experience of the developing countries, at which production for household consumption or for barter gives way on a large scale to production for a cash market. Yet even with all necessary caution and qualifications, the theoretical and practical importance of such growth figures is very great indeed. In our own country, we have seen what a difference has been made in political discussion by the development of the concept of "the performance of the economy" and by the provision of increasingly sophisticated tools for its current measurement. Similarly, the efforts in the less developed countries to create "national income accounts," rough as their first figures may be, represent a significant attempt to provide a basis for rational judgments of progress toward the accepted ideal of economic development.

To this statement of the importance of the quantitative work, I would like to add a plea for its co-ordination with the more traditional, largely qualitative types of inquiry. The study of economic growth should not be regarded as something different from, and outside, the study of economic history. It would be an intellectual anomaly, and a great handicap to useful work, if the study of past economic change should come to be divided between two separate disciplines--one presenting its findings in words and calling itself economic history and the other presenting its findings in figures and calling itself economic growth. Certainly the prose historians have much to learn from the newer quantitative work, sometimes by way of correction of earlier judgments based on insufficient evidence and perhaps more often by the opening up of new hypotheses to explore; but surely also the contrasts, comparisons, and patterns of change that are being discovered and displayed by the pioneers of growth study raise questions on which they will need to turn to the methods and insights of more general economic history for interpretation and understanding.

A third way in which economic history can take a more effective part in the common task is by devoting greater attention to the history of development policy. Economic development in the currently popular sense, in the sense that I am sure was intended by the organizers of this Conference, is a policy question. Its object is the practical one of providing a sound basis for the actions to be taken by the governments and peoples of the underdeveloped countries in their efforts to achieve economic progress. If that is so, it appears particularly relevant to ask to what extent development has been promoted in the past by policies consciously devoted to this end, and to re-examine in relation to this purpose the traditional interpretations of public policy in the developed countries.

An obvious starting point is the study of public efforts to provide the basic transportation facilities. In development parlance, this is a problem of providing the "public overhead capital" of the economy, or in the opposite but neater French term, its "infrastructure." In the language of the political history of the United States, it is the question of "internal improvements." Here the purpose was unmistakably developmental, at least in the broad sense, and the relevance is immediately apparent. The construction of the American canals and railways in the nineteenth century offers a particularly rich field for study because of the size of the transportation network created, the

amount of public investment, and the extraordinary variety of devices
by which public and private and semipublic efforts were brought into
combination. Another characteristic of the American experience was
the dispersion of the public effort over so many instrumentalities at
different levels, not only of the federal government and almost all
state governments but of well over a thousand cities, towns, villages,
and other local-government authorities. The underdeveloped countries
are not likely to imitate this unco-ordinated profusion of agencies, but
they would be fortunate if their own processes of development could
receive some of the impetus which those of the United States derived
from the fierce rivalry in the states and cities.[20]

An undertaking of particular value for students of development
would be a comparative study of the ways in which the nations of the
world obtained their railroads during the nineteenth century. Outside
Great Britain, relatively few railroads were built by unaided private
enterprise; and the exceptions were often cases in which there was an
obvious and immediate opportunity to be exploited, like the transport
of sugar from the fields to the Cuban ports or of coffee to Santos.[21]
State enterprise was widely employed, as for example in Australia and
New Zealand; but the record also includes a great variety of expedients
by which governments induced private investors to undertake enterprises considered essential to development and by which private investors in difficulties managed to shift their burdens onto the shoulders
of governments. Such a study would certainly show cases in which the
building of railroads that could not possibly have earned immediate
profits made significant and indeed indispensable contributions to economic development, but it would also throw light on the difficult and
highly pertinent problem of applying rational comparisons of long-run
benefits and costs in the selection or rejection of projects for state
construction or subsidy.

Of similar pertinence would be the study of measures taken for the
encouragement of manufactures. In the American case such a re-
examination would naturally start from that notable example of developmental planning, Alexander Hamilton's Report on Manufactures.
Its main concern would be to ask what became of the broad developmental purpose in the tangled history of American tariff policy and to
attempt to reappraise the development results of the policies adopted.
But it should also raise the question of why so little attention was paid
to Hamilton's proposals for promoting the importation of foreign techniques and the immigration of technicians and skilled workers, since
the answer appears to have such direct relevance for the current attempts of the developing countries to acquire the techniques and the
know-how of the industrial countries.

An approach by way of the question of development can yield valuable results in its application to other major economic decisions in

the American past. The great debates over land policy in nineteenth-century America were not concerned with "land use," in the sense that a modern agricultural-land planner would use the term, and still less with conservation, and not with "land reform" in the dramatic and controversial sense of the break-up of existing large estates. The primary question was the manner in which the tremendous national domain of the United States--and also the very large landholdings of the state of Texas--were to be turned over to individual and corporate use. Yet the purpose of promoting rapid development played a large and increasingly dominant role in the governmental decisions, and from this viewpoint such diverse elements in land policy as the Homestead Act and the railway land grants may not appear as "incongruous" as they have often seemed.[22]

It is perhaps more difficult to relate American money and banking policy to the question of development. On the one hand it is possible to see in Hamilton's Funding System an early example of a new and underdeveloped nation creating a favorable climate for foreign investment, and on the other hand it is easy to point out the absence in nineteenth-century America of any such developmental instruments as Corporaciones de Fomento or National Investment Funds. What is difficult, but very much worth attempting, is to untangle the developmental motives and the developmental implications in the bitter disputes over the Second Bank of the United States and over the various schemes of state regulation of banking which were fought out in their own day, and are still debated in our own, in terms of quite different slogans and purposes.

Two recent studies suggest that the results of such an examination might be disturbing to accepted views. The first is that of Carter H. Golembe, "State Banks and the Economic Development of the West, 1830–1844."[23] This deals with exactly the area and the time most often condemned for addiction to the practices of wildcat banking, and yet the author arrives at the conclusion that the Middle Western banks of the period made a great positive contribution to economic development. The second study is the chapter on banking in a book by Alfred G. Smith, Jr., on the economic readjustment of South Carolina to the opening of better cotton lands farther to the West. The story of South Carolina's banks is recorded with great approval in the standard accounts; up to the time of the Civil War only one small bank had ever failed. But Smith applies to this record a different question and concludes "that while the banking system of South Carolina was both 'sound' and solvent at all times, it was inadequate as far as the credit needs of the economy were concerned, particularly in meeting the requirements of economic expansion and development."[24] If these men are right, if impeccably orthodox banking in South Carolina is to be condemned and highly unorthodox banking in the Middle West is to be praised in terms of the criteria of development, it would appear that applying the new touchstone may well force economic historians in this and other fields to reconsider some of their long-held opinions.

Economic historians have much to learn--and perhaps some things to unlearn, or at least reconsider--if they are to make their full contribution. They will, I believe, gain greater vigor in their own work by giving more conscious attention to the problem of economic development. By so doing they will be able to take a more effective part in the common task which, in its application to the aspirations of the less developed countries, seems to me the most intellectually challenging and the most generously directed concern of the economists of our day.

NOTES

[1] " These economic developments are precisely the ones which those countries which have not experienced them want to emulate." David S. Landes, in an unpublished memorandum, 1955.

[2] Henry G. Aubrey, "Deliberate Industrialization," Social Research, Vol. XVI (June, 1949), pp. 158–182. For Japan, see also Ragnar Nurkse, Problems of Capital Formation in Underdeveloped Countries (New York, Oxford University Press, 1953), pp. 15–16.

[3] W. W. Rostow, "The Interrelation of Theory and Economic History," Journal of Economic History, Vol. XVII (December, 1957), pp. 509–523.

[4] W. W. Rostow, The Process of Economic Growth (New York, Norton, 1952), p. 13.

[5] Nurkse, op. cit., esp. p. 142.

[6] This is one of the paradoxes noted long ago by J. M. Clark in his "Soundings in Non-Euclidean Economics," American Economic Review, Vol. XI Suppl. (March, 1921), pp. 132–147.

[7] W. Arthur Lewis, The Theory of Economic Growth (London, George Allen & Unwin, 1955), pp. 141, 276, 283. Nurkse, op. cit., pp. 11–14.

[8] Forest G. Hill, "The Shaping of California's Industrial Pattern," Proceedings of Western Economic Association, 1955, pp. 63–68.

[9] Joseph A. Schumpeter, The Theory of Economic Development (Cambridge, Harvard University Press, 1934), esp. Chaps. II and VI. The quotations are from pp. 223 and 229.

[10] In a paper presented at a joint meeting of the American Economic History and the Economic History Association in December, 1958. Professor Hughes called my attention to this question and greatly influenced my treatment of it in conversations during his tenure as a visiting member of the Columbia University Department of Economics.

[11] An enthusiastic newspaper editor in Cochabamba predicted that the road would do for his country what the Union Pacific Railroad had done for the United States. His comparison does better justice than mine to the formidable ranges of mountains that had to be crossed, but the Canal offers a close analogy with respect to the resources to be developed. See also Carter Goodrich, "The Economic Transformation of Bolivia," New York State School of Industrial and Labor Relations, Bulletin 34 (October, 1955).

[12] I have suggested an approach to the examination of some of these differences in a paper "The Case of the New Countries," in Douglas F. Dowd (ed.), Thorstein Veblen: A Critical Reappraisal (Ithaca, Cornell University Press, 1959).

[13] In a book review in the Journal of Economic History, Vol. XVII (September, 1957), p. 489. "To assess the speed and extent of economic change," he says, is one of the functions neglected in the earlier work.

[14] Karl Polanyi, The Great Transformation (New York, Farrar & Rinehart, 1955).

[15] The Miner's Freedom: A Study of the Working Life in a Changing Industry (Boston, Marshall Jones, 1925).

[16] John Jewkes, David Sawers, and Richard Stillerman, The Sources of Invention (London, Macmillan & Co., 1958).

[17]John H. Dales, Hydroelectricity and Industrial Development. Quebec 1898-1940 (Cambridge, Harvard University Press, 1957).

[18]Lance E. Davis, "Sources of Industrial Finance: The American Textile Industry, A Case Study," Explorations in Entrepreneurial History, Vol. IX (April, 1957), pp. 189-203.

[19]"Measurement," Journal of Economic History, Vol. VII (Suppl., 1947), pp. 10-34. Moses Abramovitch expressed a more skeptical view in a paper, as yet unpublished, that was presented at the National Conference on Income and Wealth, held at Williams College in September, 1957.

[20]Carter Goodrich, "American Development Policy: The Case of Internal Improvements," Journal of Economic History, Vol. XVI (December, 1956), pp. 449-460; "Local Government Planning of Internal Improvements," Political Science Quarterly, Vol. LXVI (September, 1951), pp. 411-445.

[21]Julian Smith Duncan, Public and Private Operation of Railways in Brazil (New York, Columbia University Press, 1932). Rondo E. Cameron, "Le rôle de la France," Annales (April-June, 1957), pp. 243-257, emphasizes the competition of the Credit Mobilier and the House of Rothschild in stimulating both governmental and private railroad investment in Europe.

[22]See Paul W. Gates, "The Homestead Act in an Incongruous Land System," American Historical Review, Vol. XLI (1936), pp. 652-667.

[23]Unpublished doctoral dissertation, Columbia University, 1952.

[24]Economic Readjustment of an Old Cotton State. South Carolina, 1820-1860 (Columbia, University of South Carolina Press, 1958), p. 217. This book is the revision of a Columbia University dissertation.

The developmental purpose of the state-owned banks of some of the Southern states was fully recognized in G. S. Callender's well-known article "The Early Transportation and Banking Enterprises of the States in Relation to the Growth of Corporations," Quarterly Journal of Economics, Vol. XVII (November, 1902), pp. 111-162. Milton S. Heath, Constructive Liberalism: The Role of the State in Economic Development in Georgia to 1860 (Cambridge, Harvard University Press, 1954), Chap. IX, contains a reappraisal in development terms of the role of the Central Bank of Georgia.

PRESENT UNDERDEVELOPED COUNTRIES AND PAST GROWTH PATTERNS

Simon Kuznets

The Johns Hopkins University

I.

By underdeveloped countries we mean those with a per capita product so low that material deprivation is widespread and reserves for emergency and growth are small. The number and identity of such countries depends, of course, upon the level at which marginal per capita income is drawn. For present purposes I prefer to set the dividing line low in order to bring the problem into sharp focus. Specifically, using the per capita national-product estimates for 1952–54 (and some earlier years) prepared by the United Nations, I have placed the maximum income for underdeveloped countries at roughly $100 (in purchasing power of 1952–54).[1] By this criterion, most of the populous countries of Asia (China, India, Pakistan, Indonesia, Burma, South Korea) and many in Africa would fall within this group. It is significant to note that not a single reported Latin American country falls below $100 per capita. Close to half of the world population is in this group and still would be if other criteria were used--not only today, but in the 1930's, and for some time back in the past.

That we have come to designate these countries as "underdeveloped" implies that their current low rates of economic performance are far short of the potential. This, as distinct from actual rates of per capita production (no matter how crude) is a presumption rather than a statement of fact. However, it seems plausible to us because in many other countries rates of economic production are at much higher per capita levels; because strikingly high rates of growth have been attained over varying long periods within the last two centuries; and because the stock of tested useful knowledge at the disposal of mankind is large and has been increasing apace. But it is, nevertheless, a presumption and we should be wary of applying patterns of economic growth observed in only a limited number of countries--accounting for at most a fifth of mankind--to the large population masses included in the underdeveloped countries as defined above. Indeed, our main purpose in stressing certain basic characteristics of these underdeveloped countries is to point up the differences between them and comparable characteristics of the presently developed countries in the decades preceding their industrialization and growth.

In such an attempt, statistical evidence, even if available, has to be treated summarily; and the choice of characteristics necessarily reflects implicit notions of factors important in economic growth, without providing explicit exposition, analysis, and defense. Nevertheless, the attempt seems to me worth while. Much of the writing and thinking on problems of economic growth in underdeveloped countries is unconsciously steeped in the social and economic background of the developed Western nations; and there is a temptation to extrapolate from the past growth patterns of these nations to the growth problems and potentials of the underdeveloped areas. An emphasis on the differences, viewed as obstacles to such extrapolation, may contribute to a more realistic appraisal of the magnitude and recalcitrance of the problems.

II.

1. The present levels of per capita product in the underdeveloped countries are much lower than were those in the developed countries in their pre-industrialization phase.

This statement can be supported by a variety of evidence, and appears to be true--except in reference to Japan only, where per capita income prior to industrialization was as low as in most of Asia today. The pre-industrialization phase may be defined either as the decade when the share of the labor force in agriculture was at least six-tenths of the total and when this percentage was just ready to begin its downward movement, or as the decade just before those which Professor W. W. Rostow characterizes as the "take-off into self-sustained growth."[2] In either case, the evidence that we have on the presently developed countries--in Western and Central Europe, in North America and in Oceania--shows that the per capita incomes in their pre-industrial phases were already much higher than those now prevailing in the underdeveloped countries. They ranged well above $200 (in 1952–54 prices) compared with the present well below $100 for the populous underdeveloped countries of Asia and Africa. Even in Russia, per capita income around 1885 was probably more than $150 (in 1952–54 prices), on the assumption that the present level is about $500.[3]

2. The supply of agricultural land per capita is much lower in most underdeveloped countries today than in most presently developed countries--even today, and the difference was even greater in their pre-industrial phase. Comparison of the supply of agricultural land per agricultural worker would yield similar findings.

This statement conforms to our general knowledge of the higher density of population settlement and the greater pressure of population on land in such countries as China, India, Pakistan, and Indonesia than in the older Western European countries now or even more before their industrialization--not to mention the vast empty spaces of Canada, the United States, and other Western European offshoots overseas or for that matter of the U.S.S.R. Statistical evidence assembled by Colin Clark relates agricultural land (reduced to standard units) to male workers in agriculture, and yields ratios of 1.2 workers per land unit for the United States, slightly more than 3 in the U.S.S.R., about 10 in Germany and France, and as many as 31 in India and Pakistan, 25 in China, and 73 in Egypt (post Second World War).[4] More directly relevant are the data provided by Professor Bert F. Hoselitz on the density of agricultural settlement in countries with more than half of the active labor force in agriculture--which show that in England and Wales in 1688 and in many European countries in the mid-nineteenth century the number of hectares per male worker (or household) ranged mostly between 5 and 10, whereas similar calculations for Asian countries and Egypt today show a range from well below 1 to at most 2 1/2 hectares.[5]

3. The lower per capita (and per worker) income in the underdeveloped countries--relative to that in the pre-industrialization phase of the presently developed countries--is probably due largely to the lower productivity of the agricultural sector.

We have no direct confirmation at hand, but several items of indirect evidence strongly support this statement. First, and most telling, is the lower supply of agricultural land per worker noted under Point 2. Second, cross-section comparisons for recent years indicate that the shortage of per worker income in the agricultural sector relative to that in the nonagricultural sector is negatively associated with real national product per capita or per worker. This association suggests that the shortage of per worker income in the agricultural sector relative to that in the nonagricultural sector in the underdeveloped countries today is greater than it was in the pre-industrial phase of presently developed countries. Third, the nonagricultural sector in even the underdeveloped countries includes some modern industries that were nonexistent in the mid-nineteenth century or earlier; and it may well be that the per worker income in the nonagricultural sector of the underdeveloped countries is today as high as per worker income in the nonagricultural sector in the pre-industrialization phase of currently developed countries. On this possibly extreme assumption, per worker income in the agricultural sector in the underdeveloped countries must be one-fourth or one-third of per worker income in agriculture in the currently developed countries in their pre-industrialization phase (much lower than the one-third to one-half for total income per worker).

4. Inequality in the size distribution of income may be wider in the underdeveloped countries today than it was in the presently developed

countries in their pre-industrialization phase; it is at best at least as wide.

Here again we have only indirect evidence. First, limited statistical data suggest that today the inequality in income distribution in the underdeveloped countries is distinctly wider than in the developed countries;[6] and while this may be due in part to the reduction in income inequality in the process of growth of the developed countries, there is some indication that with industrialization, inequality first widened and then contracted--so that inequality in the phases preceding industrialization may not have been as wide as that during the early phases of industrial growth. Second, the very wide difference suggested under Point 4 between per worker income in the agricultural and nonagricultural sectors in the underdeveloped countries, a difference wider than that in the pre-industrialization phase of currently developed countries, also suggests wider inequality in the size distribution of total income.

Even if relative inequality in the size distribution of income in the underdeveloped countries today were no wider than it was in the pre-industrialization phase of the currently developed countries, or even if it were slightly narrower, the appreciably lower income per capita in the underdeveloped countries would aggravate the economic and social implications. For if average income per capita is so low, the majority of the population with incomes significantly below the country-wide average must exist at distressingly low standards of living, and the contrast must be striking between, on the one hand, these large masses of agricultural cultivators and of low-paid lumpen proletariat in the few cities and, on the other, the small groups that, either by control of property rights or by attachment to a few economically favorable sectors, manage to secure relatively higher per capita incomes.

5. Social and political concomitants of the low-income structure of the underdeveloped countries today appear to constitute more formidable obstacles to economic growth than they did in the pre-industrialization phase of presently developed countries.

The vast array of diverse evidence on the point can hardly be summarized here; nor do we claim that these social and political patterns are necessarily consequences of the low-income structure and attributable to it alone. But, at the risk of being accused of "economocentricity," it can be argued that the low economic base was a factor in producing the social and political results; and a few illustrations will elucidate the point.

First, the crude birth rates in underdeveloped countries even in recent years, are at least 40 per thousand, and in many cases well above.[7] Rates as high as these or even higher apparently characterized the United States in the early decades of the nineteenth century, possibly Canada, and other "empty" lands overseas. But in the older countries in Western, Central, and Northern Europe, the birth rates in the pre-industrialization phase were already down to the middle 30's, and in some cases close to 30 per thousand. In other words, part of the process of demographic transition had already taken place; and birth rates were as high as those in underdeveloped countries today only when the ratio of population to resources was extremely favorable. Obviously, rapid population growth under the conditions prevailing in underdeveloped countries today is an obstacle to accumulation of capital and to economic growth, and was also in the older European countries in their pre-industrialization phase.

Second, let us disregard for the moment literacy rates, which are distressingly low in the underdeveloped countries today, probably well below those in the currently developed countries in their pre-industrialization phase. An even more important problem for many is linguistic and cultural disunity--a problem particularly acute for both the large population units like India and China, and the smaller ones in which groups with different antecedents have been brought together. Without claiming that economic factors predominate, one can argue that the persistingly low level of economic performance, and as part and parcel of it, of communication and transportation in these countries, has played an important role. No such major problem of linguistic and cultural unity or literacy appears to have plagued the currently developed countries during their pre-industrial phase.

Third, a weak political structure is in large measure predetermined by low and unequal incomes, backwardness of transportation and communication, and linguistic and cultural disunity--if by a strong political structure one means a complex of associations culminating in an efficient sovereign government, checked and guided by a multiplicity of underlying voluntary organizations. The cleavage between the masses of population struggling for a meager subsistence and the small groups at the top--precluding a widely graded bridge of "middle" classes--certainly militates against such a strong political structure, and easily leads to dictatorial or oligarchical regimes, which are often unstable and most unresponsive to the basic economic problems of their country. In all these respects, the situation in the pre-industrial phase of the currently developed countries, again with the possible exception of Japan, was far different in the effective interplay between the government and the interests of the population; and in the much greater influence of the various groups in the population upon the basic decisions made by the state in order to facilitate economic growth.

6. Most underdeveloped countries have attained political independence only recently--after decades of either colonial status or political inferiority to the advanced countries that limited their independence. This was not true of the currently developed countries in their pre-industrial phase; industrialization followed a long period of political independence.

This statement is a partial explanation of the weaknesses in the social and political structure of underdeveloped countries today and to that extent is only a corroboration of Point 5. But there is an important additional element in it. In so far as their political independence has recently been won only after a prolonged struggle--and is thus an outcome of decades of opposition to the advanced countries, viewed as imperialists and aggressors--not only were economic problems neglected but the native leadership was trained in political conflict rather than in economic statesmanship. There was also a negative association between the forms of advanced economic operation, as practiced by the invaders and aggressors, and its products as reflected in a higher material standard of living: the higher standard was favored, but the forms of organization which made it possible were hated. A similar condition may have existed in the development of some of the presently developed countries: e.g., a distinctive minority may have been associated with a revolutionary economic process that necessitated disruptive changes and adversely affected established interests. But such an association could not possibly have been so widely and distinctly felt as are those in the underdeveloped countries, which have had such a long history as colonies or inferior political units. Neither could the disruptive effects of the advanced elements in the economy have been as great, nor in some respects as painful, as those resulting from the introduction of Western methods and practices into a social and political framework whose historical roots were radically different from those of the West.

7. The populations in underdeveloped countries today are inheritors of civilizations quite distinctive from, and independent of, European civilization. Yet it is European civilization that through centuries of geographical, political, and intellectual expansion has provided the matrix of modern economic growth. All presently developed countries, with the exception of Japan, are either old members of the European civilization, its offshoots overseas, or its offshoots on land toward the East.

This statement is again part of the explanation of the weaknesses in the social and political structure of underdeveloped countries today. But it is useful to recall that the European community went through a series of revolutions spanning from the fifteenth century (to set the initial date as late as possible) to the eighteenth--antedating the agricultural and industrial revolutions in eighteenth-century England which ushered in the industrial system, the vehicle of modern economic growth. The intellectual revolution with the introduction of science, the moral revolution with the secularization of Christo-Judaic religions, the geographical revolution with expansion to the East and the West; the political revolution with the formation of national states--all these occurred within the context of European civilization, not of those in Asia, Africa, or the Americas; and they occurred long before the modern industrial system was born. Whether or not these antecedents

were indispensable is unimportant here since we are not concerned
with a general theory of the causes of modern economic growth. Our
point is simply that participation in this long process of change before
the emergence of the industrial system, meant gradual adaptation, an
opportunity to develop within the existing social and political framework the new institutions necessary to exploit the potentials provided
by these intellectual, moral, geographical, and political revolutions.
Thus when the presently developed countries within the European orbit
reached their pre-industrialization phase, they already possessed a
variety of social, political, and economic institutions, and particularly
a prevailing set of views and scale of values which were extremely
valuable in that they permitted these societies to make the further adjustments which industrialization brought in its wake or which were
essential concomitants.

The present situation in the underdeveloped countries is in sharp
contrast. They are the inheritors of different civilizations, the pos-
sessors of social, economic, and political institutions with roots that
go far back and represent a heritage of adjustment to a quite different
series of historical events, lacking the same kind of geographical, intellectual, and political revolutions, yet possibly containing a wide
variety of other marked changes. These changes, however, are not
the matrix out of which modern economic growth emerges. Consequently, there is no continuity between the adjustments that may have
occurred in these underdeveloped areas before their invasion by the
aggressive and expanding European civilization and the adjustments
that are needed to take advantage of the potentials of modern economic
growth. Some of these other civilizations did indeed reach highly impressive levels: after all, China in the seventeenth or early eighteenth
century was a political unit that, in size of population and efficiency of
administration, dwarfed even the largest European unit of the day; and
some of the accomplishments of the native Indian civilizations were
far in advance of anything that the European civilization could produce
at the time. But this very success, the specific adaptation of the social
and cultural patterns to the potential (e.g., the development in China
of the nonphonetic written language to overcome the problem of diver-
sities of spoken languages, or in India of the caste system) becomes a
serious obstacle in their response to an entirely different range of
technological potentials, calling for a markedly different set of social
and cultural behavior patterns.

III.

These brief comments hardly exhaust the important economic characteristics of the underdeveloped economies today, in comparison with
the developed countries in their pre-industrial phase. We have made

no reference to the division between participation incomes (of employees and self-employed) and property incomes; the savings and
capital investment proportions; the spread of the market economy and
the availability of credit and financial institutions; the fiscal and tax
systems; the dependence upon foreign trade. These aspects are to
some degree implicit in the comparisons already made, and for some
of them the evidence has yet to be assembled. And our comments on
the social and political framework and the differences in historical
antecedents are no more than a few broad strokes on a vast canvas,
only the barest preliminary sketch.

Yet they should suffice to convey the far-reaching and striking differences between the underdeveloped countries today and the presently
developed countries before their industrialization. Furthermore,
many of these contrasts would persist even if the dividing line between
underdeveloped and developed countries were set at an appreciably
higher level of per capita income. Political weaknesses and heritages
radically different from the European characterize many Latin American countries--even if their ratios of population to land or population
to resources are relatively favorable--and some in the Middle East
and Africa.

Before we consider further the significance of the observations
just made, a brief aside on Japan is in order. In almost all respects,
except perhaps political weakness, Japan, before its industrialization,
appeared to be similar to the populous underdeveloped countries of
Asia. Yet it managed to utilize the potentials of modern economic
growth and to forge ahead to higher levels of economic performance.
Does this mean that the characteristics of underdeveloped countries
indicated in the preceding section are not the formidable obstacles to
satisfactory economic growth that we have suggested?

The analysis of the growth of Japan in the light of this question can
hardly be presented here; and despite much valuable work in the field,[8]
the lack of much basic data precludes a firm answer. But one point
must be stressed: the per capita income of Japan today, about eight
decades after the beginning of the industrialization process, is still
low, far lower than that in any other developed country within the orbit
of European civilization. According to the United Nations (see foot-
note 1), Japan's per capita income for 1952–54 was somewhat below
$200--lower than that in any of the European countries covered (even
Greece and Portugal), or in most of the Latin American countries.
True, the comparison cannot be pushed too far, and these postwar
estimates may still reflect transient reductions below the secular
level. But in 1938, when economic levels elsewhere were drastically
reduced after the great depression, Japan's per capita income was
$86, i.e., between a third and a fifth of the per capita income in West-
ern developed countries.[9] These low levels may be due to the limited
natural resources of Japan, and cannot be extrapolated directly

elsewhere. But unfavorable ratios of population to resources also characterize the populous underdeveloped countries of Asia and the Middle East; and the point to be emphasized is that despite long participation in modern economic growth, Japan does not enjoy adequately high per capita income, and she still suffers from the pressure of population on limited resources.

But granted that the characteristics of underdeveloped countries today do constitute obstacles to economic growth--more formidable than may have been the case in the presently developed countries in their pre-industrial phase—are there not, on the other hand, substantial advantages in the very fact that these countries face the task of growth later in history? To state definitively what these advantages are calls for more knowledge than I possess. But clearly there are two major complexes: (a) the increased stock of knowledge and experience in the fields of technological and social invention and innovation; (b) the extension in the number of developed countries and in their economic attainment.

(a) It is hardly necessary to emphasize the striking additions that have been made over the last century, and are being made today, to the stock of both basic and applied knowledge of natural processes, and of techniques of production that are the substance of much economic activity. Perhaps less obvious but equally important is the wide diversity of social techniques that have evolved. The known potential of technological and social innovations available to the underdeveloped countries today is, therefore, far greater than was that at the disposal of the presently developed countries at the middle or end of the nineteenth century, let alone earlier.

There seems to be no way to gauge the direct value of this greater potential in terms of feasible economic growth, on the one hand, and to compare it with the obstacles to such growth on the other. But at the risk of playing the role of Devil's advocate, I would like to stress certain aspects of this increase in the stock of technological and social knowledge that limit its possible value as a tool in the economic growth of the underdeveloped countries of today.

In the first place, most, if not all, such additions to production and social technology originated in the developed countries and were advanced in response to the needs of these economies or were adapted to the patterns of social and economic life peculiar to them. For example, the remarkable technological changes in agriculture seem to emphasize labor rather than land-saving innovations; but land is the more limiting factor of production in the large underdeveloped countries. Likewise, many social inventions, ranging from the more limited types in the field of financial structure or business organization to such major complexes as the planned authoritarian framework of the U.S.S.R., were evolved within the contexts of the specific economies, reflecting their distinctive social setting and historical heritage.

Some of these technological and social innovations could, of course, be transferred to the underdeveloped economies of today with relatively minor modifications. But others would require major re-adaptation, for which the material and human resources may not be available; and still others may be so divergent from the historically determined, deep-seated factors in the structure of the underdeveloped economies that their availability in any meaningful sense of the term is highly questionable.

In the second place, translating any potential of technological and social innovations into reality requires an investment before returns can be expected. This investment can be defined as the input of material resources and social change required for the adoption of the technological or social innovation in more or less the form in which it is known in the developed countries. With costs so defined, this argument becomes a supplement to that stated just above as to the "specificity" of much of the invention and innovation that emerged during the last century. If costs are defined more widely, to include also those of re-adaptation and change necessary to overcome the specificity limitations, the argument would, of course, include much of what has already been said in the preceding paragraph.

If we hold to the narrower definition of costs (which is still wider than the usual one in economic analysis), the argument can be stated simply. From a review of the history of technological and economic changes since the mid-nineteenth century, one gets the impression that the stock of potential technological innovations is large--so large in fact that much of it has not been utilized because of limited supplies of capital and of entrepreneurial ability, and because of the resistance of the existing social institutions, even in the most advanced countries of the day. The time span between major innovations--from the stationary steam engine to steam railroads; from steam power to electric power; from electric power to internal-combustion engines and subsequently to nuclear power (to mention only one line of change)-- can be understood as largely due to the fact that even the most advanced nations of the day had neither sufficient stocks of skills needed for the adaptations involved in secondary and tertiary inventions, nor sufficient stocks of capital and economic entrepreneurship to be able to handle all these major innovations within a short time after the underlying scientific discoveries had been made. This means that most of the presently developed economies, indeed all but the pioneer in its early phases, had, in their pre-industrial phase, a much larger potential of technological (and correspondingly social) changes than of the means needed to apply them. If so, the larger potential of technological and social innovations of the underdeveloped countries today may be of little importance in any comparison with the presently developed countries in their pre-industrial phase. Such a potential, i.e., a stock of tested knowledge, is a permissive, necessary condition, but in itself it is not <u>sufficient</u>. Both material resources for capital input and readiness for social change are also essential. And as we mentioned in our earlier comments on the characteristics of the underdeveloped economies today, material resources for capital inputs are exceedingly scarce, and the cost of social change, given the historical heritage, is unusually heavy.

Third, some of the additions during the last century to the stock of technological and social inventions may render the task of economic growth in the underdeveloped countries more difficult rather than less difficult--if growth means simply a sustained rise in per capita product. Two illustrations come readily to mind. The first is the effect that recent discoveries and innovations in medical and public-health technology have made on the death rates. These changes have made possible in the underdeveloped countries of today far more rapid declines in mortality than occurred in the past in the currently developed countries of the West;[10] and at extremely low cost. With these rapid reductions in mortality, which require no substantial rises in economic product per capita, and with birth rates remaining high or even rising, the rates of natural increase have risen rapidly--to levels far higher than those observed in the pre-industrial phase of the older European countries. And the resulting rapid growth of population only complicates the task of attaining higher levels of income per capita. The second illustration is suggested by what has become known in economic discussion as the "demonstration" effect. The impact of technological change during the last century on communication among various parts of the world has been perhaps as great as on any sector of economic and social activity. It brought in its wake a greater awareness in the underdeveloped countries of the higher standards of living in the developed areas, and produced a pressure for higher consumption levels that may have restricted savings and capital accumulation and added to tensions of backwardness, thus making the task of orderly economic growth only more difficult. Both these complexes of technological and social innovations are major contributions to economic product and welfare in the long run; but in the short run they aggravate the economic growth problems in the underdeveloped areas.

(b) The existence of many developed and advanced economic areas today, which was not the case a century ago or earlier, may be of advantage to underdeveloped countries--and not only because they are the originators and repositories of the stock of technological and social knowledge. More directly, these advanced areas can contribute to the growth of the underdeveloped countries by demand for their products; by capital investment, by grants, and in many other ways by which the resources of one area can be placed at the disposal of another.

There is little question that over the last century, population, per capita income, and total income of the developed areas of the world have grown proportionately more than the corresponding aggregates

for the underdeveloped areas--particularly if we confine the underdeveloped areas to the lowest income units in Asia and Africa. If the
demand by developed areas for the products of underdeveloped countries could be assumed to be a constant proportion of the total income
of the former, the increase in the number of developed areas would
provide markets for the underdeveloped units that have increased
relative to their domestic output. Likewise, if capital flow from advanced to underdeveloped areas were a constant fraction of the total
income of the advanced areas, or still better of the disparity between
the two groups in per capita income, one could state firmly that such
a flow should have increased proportionately to the domestic income
of the recipient underdeveloped countries. But no such constant proportions can be assumed--as can clearly be seen from the marked
trends in the ratios of imports to domestic output in the developed
countries; or from the well-known facts that the United States was a
net capital importer during most of the nineteenth century when its
per capita income was among the highest in the world, and that today
many of the erstwhile international creditor countries in Europe are
exporting proportionately less capital than they did before the First
World War--despite the fact that their per capita incomes are much
higher.

A vast literature deals with import and export propensities, largely
of developed countries and covering all too short a time span, and with
past and current trends in capital movements among developed and
underdeveloped countries. It is hardly possible, or necessary, to deal
with that question now. No extensive documentation is needed to support the major point here, viz., that the mere rise in number and economic magnitude of developed countries relative to the underdeveloped
ones does not necessarily mean greater relative availability of markets or capital supply from abroad. It is not only that the political
conditions in the underdeveloped areas may be unfavorable to foreign
capital imports and to the assistance by foreign enterprises in developing and stimulating export potentials. It is not only that in the
large underdeveloped countries, like all large countries, capital imports can contribute only a small fraction of total capital needs. It is
also that the very increase in technological potentials may have created in the developed countries themselves a backlog of investment
opportunities attractive enough to absorb their savings despite the
presumably greater marginal yields abroad (except in the restricted
cases of capital exports needed to assure the supply of raw materials
indispensable in the domestic economy). And finally, the larger number of advanced countries, emerging out of somewhat different historical antecedents and with different complexes of social institutions,
has resulted in the all too familiar intensified international friction
and conflict which constitute a major drain upon the surplus resources
of the developed areas and lead to a greater dominance of political
than of economic considerations in trade and capital flows to the underdeveloped areas.

IV.

Two conclusions have been suggested in the preceding discussion. The first points to the major differences between underdeveloped countries today and the presently developed countries in their pre-industrial phase--and the much greater obstacles to economic growth in underdeveloped areas that these differences imply. The second questions the advantages of a late start, in the way of a greater potential of new knowledge and a larger group of developed countries to draw upon. Both conclusions are only suggested: they can hardly be demonstrated, certainly not with the evidence now available. And their bearing is wide, but cannot be sharply defined: they have been argued in terms of the very low income countries of Asia and Africa, but much of the discussion applies to other countries on these two continents and in Latin America.

If these conclusions can be accepted, at least as working hypotheses, some implications for economic analysis and policy can be drawn. These will become apparent if we envisage the process of modern economic growth as the spread of the industrial system from its origin in pioneering Great Britain to other countries--the United States and other overseas offshoots of England, Western, Central, and Northern Europe, Japan, and most recently Russia. Since the productive system that is thus spreading has a common core, both with respect to technology and the structure of human wants, some features of economic growth will be common to all countries in which it may be taking place. An agricultural revolution, i.e., a substantial rise in per capita productivity in the agricultural sector at home, or increasing reliance upon such abroad, is one important, and an indispensable, early element. The growth of the nonagricultural commodity-producing and transportation sectors is another--industrialization in the narrower sense of the term. The growth of cities and all that is implied in modern urban civilization is a third. The shift from small, individually managed, almost family-attached economic units to the big, impersonal units, whether big business corporations or the state trusts, is a fourth. The number of such trends integral to modern economic growth can be multiplied, even if confined to the purely economic aspects; and there is a host of inevitable concomitants in the demographic and social processes--birth and death rates, internal migration, literacy, skills of the labor force, and so on, ranging to changes in scales of values. These will all be found wherever the industrial system flourishes, whether in the older European countries that still retain large residues of the pre-industrial social structure or in the young and initially empty countries overseas; under capitalism or under the state-managed system of the U.S.S.R.

Yet this common core of technological and of minimum social changes associated with the industrial system was planted, as it

spread from country to country, within units with different antecedents
and historical heritage. And some of the social forms in which the
system was clothed were quite different. They were necessarily different partly because the one central complex was combined with very
diverse initial conditions in the various countries of adoption; partly
because the very fact that some one country was the pioneer, others
the immediate followers, and others came still later, in itself affected
the measures by which growth or "catching up" was attempted, and
the very spirit in which they were undertaken. Differences were also
imposed by the size of the countries, economic growth in small and
large countries being quite different in method, if not in the common
aim of using the potential of modern technology to attain higher levels
of economic performance.

This general model suggests that the aim of research on economic
growth is to establish and measure the common and variant characteristics of the process; to "explain" the interrelations of the common
and variant characteristics, that is, to integrate them into a theory of
the growth of a country's economy viewed as a system of interdependent parts combined with a theory of the spread and modification of the
process of economic growth as it occurs among pioneer and follower
nations; large and small units; and so on. Such an attempt has barely
begun--partly because interest in economic growth has been revived
only in recent decades, after a long lapse since the mid-nineteenth
century; partly because the available data are hard to come by, and
have not yet been properly organized and examined. Economic analysis alone may not be sufficient for the explanation and elucidation of
economic growth and the provision thereby of a sound basis for growth
policy. It is clear, however, that the empirical findings that we now
have, being based largely on data for a few developed countries for
insufficiently long periods, cover too narrow a range; that the functional relations established from them cannot be extrapolated too far
in time and in space; that the very conceptual structure of economic
analysis, having been geared to the Western economies and to the
short-run problems, may need substantial revision before it can effectively explain the past economic growth of the presently developed
countries--let alone be applied to the growth problems of underdeveloped countries today. The comments above on some of the distinctive characteristics of these underdeveloped countries only point up
sharply how far removed these countries are from the observable
and measurable economic experience, which is the raw material of
almost all our empirical research and theoretical analysis.

This bears also upon discussions of policy related to growth problems in the underdeveloped countries, whether by professional economists or by laymen who either eventually make the decisions or determine them by their attitudes. Such economic-policy decisions
should presumably be based upon tested knowledge of the possible

impact of various factors or measures in relation to clearly formulated objectives. That little of such tested knowledge exists can hardly
be denied; nor is it surprising that much of the technical discussion
of growth policy is based on mechanical analogies, no matter how
elaborate; and much of the discussion by laymen, particularly in the
developed countries, follows along similar lines expressed in the
cruder terms of what was good for us should be good for them.

These remarks are not meant to advocate abandoning all attempts
to formulate bases for analysis and for intelligent discussion of policy.
Failure to analyze and recommend is in itself a decision to do noth-
ing--a policy that can hardly be defended. The plea here is for greater
realization of how little is known and how much there is to be learned,
and hence for greater caution in building models and writing prescriptions; for a clearer perception, particularly on the part of policy-
makers, that the problems facing the underdeveloped countries are
far more difficult than they appear at first sight, and that these countries cannot be expected to follow the patterns of presently developed
areas which had entirely different beginnings.

NOTES

[1]See Per Capita National Product of Fifty-Five Countries: 1952-54, United Nations,
Statistical Papers, Series E, No. 4 (New York, 1957); and National and Per Capita Incomes of Seventy Countries: 1949, United Nations, Statistical Papers, Series E, No. 1
(New York, October, 1950). The countries listed in the text are from both publications,
with some allowance for maximum growth in countries covered for 1949 but not for
1952-54.
[2]See The Economic Journal, Vol. LXVI, No. 261 (March, 1956), pp. 25-83, particularly
the table of dates on p. 31.
[3]This statement is based on the long-term rates of growth shown for Russia in my
paper "Quantitative Aspects of the Economic Growth of Nations, I. Levels and Vari-
ability of Rates of Growth," Economic Development and Cultural Change, Vol. V, No. 1
(October, 1956), Appendix table 13, p. 81.
[4]See his Conditions of Economic Progress, 3d ed. (London, 1957), Table XXXIII,
following p. 308.
[5]See his "Population Pressure, Industrialization and Social Mobility," Population
Studies, Vol. XI, No. 2 (November, 1957), Table I, p. 126.
[6]See Theodore Morgan, "Distribution of Income in Ceylon, Puerto Rico, the United
States and the United Kingdom," Economic Journal, Vol. XVIII (December, 1953),
pp. 821-834; and subsequent discussion by Harry Oshima and Theodore Morgan in
ibid., Vol. LXVI (March, 1956), pp. 156-164. See also my paper "Economic Growth
and Income Inequality," American Economic Review, Vol. XLV (March, 1955), pp. 1-28.
[7]See, for example, Report on the World Social Situation, United Nations (1957), particularly pp. 6-10.
[8]See particularly W. W. Lockwood, The Economic Development of Japan (Princeton,
Princeton University Press, 1954).
[9]See W. S. and E. S. Woytinsky, World Population and Production (New York, The
Twentieth Century Fund, 1953), Table 185, p. 389.
[10]See, e.g., the incisive summary discussion by George J. Stolnitz in "Trends and
Differentials in Mortality," Proceedings of a Round Table at the 1955 Annual Conference, Milbank Memorial Fund (New York, 1956), pp. 1-9.

ELEMENTS IN A THEORY OF UNDERDEVELOPMENT

Benjamin Higgins

Massachusetts Institute of Technology

(The University of Texas)

I. Introduction

In our efforts to frame a systematic theory as a basis for policy decisions in underdeveloped areas, we are confronted with a choice between two alternative approaches. The first is to seek a truly general theory which would explain economic development both in advanced and in underdeveloped countries, and to put into this theoretical framework the institutional and behavioral assumptions which conform most closely to actual conditions in underdeveloped countries. The second is to formulate a special theory for underdeveloped countries which would take account of their peculiarities at the outset.

The classical school, Marx, and in lesser degree Schumpeter, adopted the first approach. Most general of all in scope and method was the Marxist theory; it included a theory of history, which, I suppose, a theory of economic development must ultimately be. The most satisfactory theory of the classical period was that of Malthus; he took account of the problem of effective demand as well as of problems emanating from the side of the production function; he provided a two-sector model and endeavored to analyze the relationships between the sectors; he made explicit references to the problems of the underdeveloped countries of his own day; and he treated population growth as an endogenous factor. The Schumpeter theory is more exclusively one of capitalist development, and can be applied to underdeveloped countries only by implication. Moreover, the Schumpeter theory is more an explanation of why capitalist development must take the form of economic fluctuations than an explanation of growth, stagnation, and decline. In any case, these general theories are neither precise nor systematic. We cannot proceed directly from them to policy recommendations for underdeveloped countries.

The contemporary theories of "steady growth" are more precise, but for the most part they are mere statements of conditions for dynamic equilibrium. They concentrate on the savings-investment relationship and tell us little about the basic underlying factors responsible for the rate of economic development. This stricture applies in particular to models of the Harrod-Domar type, which in themselves say nothing about causal relationships in the growth process. In my view, the most useful theory of this type is Alvin Hansen's. While it is primarily concerned with the savings-investment relationship, it also isolates some long-run causal factors behind this relationship which determine whether an economy will grow steadily, or whether it will suffer from chronic inflation, increasing underemployment, or stagnation.

We might summarize these theories of steady growth, with emphasis on the Hansen version, as follows:

$$Y = I + C \dots \dots \dots \dots \dots \dots \dots \dots (1)$$
$$I = I_i + I_a + I_g \dots \dots \dots \dots \dots \dots (2)$$
$$I_i = I_i(\overset{\circ}{Y}) \dots \dots \dots \dots \dots \dots \dots \dots (3)$$
$$I_a = I_a(\overset{\circ}{L}, \overset{\circ}{K}, \overset{\circ}{T}) \dots \dots \dots \dots \dots \dots (4)$$
$$C = Y - S \dots \dots \dots \dots \dots \dots \dots \dots (5)$$
$$S = S(Y) \dots \dots \dots \dots \dots \dots \dots \dots (6)$$

The symbols are as follows: Y equals national income; I equals investment; $\overset{\circ}{Y}$ is the rate of change in income to time (dY/dt); I_i is induced investment; I_a is autonomous investment; and I_g is governmental investment; S is savings; C is consumption; $\overset{\circ}{L}$ is the rate of growth in the population and labor force (dL/dt); $\overset{\circ}{K}$ is the rate of discovery of known natural resources (dK/dt); $\overset{\circ}{T}$ is the rate of technological progress (dT/dt). Governmental investment, I_g, is regarded as given, and $\overset{\circ}{K}$, $\overset{\circ}{L}$, and $\overset{\circ}{T}$ are treated as external factors. Thus we have six equations and six unknowns.[1]

From this system we can derive the all-important equation for the increase in income:

$$\Delta Y = \frac{I}{\Delta S/\Delta Y}[I_i(\overset{\circ}{Y}) + I_a(\overset{\circ}{L}, \overset{\circ}{K}, \overset{\circ}{T}) + I_g] \dots (6a)$$

The theory of increasing underemployment can be derived from this one single equation.[2] Let us suppose that in an economy enjoying full employment the combined effect of the growth factors ($\overset{\circ}{L}$, $\overset{\circ}{K}$, $\overset{\circ}{T}$) becomes negative, because the rates of population growth and of resource discovery are tapering off, whereas the rate of technological progress remains unchanged. Autonomous investment (I_a) will fall. However, income will still be rising, and consequently ex-ante savings will also be rising. The marginal propensity to save will be constant or rising. Thus the rate of increase in income must fall. When that happens, induced investment will also fall, and then income will drop. So far as stability is concerned, of course, it is induced investment that is the villain of the piece. Thus the effect of a weakening of growth factors will be a series of economic fluctuations around a trend which involves increasing unemployment. Full employment can be maintained, however, by raising I_g to offset the fall in ($I_i + I_a$), or by redistributing income from savers to spenders so as to reduce dS/dY.

This model can be equally well applied to underdeveloped areas. We must, however, modify it in one respect. We know that in many underdeveloped areas population growth is no longer a stimulus to investment. Labor is already redundant and population growth is no longer needed to prevent diminishing returns to capital accumulation and it is not accompanied by an increase in effective demand. We may therefore drop the $\overset{\circ}{L}$ from our investment equation.

In underdeveloped countries it is perfectly possible for the combined effects of resource discovery and technological progress on investment to be zero. The mere presence of resource discovery or technological progress does not bring an <u>increase</u> in autonomous investment; only an <u>increase</u> in the rate of technological progress or resource discovery will do that. Most underdeveloped countries have had quite substantial rates of resource discovery and improvements in technique in the past, although concentrated in the plantation, mining, petroleum, and manufacturing sector. We need a "development plan" to <u>accelerate</u> the rate of resource discovery and of technological progress.

An increase in governmental investment for development--"Ig"-- may start a process of expansion. If it takes the right form, it may also encourage increases in autonomous private investment. However, we can see from our equation that unless the marginal propensity to save or the output of final products rises immediately, the result will be inflation. Moreover, once national income begins to rise at a significant rate, the relation $I_i(\overset{\circ}{Y})$ will be brought into play. Economic fluctuations will set in around a generally inflationary trend.

Theories of this kind, centering on the savings-investment relationship, can tell us a little about the requirements for steady growth in underdeveloped countries and about the kind of monetary, fiscal, and foreign exchange policies that may be needed to make the process of growth reasonably smooth. They do not, however, tell us anything about how underdeveloped countries got that way, or how to convert a stagnant and poor economy into an expanding one.

An alternative approach, which might be called the "planning approach," centers on the capital:output ratio rather than the savings-investment relationship. Let us write

$$O = a \,^{\circ}\, Q \dots \dots \dots \dots \dots \dots \dots \dots \dots (1)$$

Here "a" is an output:capital ratio. Most of the literature refers to a capital:output ratio, and particularly to an "incremental capital: output ratio" relating increases in output to additions to the stock of capital. If the value of "a" is independent of the level of "O" and "Q," it is the reciprocal of the incremental capital:output ratio. Then,

$$\Delta O = a \,^{\circ}\, \Delta Q + \Delta a \,^{\circ}\, Q \dots \dots \dots \dots \dots \dots \dots \dots (1a)$$
$$= a \,^{\circ}\, I + \Delta a \,^{\circ}\, Q \dots \dots \dots \dots \dots \dots \dots \dots (1b)$$

This formulation has the advantage of showing that investment, and so investment decisions, is the hard core of the development process, while recognizing at the same time that there are ways of using an existing stock of capital more effectively in order to raise output.

To get closer to the decision-making process, we can once again break up investment into its three major parts and write:

$$\Delta O = \Delta a \,^\circ Q + a(\Delta I_i + \Delta I_a + \Delta I_g) \quad \dots\dots\dots\dots\dots (2)$$

For our present purposes we can ignore induced investment. Only if significantly high rates of increase in current income and demand are achieved will induced investment be quantitatively significant; in other words, if short-lived inflationary booms are avoided, induced investment will become significant only if development plans are successful. Thus

$$I = I_g + I_a(\overset{\circ}{K}, \overset{\circ}{T}) \quad \dots\dots\dots\dots\dots\dots\dots\dots\dots (3)$$

Substituting in (2)

$$\Delta O = \Delta a \,^\circ Q + a(\Delta I_g + \Delta I_a)(\overset{\circ}{K}, \overset{\circ}{T}) \quad \dots\dots\dots\dots\dots (3a)$$

This formulation tells us a good deal about the content and purpose of a development plan. An effective plan must be designed to do the following things:

1) Increase government investment, at least to the point at which opportunities for private investment are maximized. Over a very wide range public investment can provide the impulse to increased private investment. When government investment reaches a level at which it is competing for scarce resources with private enterprise, it may still be worth expanding it if the stimulating effects on the rate of resource discovery and technological progress lead to a net increase in private investment nonetheless, or if it raises the output:capital ratio so as to more than offset any net drop in private investment. The methods of financing government investment should be of a sort that will not discourage private investment or result in less effective use of existing capital.

2) Increase the rate of resource discovery and technological progress. In part this objective can be obtained through government expenditures on geological surveys, research, transport facilities, etc. In part it involves providing incentives to private exploration and development through tax policy, foreign-exchange policy, land policy, patents, etc.

3) Raise the parameter "I_a"; that is, encourage a higher level of private investment with the existing rate of resource discovery and technological progress. This might be done by training indigenous managers, entrepreneurs, and technicians; by reducing effective rates of interest and making credit more readily available; by encouraging a "long view" through promotion of confidence, assuring physical security, insurance schemes, etc.; by improved foreign-exchange policy; and by improving the climate for foreign investment.

4) Raise the output:capital ratio (reduce the incremental capital output ratio). This can be done by training managers and workers, inducing improved factor-proportions, improving the product-mix, introducing capital-saving innovations, etc.

Thus the task of financing economic development is reduced to providing funds for public investment in a manner that does not bring avoidable reductions in private investment or in the output:capital ratio, and providing incentives to increased private investment and more efficient use of the existing stock of capital.

A formulation of this kind provides us with broad outlines of development policy, but it does not provide us with an explanation of underdevelopment. Nor does it tell us how to allocate an investment budget or how to encourage and direct increases in private investment.

We might be well advised, then, to abandon the hope for a truly general theory at this stage, and to work toward a theory of underdevelopment, which could eventually be made sufficiently rigorous and realistic to provide guides for policy. There have been a few attempts at a theory of underdevelopment, notably the Boeke theory of dual societies. While the notion of dualism is a useful one, this theory was not presented in systematic form, and it contained basic errors.[3] However, the intensive study of the problem of underdevelopment during the last decade has produced a number of carefully-stated partial theories. If we select from these partial theories those which best fit the facts, and weave them together into a general theory, we can even now take a very long step toward the construction of a general theory of underdevelopment.

No part of what follows is completely original. I have selected components of my theory from the available literature, in terms of my own experience in underdeveloped countries. However, I have altered and interpreted the theories to suit my own purposes, and I have added them together in a way that may be quite unacceptable to their authors. Thus none of the writers whose theories I have utilized can be held responsible for the general conclusions I reach.

II. The Population Multiplier

In many underdeveloped countries the initial favorable impact of industrial investment (including investment in plantations as well as in mines, petroleum, etc.) was swamped by population growth, in a way which was not true in the now advanced countries. The first wave of rapid industrialization was sometimes followed by an initial increase in per capita income. In the advanced countries of the West the rise in per capita income was sustained long enough to bring subsequent drops in fertility rates, permitting economic growth to be sustained. Why was the process in underdeveloped countries different?

When the colonial powers first came into contact with countries of Asia and Africa, the populations of the latter countries were apparently not much higher, relative to natural resources, than those of European countries. Even at the beginning of the nineteenth century, populations of many Asian countries were still small relative to resources, and prospects for economic growth would still have been good. By the end of that century, however, the population growth in countries like Indonesia, India, Japan, and the Philippines was already such that launching a steady rise in per capita incomes had become a difficult problem.

The major impact of industrial investment on the rate of population growth probably came through the accompanying reduction in mortality rates. As the colonial powers shifted from trading to settlement, in order to exploit more effectively their new interest in plantations and mines (and later in petroleum) they became more interested in the maintenance of law and order. In maintaining law and order they hampered the freedom of the native peoples to kill each other. As settlers they also became interested in a higher level of public health. In protecting themselves from malaria, plague, and other diseases, they reduced the incidence of these diseases among the native peoples as well. Improved transport reduced the danger of famine. Educational standards also rose, which may have had an indirect effect on mortality rates. Finally, the initial rise in per capita incomes of native peoples permitted--if it did not cause--a more rapid rise in the size of the population.[4]

There is some evidence that the drop in fertility rates in Europe and the New World was a concomitant of urbanization. Development in Asia and Africa, centered as it was on plantations, mines, oil fields, and exports of raw materials, brought more industrialization than urbanization; the checks on family size brought by the urban industrialization of Europe and the New World operated less effectively in the underdeveloped countries. The drops in fertility rates did eventually come in most of these countries, but too late to prevent serious population pressure from arising before planned economic development began.

Role of Colonial Policy

In part, the difference in the pattern of development in the Asian-African countries and in that of Europe reflects colonial policy. Initial investment in Europe and the New World was also directed in large measure toward agricultural improvement, mining, and the production of raw materials for export. However, this investment gave rise in advanced countries to subsequent marked expansion of the secondary and tertiary sectors of the economy. It was no part of colonial policy in most of the Asian and African countries to permit development of the secondary and tertiary sectors in the colonies themselves. Where domestic entrepreneurship appeared in the "western" sector it was usually discouraged.[5] Thus the secondary and tertiary sectors associated with industrial investment in the colonies developed in the metropolitan countries rather than in the Asian and African countries themselves. The financing, transporting, storing, insuring, and processing of industrial raw materials took place mainly <u>outside</u> the colonial country.

Industrialization which is confined to the production of raw materials does not lead to urbanization. Indeed, it can proceed quite far without disrupting very much the pattern of village life in which the bulk of the people live. There is good reason to suppose, then, that the disastrously long lag between the initial drop in mortality rates and the subsequent drop in fertility rates is associated with the peculiar form of industrialization in underdeveloped countries, a form which did not bring with it rapid urbanization.[6]

We might express the "population multiplier" principle in systematic form as follows: Let "K" be a constant number (say five); "N" is total employment; "N_a" is employment in "agriculture" (the rural sector); "N_i" is employment in "industry" (plantations, mines, oil fields, and manufacturing); and "j" is a capital:job ratio. We assume that the total population in each sector (L_i, L_a) bears a fixed relationship to employment in that sector, expressed by the constants "i" and "a."

$$L = L_i + L_a \dots \dots \dots \dots \dots \dots \dots \dots \dots \dots (1)$$

$$= i \circ N_i + a \circ N_a \dots \dots \dots \dots \dots \dots \dots (2)$$

$$\Delta N_i = \frac{I_i}{j_i} \dots \dots \dots \dots \dots \dots \dots \dots \dots \dots (3)$$

$$\Delta L_i = i \circ \frac{I_i}{j_i} \dots \dots \dots \dots \dots \dots \dots \dots \dots (3a)$$

$$\Delta L = K\Delta L_i = Ki\Delta N_i = Ki\frac{I_i}{j_i} \dots \dots \dots \dots \dots (4)$$

$$\text{and } \Delta N_a = Ki\left(\frac{I_i}{j_i}\right) - i \circ \frac{I_i}{j_i} \dots \dots \dots \dots \dots \dots (4a)$$

$$\text{and } \Delta N_a = K\left(\frac{I_i}{j_i}\right) - \left(\frac{I_i}{j_i}\right) \dots \dots \dots \dots \dots \dots (4b)$$

In this simplified model, industrial investment leaves the ratio of industrial to agricultural employment (and population) unchanged. If "K" is equal to five, industrial population remains at 20 per cent of the total throughout the growth process, and we have what Professor V. K. R. V. Rao has called "a static economy in progress"; that is, after the initial impact, industrial investment brings no further structural change.

III. Technological Dualism

If the industrial investment which launched the "population explosion" in Asia and Africa had provided opportunities for productive employment for the whole of the population increase, per capita incomes could still have risen. But industrialization in the form common to underdeveloped countries did not provide a proportionate increase in job opportunities. The Eckaus analysis of factor proportions applied to the case of two sectors--two factors of production and two goods--is enlightening in this regard.[7] While such a model is necessarily a simplified one, it is a close enough approximation to reality to provide significant results. The two sectors are the industrial sector (plantations, mines, oil fields, refineries, etc.) and a rural sector engaged in production of foodstuffs and in handicrafts or very small industries. The first of these sectors is capital-intensive. Moreover, it either is characterized in fact by relatively fixed technical coefficients (fixed proportions in which factors of production must be combined), or is assumed by entrepreneurs to be so. The effect on employment patterns is much the same in either case. The rural sector has variable technical coefficients; that is, the products could be produced with a wide range of factor proportions. The two factors of production are labor on the one hand, and capital, including improved land, on the other. The two products are industrial raw materials for exports, and necessities for domestic consumption.

At the beginning of the expansion process, no factor of production was relatively abundant or scarce. However, once the "population explosion" occurred, labor became a relatively abundant factor of production. In some periods the percentage rate of increase in population probably exceeded the rate at which capital was accumulated in the industrial sector. Because of the relatively fixed technical coefficients in that sector, employment opportunities were not provided at the same rate as that at which the population grew. Far from bringing a shift from the rural sector to the industrial sector, industrialization, after its first impact, may well have brought a relative decline in the proportion of total employment in that sector.

Thus the increased population had to seek a livelihood in the other, variable coefficient sector. The ratio of labor to capital available in that sector rose steadily, and since technical coefficients were variable, techniques in that sector became increasingly labor-intensive. For a while, the response to population growth was to bring additional land under cultivation, in order to keep the ratio of labor to land relatively constant; but since other forms of capital were not available in any quantity, the amount of land that could be effectively worked by one family was limited. Eventually, good land tended to become scarce. Where possible, more and more labor-intensive techniques--such as irrigated rice culture--were undertaken. Finally, the point was reached where the marginal productivity of labor fell below subsistence level, if not to zero, even with the most labor-intensive techniques. Disguised unemployment began to appear.

Under these conditions, there was no incentive for groups of individual farmers or small enterprises to make marginal and unrelated

investments of capital in the labor-intensive sector, nor to introduce
labor-saving innovations. And as yet there is no technology designed
to raise output per manhour without also raising the ratio of capital to
labor. Nor was there any incentive for labor as a group to increase
its efforts, since the labor supply was already redundant. Thus methods remained labor-intensive, and levels of technique, manhour productivity, and economic and social welfare remained low.

The tendency toward disguised unemployment in the rural sector
will be enhanced if technological progress takes a form favoring the
capital-intensive sector. There can be little doubt that this process
is what in fact occurred. Indeed, during the last two centuries there
has been little or no technological progress in peasant agriculture
and handicrafts, whereas technological progress in the plantations,
mining, and petroleum sector has been rapid. The tendency toward
disguised unemployment in the rural sector will also be aggravated if
wage rates are kept artificially high by trade union activities or by
government policy. Industrial wage rates which are high relative to
productivity provide an incentive for the introduction of labor-saving
devices, and consequently diminish still further the capacity of the
industrialized sector to absorb the population growth.[8]

Conflict between Output and Employment

Dr. Eckaus' analysis also shows that there can be a conflict between full employment and the maximization of output in an underdeveloped economy if the pattern of demand does not fit the factor en-
dowment. Unless the indifference maps for the two "commodities"
are such that a relatively large share of income is spent on the commodity produced by labor-intensive methods, the allocation of resources that would provide an optimal output may imply unemployment
if the labor supply is large relative to the supply of capital. When we
put the underdeveloped countries into their world setting, it is clear
that the actual pattern of demand was such as to bring increasing conflict between the objectives of optimal output and full employment.
For the output of underdeveloped countries is comprised of a world
market for export goods, and a domestic market for the produce of
the rural sector. Whatever the pattern of demand was when the expansion process began, it is apparent that in the course of time the
demand for exports grew at a much higher percentage rate than the
demand for domestic products. Indeed, under the conditions described
above, the demand for output of the rural sector grew only at the rate
at which the total population increased, if not more slowly. The demand for exports, geared to the much more rapidly expanding European economy, increased at a much faster rate. Moreover, the demand from the world market rules in the political as well as the economic sense; achieving the optimal allocation of resources from the

standpoint of the <u>European</u> entrepreneurs and administrators meant an increasing conflict of that goal with the maintenance of full employment in the rural sector of underdeveloped countries. No such conflict arose in the advanced countries. Thus the market forces were such as to bring increasing discrepancies between the standards of living of the rapidly industrializing European countries and those of the underdeveloped countries.

The Solow Model of Economic Growth

The primary aim of Solow's growth model was to show the limitations on the Harrod-Domar formulation of requirements for steady growth in advanced economies. He demonstrates in his article that "this fundamental opposition of warranted and natural rates turns out in the end to flow from the crucial assumption that production takes place under conditions of fixed proportions."[9] However, his model can also be used to analyze underdevelopment. If we select from his various cases those which seem to conform most closely to the actual conditions of underdeveloped countries, we can show that our thesis regarding technological dualism need not rely on the assumption of fixed technical coefficients in the capital-intensive sector.

Solow demonstrates that with variable technical coefficients there will be a tendency for the capital-labor ratio to adjust itself through time in the direction of an equilibrium ratio. If the initial ratio of capital to labor is above the equilibrium value, capital and output will grow more slowly than the labor force. Applying this analysis to the rural sector of underdeveloped countries, we begin again with a small population and a substantial amount of "capital," which here includes land. The ratio of capital to labor, while low, is nevertheless above the <u>equilibrium</u> ratio. After the initial increase in the labor force, there would be a move toward more labor-intensive techniques. The ratio of capital (including improved land) to labor would then be held constant at the equilibrium rate until land began to give out. From there on, to maintain the equilibrium ratio would require the allocation of more capital, either in the form of land or in some other form, to the rural sector; but under the conditions of technological dualism this will not happen. Instead, once the land gives out, the marginal productivity of labor will fall below minimal real wage rates, and unemployment will begin to appear.[10]

Solow's Figure 2 (p. 71) indicates the possibility of multiple equilibrium, with one unstable equilibrium between the rate of growth and the ratio of capital to labor, and with two stable equilibrium points, one with a high ratio of capital to labor and one with a low ratio of capital to labor. If the expansion process begins with a relatively high ratio of capital to labor, the system will tend toward a high rate of growth with capital-intensive techniques. If, on the other hand, the expansion begins with a low ratio of capital to labor it will move toward an equilibrium rate of growth with labor-intensive techniques. Applying this analysis to our two sectors, we see the strong likelihood that the industrial sector, which starts with a relatively high ratio of capital to labor, would move toward an equilibrium expansion path with a high ratio of capital to labor, even if technical coefficients were not fixed. In the rural sector, on the other hand, beginning as it did with a high ratio of labor to capital, the tendency will be toward an expansion path which will retain a still lower ratio of capital to labor.

In his Figure 3 (Fig. 1 below) Solow[11] indicates the possibility of the absence of equilibrium, which comes still closer to our historical case. In this diagram the ray nr represents steady growth equal to

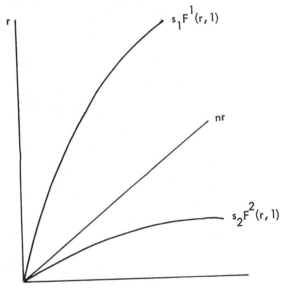

Figure 1 (Solow Figure 3)

both the warranted and natural rates, with a constant ratio of capital to labor and continuous full employment. The curve $s_1F^1(r,1)$ represents a system which "is so productive and saves so much that perpetual full employment will increase the capital labor ratio (and also output per head) beyond all limits; capital and income both increase more rapidly than the labor supply." The curve $s_2F^2(r,1)$ represents a system which "is so unproductive that the full employment path leads only to a forever diminishing income per capita. Since net investment is always positive and labor is increasing, aggregate income can only rise." Clearly, the first system conforms closely to the industrial sector of underdeveloped countries; the effective labor supply expands less rapidly than the capital inflow to that sector, for reasons elaborated below. Entrepreneurs never reach the point of considering it worth while to train skilled labor, and real income remains so low that even the supply of unskilled labor may be limited from their point of view.

Of course population grows and the number of the people in the rural sector continues to grow with it. The second system thus conforms to the rural sector, where population growth ultimately brings a conflict between maximizing output and full employment.

Unfortunately, Solow felt that "it would take us too far afield to go wholly classical with a theory of population growth and a fixed supply of land" (pp. 87-88)—unfortunately, since this classical model is the one which would conform most closely to the rural sector of underdeveloped countries. Solow does indicate that in such a model, where savings can fall to zero with income still positive, net investment might cease and the capital stock become stationary while the labor force still grows. He shies away from this case; but it is clear that in such circumstances disguised unemployment must appear as soon as marginal productivity of labor falls below minimal real wage rates. Obviously, too, with fixed techniques, a fixed supply of land, and continuing population growth, per capita income in the rural sector must eventually decline.

Professor Solow's Figure 9 (Fig. 2 below) is also interesting in this context. Here he treats population growth as a function of per capita income (and so of the capital-labor ratio) instead of treating it as an autonomous variable. The pattern of population growth implied in this diagram is that "for very low levels of income per head or real wage population tends to decrease; for higher levels of income it begins to increase, and that for still higher levels of income the

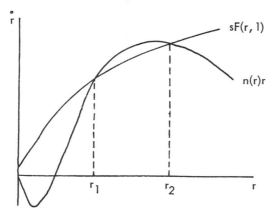

Figure 2 (Solow Figure 9)

rate of population growth levels off and starts to decline." The result
is something close to Leibenstein's "minimum effort thesis," to be
discussed more fully below. At any initial ratio of capital to labor
below r_2, the system will revert to equilibrium at the low ratio of
capital to labor r_1, with the correspondingly low rate of increase of
output. If we start with a capital-labor ratio anywhere below r_2, the
only way to assure cumulative growth is to make a sudden jump to a
ratio of capital to labor above r_2. Combining this analysis with our
discussion of population, we can readily see that because of the tendency for increases in investment confined to the industrial sector to
accelerate population growth, a <u>gradual</u> approach to r_2 is unlikely to
be effective.

Finally, Professor Solow introduces rigid wage rates, and concludes that if the ratio of wage rates to price corresponds to a capital-
labor ratio that would normally tend to decrease (or drop to less than
zero), unemployment develops and vice versa. Once again, these are
the conditions in the rural sector of underdeveloped countries; once
the first wave of population growth takes place and land becomes relatively scarce, the "fixed" real wage rate, which is a customary subsistence level, tends to be above the marginal productivity of labor.
With a low initial ratio of capital to labor and rapid population growth,
this relationship is precisely what emerges. Thus the Solow analysis,
while starting from a quite different point, tends to corroborate the
conclusions derived by applying the Eckaus analysis of factor proportions.

The Myint Model

Professor Hla Myint presents his own version of the dualistic
theory of underdevelopment.[12] He proposes the following model.
(1) The country starts its period of expansion, resulting from its being
opened up to economic relations with the outside world, "with a fairly
sparse population in relation to its potential natural resources."
(2) Its natural resources are then developed in the direction of a few
specialized lines of primary production for export. This development
is generally carried out by foreign private enterprise, assisted by
government policy, and is limited by the expansion of the world market
for the export goods. (3) The native inhabitants of the country enjoy
legal equality with other people in their economic relations, including
the right to own any type of property and to enter into any type of oc-
cupation. (In some colonial countries this assumption did not hold;
but it is all the more interesting that the Myint model does not <u>need</u>
discrimination against native people to show the tendency toward
technological dualism.) In such a model, Professor Myint points out,
"The disequalizing factors must be considered as operating not only
between the backward and the advanced countries as aggregate units,

but also between the backward and advanced groups of peoples within the same backward country itself" (p. 146). The usual "country A and B" approach "is seriously inadequate for our purpose." Disaggregation, at least to the extent of recognizing the two major sectors, is necessary if we are to obtain useful results.

Professor Myint suggests that before the underdeveloped countries were "opened up," they were "primitive or medieval stationary states governed by habits and customs. Their people might have lived near the 'minimum subsistence level,' but that standard, according to their own lights, did not appear too wretched or inadequate. Thus in spite of low discontent and frustration: wants and activities are on the whole adapted to each other and the people were in equilibrium with their environment" (p. 149).

He then moves on to the second stage, "particularly in the second half of the nineteenth century," when "these stationary backward societies were opened up to the outside economic forces. . . . Measures for economic development then consisted mainly in attempts to persuade or force the backward people into the new ways of life represented by the money economy--for example, by stimulating their demand for imports and by taxing them so that they were obliged to turn to cash crops or work in the newly opened mines and plantations."[13] The yardstick of development of such countries was their export and taxable capacity. However, the "opening up" process drew increasing numbers of the native peoples into a new elite, in which the values of Western society were increasingly accepted. This gave rise to "a sense of economic discontent and maladjustment." It was in this third stage that the political problems associated with underdevelopment appeared.

The form of development in such dualistic economies was not such as to require a high degree of specialization among the native peoples:

In spite of the striking specialization of the inanimate productive equipment and of the individuals from the economically advanced groups of people who manage and control them, there is really very little specialization beyond a natural adaptability to the tropical climate, among the backward peoples in their roles as unskilled labourers or peasant producers. . . . Thus all the specialization required for the export market seems to have been done by the other co-operating factors, the whole production structure being built around the supply of cheap undifferentiated labour. . . . Even where a new cash crop is introduced, the essence of its success as a peasant crop depends on the fact that it does not represent a radical departure from the existing techniques of production (e.g., yams and cocoa in West Africa).[14]

Indeed, Professor Myint goes so far as to suggest that the process of specialization of a backward economy for the export market is most rapid and successful when it leaves the backward peoples in their unspecialized roles as unskilled laborers and peasant producers using traditional methods of production.

Dual or Plural?

Professor Myint also draws attention to another characteristic of the dualistic--or more properly in this context, plural--economy, which has been noted by other observers as well: that the middlemen between the big European concerns and the indigenous population are very often foreigners also. He mentions the Indians and Chinese in Southeast Asia, Indians in East Africa, Syrians and "Coast Africans" in West Africa, and so on. He might also have mentioned the Indians in his own country of Burma. These middlemen collect produce from peasant farmers, distribute imported articles to the indigenous consumers, and act as money lenders.[15] They act as a buffer between the indigenous population and the advanced Western society, thus robbing them of "the educating and stimulating effect of a direct contact." Even skilled labor was brought in from abroad. Professor Knowles has said that in the British Empire of the nineteenth century there were three "mother countries": the United Kingdom, India, and China. Immigrant labor from India and China was deliberately introduced into Southeast Asia, Fiji, the West Indies, and part of East and South Africa.

True, some opportunities for the acquisition of skills did occur on the plantations and in the mines, but these were diluted by the high labor turnover. The backward peoples are unused to the discipline of the mines and plantations, and have one foot in their traditional, tribal, and village economies. They look upon wage labor "not as a continuous permanent employment but as a temporary or periodical expedient to earn a certain sum of money." Thus, "even after many decades of rapid economic development following the opening up process, the peoples of many backward countries still remain almost as ignorant and unused to the ways of modern economic life as they were before."

The Asian type of middleman, selling consumers goods, advancing seed and simple tools on a share-cropping basis, and lending money, was by no means unknown to the West. In the American South or the Canadian West, such middlemen were also buffers between the small farmers and the advancing technology of the big cities. The difference is that at a certain point it paid the middlemen as a class to take over the land altogether in the West--to foreclose on their tardy debtors--and to amalgamate small holdings into units large enough to permit large-scale, extensive, mechanized, and commercial agriculture. From there on, the advance of technology spread to agriculture as well as to industry.

The question is, then, why this process did not take place in underdeveloped countries. Why have the middlemen in Asia and Africa continued to squeeze the peasants, rather than maneuvering them into a position where they could foreclose on their land?

To find an answer to this question, the Myint point must be added to the analysis presented above. In Europe and the New World, a time came when manpower was obviously scarce in the agricultural sector, making it profitable for individual farmers to increase the size of their holdings and to use more capital-intensive methods. The barrier to agricultural improvement in the underdeveloped countries has been the fact that labor never became scarce in the rural sector. The "population explosion," brought by industrial investment in the capital-intensive sector, meant that there was an adequate supply of labor, and later a superabundance of it, in the peasant-agriculture sector. Thus in Asia and Africa the middleman has continued to play his traditional role, directing his efforts to maximizing his share of the output obtainable through labor-intensive methods, rather than endeavoring to get the peasant off the land in order to cultivate it himself by more land-and-capital-intensive methods. [16]

IV. International Trade as an Aggravating Factor

There is some evidence that engagement by underdeveloped countries in international trade, far from encouraging their growth, has actually retarded it by aggravating the dualistic nature of the economy. The argument has been cast in terms of a long-run tendency for the terms of trade to turn against countries exporting raw materials and foodstuffs, and in terms of a tendency for "backwash" (unfavorable) effects to outweigh "spread" (stimulating) effects.

Trends in Terms of Trade

Two arguments have been made concerning a tendency for the terms of trade to turn against underdeveloped countries. One of these arguments relates to the external terms of trade of the country as a whole with the rest of the world; the second relates to the terms of trade between the rural sector, in which the great bulk of the indigenous people live, and the advanced industrial sector (including importers) of the same country.

Of the two arguments, the one relating to the internal terms of trade is most clear cut. Not only has technological progress been confined mainly to the industrial sector, as shown above, but the industrial sector has developed increasingly powerful monopoly positions vis a vis the rural sector. In a typical process of development, Myint points out:

The backward peoples have to contend with three types of monopolistic forces: in their role as unskilled labor they have to face the big foreign mining and plantation concerns who are monopolistic buyers of their labour; in their role as peasant producers they have to face a small group of exporting and processing firms who are monopolistic buyers of their crop; and in their role as consumers of imported commodities they have to face the same group of firms who are the monopolistic sellers or distributors of these commodities. [17]

In advanced countries, such tendencies toward monopolistic exploitation are offset by the development of "countervailing power," to use Professor Galbraith's term. No such countervailing power emerged in the underdeveloped countries prior to their achieving independence. Even now the workers and peasants have a long way to go before their organization will give them really effective bargaining powers. "The first lesson," says Professor Myint, "is that some sources of countervailing power, like the co-operative societies, themselves need a fairly high degree of business-like behaviour and 'economic advance' and can only be fostered very slowly in the backward countries. The second lesson is that it is easier to redistribute existing income than to redistribute and stimulate economic activity by the use of countervailing power."[18] Moreover, he points out, countervailing power is sometimes sought in the preservation of traditional social institutions, which do not provide equivalent bargaining power in an economic sense.

The deterioration of the terms of trade of the rural sector, in its relations with the industrial sector of the same country, must of course be reflected in the terms of trade of the rural sector with the rest of the world. Obviously, it is the terms of trade of the rural sector with the rest of the world that is important to the great majority of the people in the country. In advanced countries the primary sector accounts for a small share of income and employment, and agricultural productivity is several times as high as in the rural sector of underdeveloped countries. It seems highly likely, then, that there has been--and is still--a trend toward deteriorating terms of trade of the rural sector of underdeveloped countries with the rest of the world.

The case is less clear concerning the export sector of underdeveloped countries, and it is on this question that controversy has been most keen. There is some evidence that over recent decades the terms of trade of countries exporting raw materials and importing manufactured goods have deteriorated; there is no assurance that this trend must continue in the future. So long as we think in traditional terms of relative prices of exports and imports, we are hampered in calculating terms of trade by the increasing prevalence of multiple exchange rates and the difficulty of deciding what exchange rate is appropriate for such a calculation. On the other hand, if we think in terms of manhours, and calculate how many manhours' production in the export industries of other countries can be purchased by "x" manhours' work in the export industries of underdeveloped countries, there is indeed good reason to suppose that the terms of trade have been moving against underdeveloped countries, and will continue to do so until means are found of raising manhour productivity in industries producing agricultural raw materials and foodstuffs.

Professor Myint has suggested that the shift of terms of trade in their favor was a major factor in accelerating economic growth of the now industrialized countries.[19] It meant that "x" manhours' worth of imports of raw materials and foodstuffs could be purchased with a smaller number of manhours' worth of exports; thus, in effect, it released manhours which could be diverted to building up the capital structure without an increase in domestic saving. In this sense it meant that the saving was done for the advancing countries by the peoples in the stagnant ones. If this argument is correct, it applies also in reverse; the deteriorating terms of trade made it increasingly difficult for the underdeveloped countries to accumulate capital, without sacrificing consumption from the already low levels.

Backwash versus Spread Effects

Myint also argues that the growth of foreign trade failed to bring overall economic growth. It is not as though these countries had no development of any kind. During the nineteenth and twentieth centuries the countries of Asia and Africa had very rapid development of the export sector. Capital was not especially scarce in the export sector of underdeveloped countries: "The foreign firms in the export sectors were normally able to borrow capital on equal terms with firms of comparable credit worthiness in the advanced countries." Why did the growth in value of exports have no multiplier effects on per capita incomes in the rest of the economy?

Myint lists as factors operating against "spread effects" the high turnover of labor, their willingness to accept very low wages, the conviction among employees that the supply curve of labor was backward sloping, and the general lack of industrial skills, which made entrepreneurs feel that recruiting an adequate labor force was a difficult affair. Wages were low, but were not considered low relative to estimates of efficiency. "The attempt to switch over from the cheap labor policy to a policy of higher wages and more intensive use of labor usually involved taking decisions about 'lumpy investments' both in the form of plant and machinery and in the form of camps and villages where it was necessary to change over from a casual to a permanent labor force."

Professor Myint stresses the reluctance of European entrepreneurs to make heavy investments of a kind which would require a large supply of skilled workers, and their preference for simple labor-intensive techniques which left labor productivity low and afforded few training facilities. As we have already seen, however, the factors cited by Myint also provided an incentive for a shift to wholly capital-intensive techniques, requiring relatively few workers of any level of skill, where these were technically possible. The result was some of each. Thus we find on the same plantation labor-and-land-intensive methods, of a sort that give little generalized training, in the agricultural side of the operation, combined with capital-intensive techniques in the

processing part of the operation. It is the intermediate kind of technique, requiring fairly large numbers of workers in skilled occupations, which were shunned by entrepreneurs in underdeveloped countries; and, as Professor Myint suggests, it is these intermediate
techniques that provide the best means of training large numbers of
workers.

Finally, Professor Myint explains the lack of spread effects from
development of the export sector by an appeal to the concept of "non-
competing groups":

Thus it may be possible to find an analogue of non-competing groups in the
foreign and domestic sectors of the backward countries which contributes to
a lack of secondary rounds of activities. This leads us to the second argument, that the dynamic gains from specialization in industry are likely to be
greater because it has a greater "educative" effect on the people of the country
than agriculture. Here it must be admitted that in contrast to the tremendous
stimulus to further economic development enjoyed by the advanced countries,
international trade seems to have had very little educative effect on the people
of backward countries except in the development of new wants. Apart from
the introduction of modern transport, it is difficult to observe any revolutionary changes in their methods of production and efficiency both in the peasant
and in the non-peasant sectors. The peasants specialize for international
trade simply by going on producing traditional crops by traditional methods
or new crops which can be readily produced by traditional methods.[20]

Professor Gunnar Myrdal makes a still stronger argument than
that of Professor Myint: because of "circular causation" and "backwash effects," he contends, the involvement of underdeveloped countries in international trade with advanced countries, far from bringing
a tendency toward equality of marginal productivity and incomes, resulted in a tendency away from equilibrium, a vicious spiral bringing
increasing discrepancies between productivity of advanced and underdeveloped countries.[21]

Myrdal begins his analysis with the tendency toward regional inequalities in a single country. The growing communities will exert a
strong agglomerative pull, accelerating their rate of growth and bringing increasing stagnation or decline in other parts of the country. No
offsetting forces arise to prevent the acceleration of this shift of economic activity from decadent to progressive regions. Any accident
or shock giving a momentary advantage to one region can start this
chain of disparate growth movements. Among such shifts in relative
advantages of regions of a country, Professor Myrdal singles out "a
change in the terms of trade of a community or a region" as one factor
which has historically played this role.

Among the aggravating forces, he says, will be demographic ones;
the poorer regions will be the ones with the relatively high fertility.
This factor, together with net immigration from the decadent regions,
makes the age distribution in these regions unfavorable. The poverty
in rural regions of Europe during the long period of net immigration
to industrial centers and to the United States, he says, "has a main

explanation in the unfavorable age distribution there, caused by migration and in part also by higher fertility rates."

The expansion of trade only aggravates the process. "The freeing and widening of the markets will often confer such competitive advantages on the industries in already established centres of expansion, which usually work under conditions of increasing returns, that even the handicrafts and industries existing earlier in the other regions are thwarted." He cites as a dramatic example of the growth of regional disparities following liberation of trade, the expansion of the north and retrogression of the south of Italy following political unification in 1860. For one thing, regions which "have not been touched by the expansionary momentum could not afford to keep up a good road system and all their other public utilities would be inferior."[22]

True, expansion in one region also has spread effects; the growth of industrial cities, for example, should create a demand both for agricultural raw materials and for consumers' goods. There is, however, no reason for equilibrium between backwash and spread effects. The analysis above provides some reason for assuming that the backwash effects will be predominant. The spread effects could outweigh the backwash effects only if income and employment in the leading sectors grow relative to that of the laggard sector, as it did in the now advanced countries. The historical pattern of growth in underdeveloped countries, however, has been such that spread effects were weak. The rural sector (as defined above) did not produce the raw materials for the expanding industrial sector, nor did the expanding industrial sector rely heavily on the rural sector for foodstuffs. (Rice was not the major item in the food budgets of the British, Dutch, or Spanish in their colonies.) Thus the market for cash crops of the rural sector was not much expanded by the growth of the industrial sector.[23]

These inherent tendencies toward integration in advanced countries and leading and lagging sectors in underdeveloped ones were strengthened by national policy. The poorer countries--especially the colonial ones--did not have effective policies for national integration, of the sort that have been introduced in the more highly developed ones:

> Generally speaking, on a low level of economic development with relatively weak spread effects, the competitive forces in the markets will, by circular causation, constantly be tending towards regional inequalities, while the inequalities themselves will be holding back economic development, and at the same time weakening the power basis for egalitarian policies. A higher level of development will strengthen the spread effects and tend to hamper the drift towards regional inequalities; this will sustain economic development, and at the same time create more favourable conditions for policies directed at decreasing regional inequalities still further.[24]

It is perfectly possible, Professor Myrdal argues, for international trade to have "strong backwash effects on the underdeveloped countries." The present pattern of production in underdeveloped countries reflects these backwash effects rather than true comparative advantage. Rather than increasing further production of primary goods for export the true advantage of these countries may lie in improving the productivity of the rural sector, and in the development of manufacturers. Nor can capital be expected to flow to underdeveloped countries simply because capital is relatively scarce there. On the contrary, in the absence of exchange controls, capital would flow out of the underdeveloped countries to the more advanced (and more rapidly advancing) ones. International adjustment through migration is no longer possible.

The present pattern of production in underdeveloped countries also reflects the past policies of the colonial powers, which often "took special measures to hamper the growth of indigenous industry." This colonial heritage is not dispelled by political independence alone. The "cumulative social processes holding it down in stagnation or regression" are still there. And "colonialism meant primarily not only a strengthening of all the forces in markets which anyhow were working towards internal and international inequalities. It built itself into, and gave an extra impetus and a peculiar character to, the circular causation of the cumulative process."[25]

Unlimited Supplies of Labor?

Similar conclusions are reached in more systematic fashion by W. Arthur Lewis in his well-known article "Economic Development with Unlimited Supplies of Labour."[26] This article begins with the assertion that many underdeveloped countries conform to the classical model, in which the supply of labor is perfectly elastic at current wage rates. The "widow's cruse" of workers consists of farmers, casual workers, petty traders, domestic retainers, and population growth. Since his conclusions rest on this basic observation, let us begin by examining the observation itself.

Some observers, including the present one, have pointed out that the early optimism regarding development by absorption of disguised unemployment from agriculture was unfounded; in point of fact it is not possible to transfer large numbers of workers permanently and full-time from peasant agriculture to industry without a drop in agricultural output. During planting and harvesting seasons, which together amount to several weeks per year, the entire labor force is occupied. It may even be necessary to bring back members of the village who have gone off to take casual jobs in the industrial sector. It is true that reorganization of agriculture and a shift to relatively extensive and mechanized techniques could release large numbers of workers from agriculture, but that can be done only with a certain amount of investment in the agricultural sector itself. Even the urban peddler, with three empty bottles in one basket and two right shoes in

the other, may be performing a real service if there are customers
who have left shoes and who want empty bottles. Thus in the static
sense, it may be questioned whether supply curves of labor to the
industrial sector are perfectly elastic.

If one puts the whole growth process in time, however, as he must
if he is to get meaningful results, the Lewis model is in accord with
reality in many underdeveloped countries so far as unskilled labor is
concerned. The Lewis argument does not require disguised unemployment. It requires three conditions: that the wage rate in the industrial
sector be above the marginal productivity of labor in the rural sector
by a small but fixed amount; that investment in the industrial sector
be not absolutely large relative to population growth; and that the cost
of training the necessary numbers of skilled workers be constant
through time. The first condition seems to be met in many countries.
If the "population multiplier" operates, the second condition is automatically guaranteed. But even if industrial investment does not actually accelerate population growth, the second condition can be met
if employment in the industrial sector is a small proportion of the
total and population growth is fairly high. Suppose, for example, that
the labor force is twenty million, that four million are employed in
the industrial sector, that the capital:job ratio in that sector is $2,000
per man, and that the total labor force grows at the rate of 2 per cent
per year. To employ the total increase in the labor force in the industrial sector would require net investment of $800 million next
year, or by 10 per cent of the total stock of capital. Net investment
on this scale would double the stock of capital in about eight years, a
rate of growth beyond the wildest dreams of most underdeveloped
countries. Thus for all practical purposes the supply of unskilled
labor to the industrial sector can be treated as perfectly elastic, while
in the rural sector it is already redundant in the sense that marginal
productivity there is below the subsistence standard of living.

Of course the industrial employers are interested in skilled labor,
too. Lewis argues that labor skills are only a "quasi-bottleneck"; if
you have unskilled workers you can convert them into skilled ones.

In the short run, the necessity of training or importing skilled
workers may not alter the argument very much; if the cost of training
or importing is constant, the elasticity of supply of skilled labor can
still be infinite. As we have seen already, it is possible that the cost
of training or importing technicians may be high enough to induce
entrepreneurs to use capital-intensive techniques in those parts of
their operation where skill is necessary; but this fact does not change
the argument either, unless these costs are rising. However, we have
seen that the Lewis thesis is of dubious validity even for unskilled
workers if we think in purely static terms; and if we think in terms
of long-run supply through time, the relevant question about the supply
of skills is whether or not the cost of training or importing is rising

through time. The answer will depend on the nature of technological progress; if it is of a sort which reduces both the capital:labor ratio and the capital:output ratio simultaneously, the Lewis thesis may hold for skilled labor as well as for unskilled.

Now if we accept the thesis, the process of growth will look like Figure 3. Here $\overline{w}$ is the productivity per manhour in peasant agriculture, and w is the conventional wage in the industrial sector. The

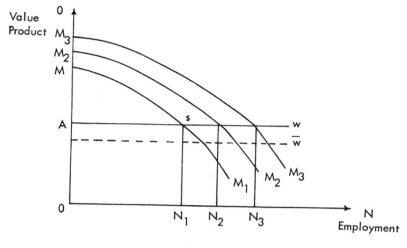

Figure 3

marginal productivity of labor in industry is MM_1, which permits the capitalist to earn a surplus, AMS. When he invests this surplus--perhaps improving techniques at the same time--the curve of marginal productivity shifts to MM_2; and so on. The per capita income of workers and peasants remains unchanged, and the entire benefits of development accrue to capitalists. Lewis suggests three ways in which the process might be halted: if the expansion of the industrial sector is rapid enough to reduce the absolute population in the rural sector, raising the manhour productivity in that sector, and so raising $\overline{w}$ and w (this will not happen if the population multiplier is operating); if technological progress in the rural sector raises productivity there, and so raises $\overline{w}$ and w; or if the terms of trade turn against the industrial sector with rising prices of food and raw materials, and so bring a rise in $\overline{w}$ and w (this is the classical model). The achievement of balanced growth and generally higher living standards requires that the process must be halted by either method one or method two, while at the same time measures are taken to continue investment in the industrial sector.

Lewis applies his analysis to the impact of international trade. First, he shows that technological progress in the export sector of underdeveloped countries helps only the workers of advanced countries. Suppose one man-day of labor in the advanced country "A" produces three food or three steel, while in the underdeveloped country "B" it produces one food or one rubber. The rates of exchange will then be one food equals one steel equals one rubber. Now assume that productivity in rubber-growing trebles. Then one steel will buy three rubber. But the wage in "B" is still equal to one food (plus the conventional surplus in the industrial sector) because the supply of labor to the rubber industry is unlimited. Thus foreign investment in the industrial sector of "B" can provide only additional employment and perhaps some taxes revenues; in itself it cannot raise per capita incomes.

Now assume a man-day in "A" produces three food or three cotton manufactures, while a man-day in "B" produces two food or one cotton manufactures. The marginal man-day in "A" produces three food or three cotton, and the marginal man-day in "B" produces zero food and one cotton. On the principle of comparative advantage, "B" should export cotton manufactures and import food. But "w" in cotton manufactures is two food in country "B"; and "w" is three to six food in country "A." In money terms, it is cheaper for "B" to export food and import cotton.

I agree wholeheartedly with Lewis in his conclusion that countries with inadequate agricultural resources relative to their population (India, Japan, Egypt, the United Kingdom) should export manufactures and import agricultural products. It is impossible to imagine India as a truly efficient agricultural country, but it is easy to imagine India as an efficient producer of steel and textiles. In my own view, this kind of misallocation of resources occurs in many underdeveloped countries. The implication is that planning must be based on "shadow prices" as they would prevail after a drastic structural change has been achieved.

Finally, Lewis indicates a way out of the vicious circle. Suppose a man-day in "A" produces five food or five cotton textiles, and a man-day in "B" produces one food or three cotton. Wages in "B" are one food, and "B" will export textiles. Wages in "A" are five food; "A" gets all the benefit from trade. Now suppose productivity is raised in "B's" cotton manufacturing industry. The wage in "B" is unchanged, and the entire benefit goes to "A," as before. But if productivity is raised in "B's" food production, "B's" wage will rise. Then cotton prices will also rise, to the benefit of "B" and the disadvantage of "A." Thus economic development requires raising productivity per man-day--not per acre--in the peasant agriculture sector. Given the rates of population growth in that sector, raising productivity per man-day almost requires a shift to more extensive and more mechanized agriculture.

One final point may be noted. The current nationalist policies, with their emphasis on training and upgrading of domestic labor, and limitations on immigration of skilled workers, managers, and technicians, may mean that skilled workers will be a more serious bottleneck to expansion in the future than they have been in the past. It is a question of whether techniques of training, as well as of production, can be improved sufficiently to keep training costs per unit of <u>output</u>, at least, from rising as industry expands.

VI. Discontinuities and the "Minimum Effort" Thesis

A number of writers have recently stressed the importance of discontinuities in the functions related to development and the consequent need for a "big push" or a "minimum effort" to launch a process of sustained growth. Dr. Rosenstein-Rodan has argued that the difference in the importance of external economies is one of the major marks of the difference between static theory and a theory of growth. In static theory external economies are indeed relatively unimportant.

In the theory of growth, however, external economies abound because given the inherent imperfection of the investment market, imperfect knowledge and risks, pecuniary and technological external economies have a similarly disturbing effect on the path towards equilibrium. While the distinction between pecuniary and technological external economies becomes practically irrelevant in the theory of growth, three different kinds of indivisibilities and external economies may be distinguished.

1) Indivisibilities in the production function, especially the indivisibility of supply of Social Overhead Capital (lumpiness of "capital").
2) "Indivisibility" of Demand (complementarity of demand).
3) "Indivisibility" (kink in the) Supply of Savings.[27]

Social overhead capital is the most important instance of indivisibility and externalities on the supply side. Its most important products "are investment opportunities created in other industries." Moreover, they usually require "a great minimum size," so that "excess capacity will be unavoidable over the initial period in underdeveloped countries." It is irreversible in time, and must precede other directly productive investment, have a high minimum durability, a long gestation period, a minimal industry mix, and its services cannot be imported.

The concept of indivisibility of demand has become widely known to workers in this field as a result of Dr. Rosenstein-Rodan's <u>Economic Journal</u> article and the discussion of the same problem by Ragnar Nurkse.[28] The indivisibility in the supply of savings is also familiar:

A high minimum quantun of investment requires a high volume of savings, which is difficult to achieve in low income underdeveloped countries. The way out of the vicious circle is to have first an increase in income . . . and to provide mechanisms which assure that every second stage the marginal rate of savings will be very much higher than the average rate of savings.[29]

I myself lay greater stress on what I have called the indivisibility of the decision-making process than on the three indivisibilities stressed by Rosenstein-Rodan. Allocation of capital on the basis of individual estimates of short-run returns on various marginal investment projects is the very process by which underdeveloped countries got where they are. The basic reason for government intervention for development purposes is that a set of individual private investment decisions may each seem unattractive in themselves, whereas an investment program undertaken as a unit may yield substantial increases in national income. True, it may be possible for the government to arrange for this lump-sum investment to be made by groups of private entrepreneurs; whether or not it should be done this way or through public investment is a matter of administrative convenience, not of economics. But the needed investment will not take place without government intervention in the decision-making process.

We turn now to Leibenstein's theory of the minimum effort.

Let us begin with an adaptation of one of Leibenstein's simple diagrams illustrating the relationships among population size, investment, and per capita income. Figure 4 (below) represents the adaptation to our own purposes of Leibenstein's Figure 3-2. Per capita income is measured on the vertical axis, population size on the horizontal axis. The straight line x = z represents the level of per capita income at which there is neither population growth nor capital accumulation.[30]

We are applying the diagram only to the rural sector of the underdeveloped economy. The curves r_1, r_2, r_3, etc. represent the relationship between average output and income and size of population for varying stocks of resources, including land. We begin with population at P_1, and per capita income at $Oa = P_1E_1$. We now introduce industrial investment in the capital-intensive sector. This investment will withdraw a small amount of population from the rural sector, and perhaps increase somewhat the resources available to the rural sector, in the form of improved roads and the like. Thus the impact effect of the commencement of industrialization is a movement to the left along the population curve, which in itself tends to raise per capita income, and a small shift in the average productivity curve to the right, r_2. On both accounts per capita income tends to rise. However, the result (or at least the accompaniment) of rising per capita income is an increase in population. Some net investment will now take place, mainly in the form of clearing new land, perhaps accompanied by some shift from "slash-and-burn" to irrigated agriculture.[31] Thus the average productivity curve shifts further to the right, to r_3.

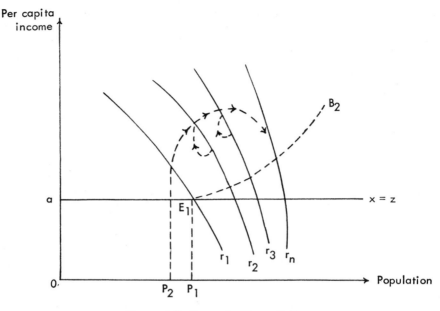

Figure 4 (Leibenstein Figure 3-2)

As population grows, per capita income will tend to move downward along this curve. However, with the next wave of industrial investment, the process is repeated. Here is a new shift to the left along the population curve, a new increase in amount of resources immediately available, and a new incentive to occupy new land and improve agricultural techniques.

This process continues so long as the industrial investment takes place, and so long as good new land is available or not all land has been converted to the more productive of the known (labor-intensive) agricultural techniques. However, there will be some tendency for the average productivity curve to become steeper as we move to the right and the possibility of adding to agricultural resources diminishes. Eventually we reach the point where all land is occupied and converted to the more efficient technique. The average productivity curve then becomes a rectangular hyperbola. That is, as population grows, total income remains unchanged, and is simply divided among more people. From this point on, the sole effect of industrialization can only be further increases in population, declining per capita income, and a consequent movement along the curve rn. The process will stop when rn cuts the zero population growth line.

It is possible, of course, that the zero population growth line will rise as population rises. If we consider the whole process in time, and imagine that we move through time as we move to the right along the population curve, there is some reason to believe that the curve would take the form of B₂. The significance of this pattern of growth is that with sufficiently large initial increases in resources (implying that financial capital is directed toward the rural sector as well as new land being occupied) the rate of population growth would fall below the rate of indigenous net investment, permitting cumulative growth. Better still, as will become more apparent below, would be an initial rate of investment in both sectors that would permit a jump to levels of per capita income at which steady growth could be maintained from a domestic savings and investment.

This point can be illustrated by an adaptation of Leibenstein's Figure 3-5 (Fig. 5 below). It is here assumed that as income rises and population grows beyond the present level, the per capita income

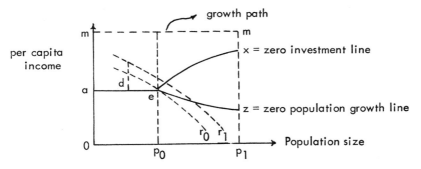

Figure 5 (Leibenstein Figure 3-5)

at which population growth falls to zero also falls--a quite reasonable assumption from a demographic point of view. At the same time, the zero-investment line is considered to rise with capita income and population. If the "demonstration effect" is operative, this assumption is also reasonable; after a lag, consumption patterns are adjusted to the higher-income levels, and when income falls again, zero saving is reached at higher levels of income than before. The line mm represents the level of per capita income at which the rate of population growth falls below the rate of capital accumulation, permitting cumulative growth.

It is apparent that any initial displacement through industrial investment which leaves the system within the area ezx or within the area exmn involves a return to the initial equilibrium position e. The former area is one of net disinvestment, which must lead eventually to net decline in population and a return to e. The latter area involves net investment, but at a rate slower than population growth, so that per capita incomes fall after the initial rise, forcing the system back to e.

On the other hand, a simultaneous reduction in the population of the rural sector, such as is involved in the movement from e to d, combined with an increase in investment in the rural sector which would raise the average productivity curve to r_1 would bring the rural sector into the range of cumulative growth.

Leibenstein also shows that at low levels of income the optimum degree of specialization is rather low. "It is the highly efficient special-purpose equipment that, for the most part, is subject to indivisibilities at points where cost per unit of capital is quite high. It is the degree of indivisibility per unit of efficiency that matters." This relationship complicates the problem of finding efficient techniques for the degree of specialization called for at the low levels of income in the rural sector.

One of Leibenstein's most interesting diagrams is his Figure 15-1 (Fig. 6 below). We start with per capita income at oa. If enough investment is injected into the system to raise per capita income immediately to om, sustained growth will occur. However, it would be

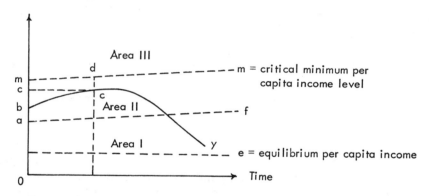

Figure 6 (Leibenstein Figure 15-1)

cheaper for the investor (which might in this context be a foreign government undertaking a foreign-aid program) to make the injection in two stages. The initial injection might be enough to raise income to ob; then at time (t) the second injection could be made to raise per capita income by cb, to the critical minimum.

Leibenstein readily admits that this theory of the critical minimum effort is an empirical one. In his Figure 8-1a (Fig. 7, below), the relationship of income-raising and income-depressing forces is such that starting from an equilibrium position e, no investment program which fails to raise per capita income to the level g will produce sustained economic growth. It is of course possible to construct diagrams to show cases in which no growth is possible at all, or in which any initial shock bringing a small increase in per capita income would

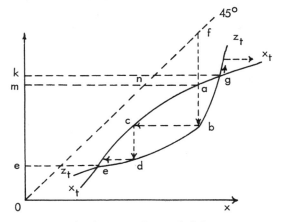

Figure 7 (Leibenstein Figure 8-1a)

produce steady growth. The reason for assuming that underdeveloped countries in fact face a position where a substantial increase in investment is necessary to yield steady growth relates to the underlying theory of population growth, and actual evidence with respect to internal economies of scale due to indivisibility of the factors of production, other indivisibilities with regard to investment decisions, external economies due to external interdependencies, and the like. Leibenstein has also shown, however, that there is a biological maximum to the rate of population growth, in the neighborhood of 3 per cent. Consequently, given a sufficiently large volume of technical and capital assistance, it is always possible to produce some initial increase in income that will become cumulative.[32]

VI. Conclusions

If the foregoing analysis is correct, the economics of underdeveloped areas must differ in scope and method from the traditional economics of the advanced countries. The chief differences are as follows:

1) The strategic functions are discontinuous. The discontinuities may take either of two forms. If "A" is a function of "H," instead of a smooth curve relating the two variables, there may be a sudden jump in the value of "B" at a critical value of "A"; or the functions may have sharp points. Both the first and second derivatives may have positive signs within one range of "A," and negative signs in another value of "A." These discontinuities are particularly important in the relationship between capital accumulation and output, in the supply of labor effort, the supply of risk-taking, in decision-making, and in production functions.[33]

2) In underdeveloped countries intersectoral and interregional relations, instead of being a frill to be superimposed on a more or less
complete system, are the very core of the analytical framework.[34]

An intersectoral model somewhere between the Leontief input-output matrices and Keynesian aggregates is needed. Even a two-sector
model takes a big step toward an understanding of underdeveloped
countries, and the addition of three or four more sectors would bring
us considerably closer to reality. Discontinuous structural change is
the essence of development policy, and to reach the right policy decisions, we must have an analytical framework designed to deal with
such structural changes.[35]

3) Cumulative movements away from dynamic equilibrium, or balanced and steady growth, are typical of underdeveloped countries.[36]

4) In a theory of economic development, population growth and
technological progress cannot be treated as exogenous variables but
must be worked into the system. Technological progress in this context includes resource discoveries and the spread of managerial,
technical, and entrepreneurial skills. The relationship between these
factors and economic growth is a circular one and must be treated
only as such; that is, population growth and technological progress
cannot be treated only as factors influencing the rate of growth; the
system must include the factors which determine them in turn. It is
unfortunate that such is the case, since we know relatively little about
the causes of technological progress and the population growth; but by
leaving them out we produce theories which are not solid foundations
for policy recommendations.

5) "Psychological individualism" is of limited use as a method of
analysis--not because "people are different" in underdeveloped countries, but because so many of the important decisions are group decisions rather than individual decisions. What may be bad policy for
each of one thousand entrepreneurs may be good policy for the thousand entrepreneurs together; what is unattractive to an individual
worker may be very attractive to a trade union or to a village.

6) For the decisions important to development policy, the market
no longer provides an adequate guide. It is not a matter of estimating
cost-benefit ratios of a 10 per cent or even 50 per cent expansion of
existing industries, during a period when per capita income is rising
by, say, 20 per cent. It is a matter of estimating cost-benefit ratios
as sudden increases in output ranging from several hundred per cent
to infinity, with no previous experience, while national incomes double
or triple. We are concerned, not with the increase in output to be
brought next year by investment of $100,000 in this way or that, but
with the aggregate national income between (say) the year ten and the
year twenty, with this complex of investment or that. It is not merely
a matter of monopolistic distortion of the allocation of resources in
the market; the marginal choices reflected in the market are almost

totally irrelevant to the decisions that are important for economic development.

7) The analytical framework must be a general equilibrium system, not a partial equilibrium one. It is the conjuncture of forces causing economic growth that is important, and no one of them alone will have the same effect as it does in conjunction with others. The system is bound to be rather complicated; it is doubtful whether the method of "successive approximations" will give the right answers. Dealing with the whole system at once enormously increases the intellectual difficulty of dealing with the problem.

8) The whole process must be put into time; the shape of functions at a point of time is less important than their shape through time.

9) Considering the enormous complexity of the problem and the overweaning importance of the empirical framework, we may be wise to abandon the purist approach I have myself suggested on an earlier occasion,[37] and content ourselves with the relatively "sloppy" methods of the physicists.[38] That is, instead of insisting on having explanations that are both necessary and sufficient, we might adopt explanations that are merely sufficient, until they prove inconsistent with observation. This method has, after all, worked well for the physicists. At this stage of development of the theory, any refutable hypothesis is well worth stating. Let us be bold in stating them, and not wait until we can set forth irrefutable ones, which are quite likely to be fruitless anyhow. And of course, if we adopt this approach, we must devote a good deal of our time and energy to empirical testing.

Policy Implications

It seems to me that the theory of underdevelopment presented above provides a satisfactory explanation of how underdeveloped countries got that way. When we weave together the population multiplier, technological dualism, elastic supplies of labor to the industrial sector, the "backwash effects" of foreign trade, and discontinuities requiring a "big push," we can readily see why substantial industrial investment failed to bring widespread and continuing increases in income in Asian, African, and some Latin American countries.

The theory I have presented does not, of course, tell any particular country exactly what it must do to achieve "a take-off into sustained growth." Every country is to some degree a special case, with its own pattern of natural and manpower resources, savings-investment potential, etc. The theory does, however, suggest the broad framework of development policy, and the conclusions to which it leads seem to me significant:

1) The present allocation of resources in underdeveloped countries may be no reflection of comparative advantage, either domestically or internationally, and could well be just the reverse of what is required.

2) By the same token, further expansion of international trade without a drastic change in its pattern is no guarantee of a take-off, and could even delay a take-off.

3) The "calculus" involved in economic development is one of comparing the effects of one gestalt of investment with another over a period beginning at least ten years hence and extending well into the future. The market provides very limited guidance in allocating resources so as to maximize the degree of development. For this reason development planning is necessary. The need for a plan has nothing to do with the relative importance of the public and private sectors; intervention to alter the decisions of private entrepreneurs is still a plan.

4) The plan must be a long-run one, extending for at least three or four five-year plans. What goes into the current five-year plan must be determined in large measure by the pattern of production established as a goal for the end of the third and fourth five-year plans.

5) In drawing up such a long-run plan, careful studies must be made of the natural resources, manpower resources (including management and technical skills), and capital resources, as they are and as they might be over the plan period. An effort must then be made to estimate the best allocation of these resources after a take-off has been accomplished and substantial structural change has been achieved.

6) A gradualist approach is almost certain to be self-defeating. In our foreign-aid policy we should be urging the governments of underdeveloped countries to be more ambitious, not less ambitious, in their planning. The targets for investment and increase in income must be high enough to outrun population growth and bring the needed structural change.

7) If the structural change brought by the development program does not in itself bring a drop in fertility rates, to offset the probable drop in death rates, it may be necessary to attack the population problem directly as a part of development policy.

8) It is essential to break through the vicious circle of technological dualism. Doing so means planning for increased productivity in the rural sector. In the phase when "pre-conditions" for take-off are being established, it may make good sense to seize remaining opportunities for raising productivity through fertilizers, seed selection, etc. But a take-off requires a shift to more extensive and more mechanized agriculture, which means getting people out of the rural sector and getting capital into it.

It has long been recognized that there is a high correlation between the ratio of nonagricultural employment to agricultural employment and per capita income. Similarly, it has long been known that rising per capita income has been accompanied historically by a relative decline in the share of output and income generated in the primary sector of the economy. The theory of underdevelopment presented above shows why this relationship is so inescapable. With a large proportion of the population engaged in labor-intensive agriculture on very small holdings, the rural sector acts as an anchor sunk deep in the sands of time, so that the ship of state can never move far from its present state of rest, with low levels of productivity and of income. It cannot accumulate capital at a rate fast enough to outrun population growth, and it cannot improve its agricultural techniques very much.

Moreover, a consideration of true comparative advantage suggests that leaving large numbers of people in peasant agriculture means continuing to engage in activities for which the economy is not well suited. It seems unlikely that fertility will drop significantly in such societies unless there are further reductions in per capita income. If small-scale developmental efforts raise productivity faster than they reduce mortality there is every reason to suppose that fertility may rise again in such societies.

There is no automatic tendency to adjust, either internally or internationally, to the glaring discrepancies in productivity between the rural sector and the industrial one, or between average productivity of the economy as a whole and that of advanced countries. Foreign trade may only aggravate these disparities. Only a rapid change to extensive, mechanized agriculture, with enough industrialization to absorb the population displaced from the rural sector, will assure a take-off into steady growth.

Indeed, economic development is tantamount to getting people out of agriculture. Cumulative growth comes spontaneously only when labor becomes scarce in agriculture, so that a shift to more land-and-capital-intensive techniques becomes profitable from the standpoint of individual farmers. In brief, what is needed is a planned substitute for the constellation of plague, enclosures, reformation, discoveries, and industrial revolution which launched the process of cumulative growth in Europe.

At the same time, industrialization alone is unlikely to produce the desired results. Concentration of a limited capital budget in the capital-intensive sector will merely continue the process which prevailed for two centuries under colonial administrations. It is not a question of balanced growth or unbalanced growth, but one of balanced growth or no growth at all.

There is no reason why policies of this kind should not be carried out by democratic governments. There is no reason either why they should not be pursued in countries where private enterprise predominates, if that is the preference of the people concerned. Development planning of this kind does not mean that the market is totally replaced by bureaucratic decisions. On the contrary, the more the market can be used, the better. The basic decisions regarding the framework of private decision-making and the scale and nature of public investment cannot be left to the market, any more than the

maintenance of full employment without inflation can be left to the
market alone. But once the framework is established, "consumer
sovereignty" can reign with respect to all <u>other</u> decisions. Indeed a
"mixed economy" is most likely to succeed, in development as in
stabilization. Laissez faire will not do the job, and totalitarian physical planning will not do the job well. It is the essence of good development planning that the government should take those decisions which
it alone can make effectively, leaving to the market the decisions that
can be made more effectively there.

NOTES

[1]It would be possible to bring K and T into the system, as Schumpeter does, by making
them a function of the supply of entrepreneurship. However, this procedure would
complicate the system unnecessarily for our immediate purpose and would be a departure from the usual form of contemporary theories of steady growth.

[2]Those who prefer a lengthy and cumbersome presentation of the theory can find one in
my two articles in the <u>Economic Journal</u>, "The Theory of Increasing Under-Employ-
ment" (June, 1950) and "Interactions of Cycles and Trends" (December, 1955).

[3]See B. Higgins, "The 'Dualistic Theory' of Underdeveloped Areas," <u>Economic Development and Cultural Change</u> (January, 1956).

[4]It may also be that in some countries industrial investment provided incentives for
raising larger families. In Indonesia, for example, after the shift from trading to the
"culture system," involving compulsory deliveries of plantation products to the colonial
authorities, the easiest way for the people to maintain their standards of living and lei-
sure while meeting the levy of the colonial government was to have more children, to
occupy more land, and to devote a larger proportion of the land to irrigated rice culture, as distinct from the slash-and-burn shifting agriculture. Something similar may
be true of other countries as well. Leibenstein, who has devoted much more attention
to the demographic aspects of economic development than I have, is quite ready to
generalize on this relationship and to argue that initial rises in per capita income will
tend on balance to bring initial increases in the "demand for children."

[5]For example, when the development of the sugar plantations and refineries in the mid-
nineteenth century in Java led to a shift from rice cultivation to sugar planting by
Javanese landowners, the Netherlands East Indies government sought to nip this local
industrialization in the bud by imposing a regulation forbidding the sugar refineries to
buy cane from native growers. Since the Javanese did not have the capital or the technical skills for large refineries, they had to be content with simple refining methods,
producing brown sugar for the local market. Similarly, when smallholders' rubber
became an active competitor of plantation rubber, the Netherlands East Indies administration imposed a discriminatory tax on smallholders' rubber (in this case without
success).

[6]Dr. Hagen attaches importance not to urbanization as such but to "built-in technological progress." Wherever and whenever technological progress becomes built into the
behavior patterns of a society, he argues, it will bring not only steadily rising productivity but also, after a lag, falling fertility. For our purpose, Dr. Hagen's variant adds
up to the same thing. Industrial development in Asia and Africa did not bring "built-in
technological progress" to indigenous society. The new techniques were not the product
of their own society and had relatively little impact upon it. Few native people were
in direct contact with the advancing technology, and the methods of production of the
masses of the people were unchanged by it, for reasons that will become more clear
in the next section. Thus from the Hagen thesis as well as from the urbanization
thesis, a long lag between the initial drop in mortality rates and the subsequent drop
in fertility rates could be expected in underdeveloped countries.--Everett Hagen,
<u>Population and Economic Growth: Making the Theory Fit the Facts</u>, Center for Inter-
national Studies (Cambridge, Massachusetts Institute of Technology, August, 1957).

[7]R. S. Eckaus, "The Factor Proportions Problem in Underdeveloped Areas," American Economic Review (September, 1955).

[8]With the emergence of national states in former colonial countries after the Second World War, both trade union activity, supported by government, and direct government intervention in the labor market have tended to create artificially industrial high wage rates in a number of countries. These policies have little or no effect on real wage rates in the rural sector. Accordingly, they aggravate the tendency toward technological dualism.

[9]Robert Solow, "A Contribution to the Theory of Economic Growth," Quarterly Journal of Economics, Vol. 70, No. 1 (February, 1926), p. 91.

[10]The Philippines today seem to be in this stage of balanced growth in the rural sector, with little capital and land combined with much labor. However, with present rates of population growth, even the Philippines are approaching the point where it will no longer be possible to maintain present ratios of land and other capital to labor. Marginal productivity of labor will then begin to fall below the minimal subsistence real wage rates. In Java, this point has already been reached.

[11]Solow, op. cit., p. 91.

[12]Hla Myint, "An Interpretation of Economic Backwardness," Oxford Economic Papers, Vol. 6, No. 2 (June, 1954).

[13]Ibid., p. 150.

[14]Ibid., p. 153.

[15]It is said in the Philippines, for example, that the growth of a particular village depended entirely on the resources of the local Chinese, for it was his resources that determined the size of the cash crops of which they could dispose. Moreover, there is a continuous draining-off process. The Chinese who becomes successful in the village does not stay there, but moves on to a city, installing in his village store a relative whose talents are less striking than his own.

[16]Hla Myint, op. cit., p. 154.

[17]Ibid., p. 155.

[18]Ibid., p. 162.

[19]Hla Myint, "The Gains from International Trade and the Backward Countries," Review of Economic Studies, Vol. XXII, No. 2.

[20]Ibid., p. 140.

[21]Gunnar Myrdal, Economic Theory and Under-Developed Regions (London, Gerald Duckworth and Company, 1957).

[22]Ibid., pp. 28-29.

[23]Professor Myrdal reports two striking correlations which were discovered in the studies of the Economic Commission for Europe: first, the regional disparities are greater in poor countries than in rich ones; and second, the disparities are increasing in poor countries and decreasing in rich ones. "A large part of the explanation for these two broad correlations," he says, "may be found in the important fact that the higher the level of economic development that a country has already attained, the stronger the spread effects will usually be."--Ibid., p. 34.

[24]Ibid., p. 41.

[25]Ibid., p. 60.

[26]W. Arthur Lewis, "Economic Development with Unlimited Supplies of Labour," Manchester School of Economy and Social Studies (1955).

[27]P. N. Rosenstein-Rodan, Notes on the Theory of the "Big Push," Center for International Studies (Cambridge, Massachusetts Institute of Technology, March, 1957).

[28]Rosenstein-Rodan, "Industrialization of Eastern and Southeastern Europe," Economic Journal, 1943; and Ragnar Nurkse, Problems of Capital Formation in Underdeveloped Countries (Oxford, University of Oxford Press, 1953).

[29]This is one of the points that was well understood by Malthus, and misunderstood by his contemporaries. He stated quite clearly that the increase in savings needed to finance growth was an increase in ex post savings arising out of the increase in income, rather than an initial reduction in consumption, which could not discourage investment. --See Rosenstein-Rodan, Notes on the Theory of the "Big Push."

[30]Leibenstein presents other diagrams in which the zero investment line is above the zero population line; but we consider the assumption that complete absence of population growth is accompanied by absence of capital accumulation is more realistic for a peasant economy. Indeed, there is some evidence that in Asian countries a certain

amount of capital accumulation took place, even in the absence of population growth, in the form of simple transportation equipment, roads, housing, irrigation systems, and the like. However, for simplicity we shall assume that prior to the beginning of industrialization there is no population growth and no net capital accumulation.--Harvey Leibenstein, Economic Backwardness and Economic Growth (New York, John Wiley & Sons, Inc., 1957), p. 88.

31It is perhaps worth noting that in the tropics improved land meets Professor Hayek's definition of capital; it is a "non-permanent productive resource."

32Leibenstein has also made an attempt to estimate the actual size of the "minimum effort." He makes plausible assumptions with respect to the relationship between rates of increase in life expectation with rising income and fertility levels. He then calculates, for an ICOR of 3:1 and 5:1, the ratio of net investment to income that would be required to produce certain patterns of income rise and population growth. His projection 2b in Table 14-9 (not reproduced here), in which population growth rises to a bit above 2 per cent in the first five-year period and then rises gradually to 2.8 per cent for the fiftieth to fifty-fifth years, conforms fairly closely to what seems to have happened in Indonesia during the nineteenth century. Under these conditions, he shows, the required net investment is 13.2 per cent of national income in the first five years and rises gradually to a level of 15.72 per cent of national income. Even his pattern 4b, which shows population growth rising to 2.42 per cent in the twenty-fifth to thirtieth years and then tapering off, requires investment of 13.2 per cent of national income in the first five years, rising to 14.52 per cent, and then dropping to 13.08 per cent in the fiftieth to fifty-fifth years. These figures conform closely to the estimates of capital requirements for Indonesia made by the M.I.T. Indonesia Project.

33It is probably true that there are discontinuities in the strategic functions for advanced countries as well, but they are of relatively minor importance. For advanced countries the assumption of continuity gives a reasonably good approximation to reality, and the differential calculus is a useful tool. In underdeveloped countries, on the contrary, the discontinuities are fundamental, and the use of differential calculus can give quite wrong results. Differential equations may help, but a system of mathematics especially designed to take care of discontinuous functions might be more helpful still.

34This fact was well understood by the classical economists, who were always concerned with relations between the agricultural and industrial sectors of the economy. Intersectoral relations played a more explicit role in the Marxist analysis. Specialists like Boeke were groping toward such a framework in their theory of "dualism," but were misled by the feeling that sectoral discrepancies were based on sociological factors, whereas in fact they can be explained in purely economic and technical terms. An important part of the intersectoral relation is the relationship between shifts in location of industry and economic growth, a relationship which has been pointed out by Professor Burton Keirstead in Theory of Economic Change, but which he has not yet worked into a systematic theory of growth.

35One by-product of recognition of the importance of intersectoral relations and regional shifts is that attention must be given to the nature of the frontier. Any easy optimism about the prospects for development of the now underdeveloped countries is promptly dispelled by a consideration of the difference in the nature of the frontier in those countries now and in Europe in the eighteenth century or the New World in the nineteenth century.--Cf. Benjamin Higgins, "Economic Development of Underdeveloped Areas: Past and Present," Land Economics (August, 1955).

36Cumulative movements away from stable equilibrium are not unknown in advanced countries; but in advanced countries these cumulative movements are important mainly for the theory of fluctuations, where they are limited by a "floor" and a "ceiling," as in the Hicks model of the trade cycle. Where we are concerned with trends, however, there are no such limits, at least within very long periods. Trends in the terms and balance of trade, regional discrepancies in productivity, and the like, can continue for decades, even generations. It is this kind of destructive cumulative movement that development policy must endeavor to halt. On this point, see also Albert O. Hirshman, "Investment Policies and Dualism in Underdeveloped Countries," American Economic Review (September, 1957).

37Benjamin Higgins, What Do Economists Know? (Melbourne University Press, 1951), Chap. 1 and especially p. 27.

38This expression is Professor Boulding's.

Part II

Problems Arising From Rapid Development

Papers: Singer
                    Maynard
                    Prebisch

THE CONCEPT OF BALANCED GROWTH IN ECONOMIC DEVELOPMENT: THEORY AND PRACTICE

Hans W. Singer

New School for Social Research

I. "Balanced Growth"--Definitions

It may perhaps help to clear the ground to spend a few minutes on terminology. The concept of balanced growth, or of the maintenance of some kind of equilibrium during the process of growth, means different things to different people. Broadly, we may distinguish three classes of usage: (1) a nontechnical usage, (2) a general technical usage, and (3) a specific technical usage.

1) In the nontechnical sense, the term is often used to describe such ideas as growth without too much social disruption; broadly based growth, which spreads its benefits widely among different classes; sustained growth, which is neither of such a kind nor of such a rapidity that it turns out to be a flash in the pan. In its most watered-down versions this nontechnical usage comes pretty close to identifying balanced growth with the kind of growth with which the observer agrees; or growth which is considered ex post as having turned out to be successful and which is then retrospectively praised with the laudatory epithet of "balanced." For some economists, of course, there can be no higher term of praise than that of "balance" or "equilibrium," and the bestowal of this praise on a certain growth process may then merely amount to a general accolade for the country or period in which it occurred. Needless to say, we shall not be concerned here with this nontechnical usage, even though the problems with which we shall deal will not be found entirely unrelated to these more emotional roots of the concept.

2) In the general technical sense, balanced growth may refer to the balance between ambitions and the resources available to satisfy the ambitions, or more narrowly the balance between intended savings and intended investment. Investment is balanced if it fits in with available resources and in this sense can be carried out without inflation, or at least with only that amount of inflation which serves a useful pump-priming function and brings itself to an end. The latter qualification is necessary, although most observers would agree that in underdeveloped countries he who primes the pump will often find that he has a tiger by the tail.

Still keeping within the class of general technical usage, the term "balance" may refer not to the equilibrium between aggregate resources and aggregate demands, but to specific resources. It is well understood among the practitioners of economics that the balance of resources and ambitions may be upset not only by excessive demand in the aggregate, but also by "bottlenecks," that is, a failure to match the "mix" of resources with the "mix" of demands or claims upon these resources.

The third "balance" referred to in general technical usage is the external balance, the interrelationship between the pressure of domestic demand and the pressure from the need to equalize the inflow and outflow of foreign exchange, after taking account of intended changes in foreign reserves. It is well understood that developmental investment may be brought up short by the barrier of external balance, even before the barriers of bottlenecks and of the limitation of aggregate resources are reached. Again, underdeveloped countries may have special reason to worry about the external balance because of their chronically low foreign-exchange reserves, because of their chronically high import demand as a result of demonstration effects, because of the facts of technological life, and because of their chronic difficulties in achieving the desirable degree of export promotion. But although these problems do come nearer home to our present subject than the ones indicated by nontechnical usage, they are not the problems with which I shall be concerned.

3) The specific technical sense of the concept refers to the balance between the size of markets, the volume of supply, and the demand for capital. It is the same balance as that which concerned Adam Smith, the balance between the division of labor, the extent of production, and the extent of the market. In the more modern literature on underdeveloped countries, this concern with the balance of markets and supplies often takes the form of a discussion of the balance between different sectors of the economy--usually agriculture and industry. Or it may take the form of the need to create the necessary improvements in the efficiency of production which create new markets by a simultaneous expansion of the economic "infrastructure" of health, education, transport, power, and housing, together with the more direct expansion of supplies of final goods. Again, it may take the form of achieving these necessary improvements in the efficiency of production by broadly based simultaneous investment so that the infrastructure, external economies, economies of large-scale production, and the total supply of final goods should go forward together all along the line, and in such a fashion that at each step the increase in real income is such that it provides the market for the increased flow of final goods. The "big push," Schumpeter's "waves of investors," and the virtues of the "investment package," are all variations on this theme. It is with this specific technical use of the term that I am

concerned. Essentially, in spite of the rather different form in which this concept is expressed now, the problem is still Adam Smith's sixty-four-dollar question--the question of keeping the growth of markets and the growth of supply in balance. As if to emphasize the continuity of the problem from Adam Smith to Nurkse and other more modern writers we have Allyn Young's celebrated article[1] forming a clear bridge between the two.

II. Structural Change and the Marketing Problem

What then, precisely, is this problem of balanced growth, in its specific technical sense of the problem of "markets"? To understand, we have to construct some kind of fundamental structural picture-- "model" if you like--of an underdeveloped country. An underdeveloped country has a clearly defined employment structure: 70 per cent to 90 per cent of the employed population are engaged in agriculture. In a developed country, which has reached the national income levels of northwestern Europe or North America, about 15 per cent of the population are engaged in agriculture--more, if the country is a net exporter of agricultural products (or accumulates agricultural surpluses), and less, if the country is an agricultural net importer. However, even those developed countries that are heavy net exporters of agricultural products--Canada, Australia, New Zealand, Denmark, and, yes, even Iowa or Texas--have an employment structure which sets them well apart from the underdeveloped countries.

An underdeveloped country, then, may be defined as a country with 80 per cent of its people in agriculture and a developed country as one with only 15 per cent of its employment in agriculture, in both cases giving or taking a little according to foreign trade. Arthur Lewis has defined the process of economic growth as the problem of transforming a country from a 5 per cent saver into a 15 per cent saver. We can, with equal justice, define the process as one of transforming a country from an 80 per cent farmer to a 15 per cent farmer. Note that we are speaking here of the employment structure, not of the structure of foreign trade or of the composition of the national income.

The 80 per cent farmer economy corresponds always to the low level of productivity of the underdeveloped economy. The low level of productivity in farming decrees that the bulk of the people must be in farming in order to feed and clothe themselves, and that they have little to spare over and above their personal needs. The low level of incomes decrees, by writ of Engel's Law, that a very high percentage of the low incomes is spent on food and essential clothing. The demand for other things, particularly manufactured goods and services, is thus perforce limited to a very small percentage of a very small income. This compound effect of low incomes and Engel's Law means that the market for nonagricultural goods is exceedingly small. Productivity in agriculture, level of incomes, Engel's Law, and employment structure form an interdependent equilibrium system. The equilibrium which they determine by their interaction in an underdeveloped country is a low-level equilibrium.

The above brief description is subject to a significant but not fundamental modification arising from the existence of foreign trade. In such case the employment structure is not in direct harmony with the level of incomes and productivity, and the "rest of the world" account must appear as a further determinant. Normally, underdeveloped countries are net exporters of agricultural products and net importers of other products. Overpopulated countries or mining countries can be significant exceptions to this. But the rule remains. As we shall see later, the existence of domestic markets for manufactures presently satisfied by imports from abroad is a significant factor in applying the doctrines of balanced growth. For the moment, however, it is better to stick to fundamentals, and we may think either of the world as a whole, or of a closed economy, or of an underdeveloped country, the foreign trade of which is balanced with respect to farm products and other products.

At this point a second feature should be introduced into our simple model of employment structure. The output:labor ratio in agriculture appears in the statistics almost invariably as lower than the national average. Caution is advisable in connection with this statement. First, there are one or two exceptions to it among the more developed countries--Australia seems to be one of them; yet it remains one of the best-founded generalizations we can make for underdeveloped countries and developed countries alike. Second, the published figures may understate agricultural output, especially in connection with subsistence farming and with agricultural capital formation; hence, my proposition referred to what "appears in the statistics" rather than what is. Third, my proposition has doubtful applicability in terms of welfare: it is doubtful whether the lower value of output per employed person in agriculture is not partially offset by lower prices, lower cost, less need for keeping up with the Joneses, or other nonpecuniary factors. But when cautiously interpreted I do not think that the evidence for the lower output:labor ratio in agriculture could be contested. In fact, for a surprising number of countries, figures come remarkably close to a constant relation of the form:

$$A = \frac{2}{3}N$$

where A is output per employed person in agriculture and N is output per employed person in the economy as a whole.

From this differential between agricultural output per person and nonagricultural output per person, there follows with the force of an arithmetical identity a fact of considerable significance: if an 80 per cent farmer economy produces only two-thirds of its national per capita average in the agricultural sector, the differential between the agricultural sector and the nonagricultural sector will be much larger than will be the case in a 15 per cent farmer economy which also produces two-thirds of its national average in the agricultural sector. In fact, in the underdeveloped country, output per worker outside agriculture compared with agricultural output per worker tends to be in the ratio of 3:1. Thus, structural change in the sense of moving from an 80 per cent farmer economy in the direction of a 15 per cent farmer economy begins to look like being more than a symptom or measure of economic development; it begins to look like a method or instrument of economic development.

This impression is understandable, but it is doubly fallacious. In the first place, transfer from agriculture which is not justified by the level of productivity and the state of real demand or markets cannot possibly be maintained or beneficial. In the second place, the higher output per person outside agriculture is not in itself conclusive evidence of a more favorable capital:output ratio outside agriculture than inside, neither in the average sense nor in the marginal sense relevant for allocation of available capital. However, the magic of this differential is understandable. Moreover, in spite of the basic fallacies involved--as has just been pointed out--there is at least an element of truth in the idea that this differential could be utilized in economic development. In so far as the greater output per person outside agriculture does in fact represent greater net productivity of labor, derived from internal and external economies, and not only a greater input of capital, a cumulative or multiplier effect is introduced into the process of structural change. As the levels of productivity and of real demand and markets rise, the structural change from an 80 per cent farmer economy toward a 15 per cent farmer economy made possible by this rise will in its turn generate forces which themselves tend to raise productivity and real incomes. In this fashion the effect may become the cause--and we are in the midst of a hen-and-egg riddle. Here, in a nutshell, we have the starting point of the doctrine of balanced growth in the more modern form developed by Rosenstein-Rodan, Nurkse, and others: the self-justifying broadening of real demand and markets, the investment which looks uneconomical ex ante, but becomes economical ex post, the shipwreck which yet helps to set off the wave that will float it off the rock.

III. "Balanced Growth"--a Possible Solution of Doubtful Applicability

We have now established that a shift in the employment structure from agriculture toward nonagriculture, especially to industry, can be considered an inevitable accompaniment of economic development. This is certainly true for a closed economy and, with a certain time lag, almost certainly true for an open economy. We have further seen that in a very limited sense it might even be said that the process of transfer itself can help to promote economic development. At the same time, we have seen that the extent of the market--reflecting the state of real incomes, the institutional framework, and the state of foreign trade--sets strict limits to this required, and desired, shift in the employment structure. Industry cannot expand, because it needs expanded markets in agriculture; and agricultural marketing, in turn, is limited by the absence of employment opportunities in industry, which forces agriculture to feed too many people on the farms. Individual industries cannot expand, because other industries have not developed so as to provide markets.

The doctrine of balanced economic growth, in its specific technical sense, offers a way of solving this marketing difficulty. Perhaps it would be more correct to say that it offers a way of by-passing the marketing difficulty. What it says, in effect, is this: "Let us leave the present system alone, deadlocked in low-level equilibrium. Let us superimpose upon this deadlocked system a second, self-contained system which provides at the same time additional markets and additional supply. Let us create this second self-contained system with emphasis on the sector which would in any case have to be expanded in the process of economic growth, and which is also the sector where simultaneous projects can most readily support each other. The way to do this is by a simultaneous wave of new plants, composed in such a way that full advantage is taken of complementarities and external economies on the supply side, and of the complementarities of markets on the demand side." In this way, it is explained--to use a metaphor coined in a rather different context--a hundred flowers may grow where a single flower would wither away for lack of nourishment.

In other words, we are told that the marketing difficulty looks formidable only to our habit of thinking small, in terms of piecemeal projects. "Stop thinking piecemeal; start thinking big," we are told, "and the marketing difficulty which seemed to loom so formidable will turn out to be a paper tiger."

Let it be said at once that this doctrine must command respect and sympathy. The advice to underdeveloped countries to stop thinking piecemeal and to start thinking big is sound advice. The programing approach is better than the project approach. In a good development program, individual projects can and should mutually support each other; if proper advantage is taken of such opportunities, the productivity of investment can be significantly increased. A widespread expectation among individual entrepreneurs that the demand for their product is going to increase can do wonders with the inducement to invest, and it can be self-justifying, so far as the demand side is concerned.

Yet there remain several areas of doubt--indeed, of rather obvious doubt--about this approach. In the first place, it seems plain that a purely nonagricultural system of additional markets can never be entirely self-contained. Engel's Law may say that the demand for food increases less than in proportion to income, but it certainly does not say that the demand for food does not increase at all--and most particularly not at the low-income levels of underdeveloped countries. Moreover, it is fallacious to think of the new system of additional markets and the old deadlocked system as unrelated to each other. Where you have the institution of family subsistence farming, the demand for food per capita of those remaining on the land will increase as the employment structure changes and people are drawn off the land, with a resulting increase in real income. This increase in demand for food will be additional to the increase in the demand for food of those drawn off the land.

The implications for the doctrine of balanced growth have not perhaps been fully realized. The implications are that the big push in industry may have to be supplemented by large-scale investments in agriculture additional to the "balanced diet" element in the package. But once this is admitted, two consequences follow. In the first place, the doctrine begins to look suspiciously like the more orthodox doctrines--with which Adam Smith would not have quarreled--that structural change must rest on a foundation of raising productivity within the existing structure (and in underdeveloped countries that means mainly agriculture) until real incomes have risen to a level which justifies structural change. Even more damaging to the doctrine, at least in its practical application, is a second consequence of the admission that the widening of markets must include major additional blocks of investment in agriculture. The total resources required for the big industrial push may already be too large for an underdeveloped country. But even they are not sufficient: we must further add to the required resources not only the investment needed in agriculture to make the new system self-contained, thus removing the market difficulty, but further blocks of investment to cater to the higher real incomes of those not transferred from agriculture.

The reason why these difficulties are more clearly seen in connection with the problem of sectoral balance between agriculture and industry, rather than in their implications for the specific doctrine of balanced growth, lies probably in a lingering belief that the required changes in agricultural supplies could be brought about by institutional changes rather than by new investment. While it is true that reducing population pressure may make it easier to introduce institutional reforms, such as consolidation of holdings, introduction of commercial crops, experimentation with better farming methods, etc., yet once the subject is brought out into the open, the need for agricultural investment would be fairly generally admitted. However, the argument is often conducted along lines which seem to neglect this need.

A second obvious area of doubt about the doctrine is already implied in what has just been said. We may use the words of Marcus
Fleming: "The situation might be roughly expressed by saying that,
whereas the balanced growth doctrine assumes that the relationship
between industries is for the most part complementary, the limitation
of factor supply ensures that that relationship is for the most part
competitive."[2]

We may say that the resources required for carrying out the policy
of balanced growth--particularly when the extension to agriculture
just made is borne in mind--are of such magnitude that a country dis-
posing of such resources would in fact not be underdeveloped. A
slightly different way of putting the same point would be to say that
the doctrine may be more useful as a recipe for sustained growth in
developed countries than as a recipe for breaking the low-level equilibrium deadlock in underdeveloped countries. To justify the doctrine
as a recipe for breaking the deadlock, it would really have to be argued that the required resources, even though not initially available,
would be forthcoming under the pressure of widened markets and
balanced growth of demand. But this also would hardly be compatible
with the assumed inelasticities of factor supply in underdeveloped
countries. If pump-priming were the answer, the problems of underdeveloped countries would not be as tough as they seem to be.

It may be tempting to try to vindicate the doctrine by some argument along the following lines: "True, the balanced-investment package requires large resources ex ante. But if the balanced investment
can be physically realized in the first place, the required savings will
be provided ex post. So there is nothing to worry about, really." But
this argument presumably must assume that the marginal rates of
savings and taxation are sufficiently high to secure the ex-post identity
of savings and investment without too much inflation; unless indeed it
refers to a fleeting identity brought about as part of continued gallop-
ing inflation. In any case, however, the argument cannot vindicate the
doctrine. In so far as the additional incomes are saved or taxed away,
it is true that the insufficiency of resources no longer furnishes an
argument against the approach. But this is achieved only at the price
of removing the initial justification for the whole operation. For it
stands to reason that in so far as additional incomes have to be saved
or taxed away, these incomes are not available to provide the required
markets. Supply can create its own demand, or it can create its own
finance--but it cannot conceivably do both. Therefore, to recommend
the balanced-investment package as a device to solve simultaneously
both the marketing deadlock and the deadlock of insufficient resources
is to become the victim of a double-counting trick. Where pump-
priming can be successfully practiced--probably not a frequent case
in underdeveloped countries--that is fine, but there is no particular
advantage in pump-priming by means of balanced-investment packages.

The argument proves the doctrine of balanced growth <u>premature</u> rather than <u>wrong</u>, in the sense that it is applicable to a subsequent stage of sustained growth rather than the breaking of a deadlock. It may well be better development strategy to concentrate available resources on types of investment which help to make the economic system more elastic, more capable of expansion under the stimulus of expanded markets and expanding demand. This would draw our attention to investments designed to strengthen the economic and social foundation or "infrastructure": health and education, transport and communications, energy and power, skills and knowledge of resources. Added to this general strengthening of the foundations, there would have to be investment designed to remove specific bottlenecks that would arise as a result of previous growth and recent economic history. As before, if we assume that such a system of investment could be simultaneously undertaken with the wave of directly productive projects described by the doctrine of balanced growth, all would be well. There is certainly nothing inherently contradictory about the two areas of investment. But by thus increasing even more the required size of the investment "package" so as to include the public foundation services required for expansion, we remove the whole idea even further from the realm of practical development policy in underdeveloped countries. And if a choice has to be made, it is difficult to avoid a sequence in which, during the early stages, "foundation" investment is bound to predominate. For such investment, which is essentially promotional and does not itself produce goods sold in the final market, the marketing difficulty in the normal sense does not exist. This investment also has the purpose of <u>creating</u> markets, but by a different route than "balanced growth," namely, by creating conditions where subsequent individual projects become economically feasible as a result of lowering their real cost of production. Where the choice is between the simultaneous creation of complementary high-cost plants--high cost for lack of skills and basic services--on the one hand, and, on the other, the improvement of technology and services combined with investment in such selected individual projects as have become economical as a result of lower real cost, who can doubt what the better resource allocation in an underdeveloped country is?

To summarize: in spite of its intellectually satisfying features, the doctrine of balanced economic growth has severe limitations in its applicability to underdeveloped countries. While it rightly insists on marketing difficulties as a cause of low-level equilibrium, and while it rightly shows that the marketing difficulty can be overcome by a broadly based, balanced-investment program, it fails to come to direct grips with an even more fundamental problem of underdeveloped countries: the shortage of resources. It may be true that supply of goods--provided it is properly composed and properly balanced--will create its own demand. But supply of goods means demand for factors of production, and especially for capital; and while supply of goods may create its own demand, unfortunately in underdeveloped countries demand for factors does not create its own supply. Worse, the demand for factors implied in the broadly based investment program must be in direct competition with other investment projects and other types of expenditure whose direct objective it is to increase available re-sources. If both types of investment could be undertaken simultane-ously, all would be well and the doctrine would be fully vindicated. But in that case the concept of balanced economic growth would have to be broadened considerably beyond what is normally implied. The doctrine would then come perilously close to saying: "If only the economic problem did not exist (that is, if resources were not scarce and everything could be done simultaneously), then the problem of development could be solved." This is a somewhat unfair reductio ad absurdum, but it does bring out the severe limitations of the doctrine. The more urgent the problem of economic development, the less ap-plicable is the doctrine. The more appropriate the doctrine, the more the problem of development is likely to take care of itself.

If the doctrine has merits in pointing out the marketing difficulty and in describing a way of making investment more productive, it also has dangers in that its inherent limitations may be ignored. The in-tellectual appeal of the doctrine, together with its direct association with the desired structural change, may lead countries to apply it even in situations of resource shortage and of resource inflexibility. In that case it will lead to policies which curtail rather than increase the productivity of investment. It will either lead to inflation, or to a formulation of balanced-investment packages on a very narrow geo-graphical base, or else to costly sacrifices of other types of invest-ment on the altar of balanced growth. To return to our previous paraphrase: it is sound to advise underdeveloped countries to "Think big," that is, in terms of aggregate national income accounts--but it may not be sound advice to tell them to "Act big," or at any rate big-ger than their resources permit.

It should be emphasized that the doubts that must attach to the doc-trine of balanced growth refer to the applicability and operational value of the "wave of investments" or "balanced-investment package" in underdeveloped countries, rather than to its intellectual validity or even to its operational value in the different circumstances assumed by Schumpeter in his "Theory of Economic Development." Professor Nurkse, for instance, who took a leading part in relating the Schumpe-terian idea to the marketing deadlock in underdeveloped countries, and thus evolved the idea of expanding markets by balanced-invest-ment packages, makes it abundantly clear that he is aware of the limi-tations here suggested: "There is no suggestion here that, by taking care of the demand side alone, any country could, as it were, lift itself up by its boot-straps. We have been considering one particular facet of our subject. The more fundamental difficulties that lie on the supply side have so far been kept off-stage for the sake of orderly discussion."[3] But our problem here is not "orderly discussion": it is economic development. Our paper is called the "Concept of Balanced Growth in Economic Development--Theory and Practice." The trouble with Professor Nurkse's approach is that the remedy for the demand side that he proposes puts a particularly heavy strain on the supply side, which in any case is the "fundamental difficulty," to use his own words. It is perhaps a pity that the chapter entitled "The Size of the Market and the Inducement to Invest" should have been the first chapter of his great book rather than the last. This has given rise to some misunderstanding. Nor has this misunderstanding been confined to one side only. When Mr. Fleming raised the supply problem, Professor Nurkse objected that "the word 'growth' alone hints that something more is involved than the rules of allocating a given factor stock (which, in their proper place, are not to be disparaged). This is all the more evident if attention is paid to the context in which the balanced-growth idea has turned up in the literature. My own assumption, in Chapter I of my book, was that of a given labor force being equipped with an increased stock of capital."[4]

But Professor Nurkse's assumption, so clearly stated in his last sentence, does not remove the objections. The fact is that even though we may assume that resources are available for net investment, so that "a given labor force is being equipped with an increased stock of capital," the additional capital still has to be carefully allocated and the investment package will have to compete on its own merits together with other possible ways of utilizing "the increased stock of capital." It is by no means certain that the right strategy for an underdeveloped country is the "frontal attack of this sort--the wave of capital investments in a number of different industries"[5] that Professor Nurkse writes about. Perhaps guerrilla tactics are more suitable for the circumstances of underdeveloped countries than a frontal attack.

IV. A Balanced View of Balanced Growth

In the preceding section, the doctrine of balanced growth has been offered on the one hand as a possible solution and one with some educational merit for underdeveloped countries, but on the other hand as an incomplete, implausible, and even potentially dangerous solution. Perhaps it is well now to amplify this judgment by standing back and taking a broader view of the problems involved. For this purpose, the elementary sketch of an underdeveloped economy may be re-introduced. There are several distinct roads to economic growth.

1) In the first place and most obviously, there is the increase in productivity in agriculture. It is not unnatural that foreign missions to underdeveloped countries should emphasize this road to economic growth: any visitor to an underdeveloped country will observe, first, that the bulk of the population--about 80 per cent in our sketch--is employed in agriculture; and, second, that agriculture is carried on at a particularly low level of productivity, not only in relation to agriculture in more advanced countries, but also in relation to other occupations in the same underdeveloped country. Higher productivity in agriculture must certainly be one of the main roads to economic growth. When it occurs it would normally solve the marketing difficulty; the higher incomes of farmers will provide expanded markets for industries and, according to Engel's Law, part of the additional demand is likely to be for nonagricultural products. Note, however, that the solution of the marketing difficulty through higher agricultural productivity is by no means automatic: where the higher productivity results in a higher level of feeding for the extended family of the subsistence farmer, it is still clearly a good thing--but it does not remove the marketing difficulty from the path of structural change. Where improvements in agricultural productivity occur in relation to commercial crops, and even more so where they occur in relation to export crops, we can be reasonably certain that such improvements will create pre-conditions for growth, and enable us to dispense with the balanced-investment package as a specific remedy for marketing troubles. Where agricultural productivity rises within a system of subsistence farming, it should normally be possible for an enlightened government to link this rise in productivity with institutional changes that would utilize it as a foundation of growth. For example, where the higher agricultural productivity is accompanied by the offer of "incentive goods" to farmers which will induce them to develop a propensity to "truck, barter, and exchange" as their output increases, growth becomes possible as a result. Furthermore, an increase in agricultural productivity, in so far as it releases labor from the farms, creates part of that elasticity of factor supply which makes the balanced-investment package possible.

2) A second road to economic growth is improvement of productivity outside agriculture, specifically in industry. There is plenty of evidence to show enormous scope for such improvement. It would indeed be surprising if it were otherwise, considering the lack of experience in handling capital, the scarcity of managerial skills, the absence of supporting managerial services and of external economies, and the absence of maintenance and repair facilities. We may perhaps add to this list the fact that the technology used is an alien growth imported from abroad, and was therefore not developed in line with the requirements and resource endowments of the underdeveloped countries. The pioneer study by the United Nations Economic Commission

for Latin America[6] on cotton textile industries may be quoted as providing many illustrations of possible improvements in efficiency.
Such nonagricultural improvements may be not so obvious, especially to the outside observer, as the need for higher productivity in agriculture. But even though agriculture may employ 70 per cent to 80 per cent of the total population, it does not normally account for more than half the national income. It follows that a given degree of improvement in the nonagricultural sectors will increase total real incomes by about as much as the same degree of agricultural improvement. Investments designed to raise nonagricultural productivity, by lowering real cost curves, will create "markets" where none existed before, and they do so without the need for a broadly based investment package.

3) The promotion of export trade is a third means of stimulating economic growth. The low-level equilibrium deadlock of real incomes and markets exists only in a closed economy, or for the world as a whole. In any individual underdeveloped country with significant foreign trade--and that means nearly all underdeveloped countries--some of the markets lie abroad in highly developed countries, and hence are not limited by the low domestic incomes. These markets are, of course, also limited: by real incomes abroad, by competition from possibly lower cost competitors, and by technological changes. Furthermore, the notorious instability of world commodity prices may make markets abroad particularly hazardous for the specialized exporter. All the same, export promotion offers a historically and analytically most important method of by-passing the marketing deadlock, offering opportunities for economic growth without the balanced-investment package.

4) A fourth means of improving the economic status of an underdeveloped country is import substitution. A country engaged in foreign trade has established domestic markets presently supplied by imports from abroad. Import substitution, like export promotion, thus offers an opportunity of growth in happy disregard of the need for an investment package. The protective tariff has historically been a major alternative to the balanced-investment package, in the early stages of development. Arthur Lewis' "Report on the Industrialization of the Gold Coast" provides the locus classicus for this unbalanced, yet effective, approach.

5) In relation to the improvement of productivity, there is a fifth approach to economic growth, via building up the economic infrastructure. Here, perhaps, investment in transport facilities is most obviously an alternative to the balanced-investment package as a method of creating new markets. The absence of markets in underdeveloped countries is not merely a question of low real incomes; it is also a question of the specific economic framework and institutions in which the incomes are earned. If the division of labor depends on

the extent of the market, the market in turn depends on the extent to which certain facilities are available. Transport is the most obvious of these facilities. The doctrine of balanced economic growth is right in emphasizing the creation of markets as a key problem, but one can create markets by methods other than by inducing balanced demand.

6) Unbalanced investment, a sixth means of encouraging economic growth, and quite apart from foreign trade, appears at first paradoxical. It would be unrealistic to assume a state of perfect harmony-- even the harmony of the deadlock--between markets and supplies. The doctrine of balanced growth seems to assume that in making decisions on the allocation of resources in an underdeveloped country we start from scratch. That, of course, is not so. Rather, we start with a situation which incorporates the effects of previous investment and previous developments. This means that at any given point of time there are types of investment which are not in themselves balanced-investment packages, but which are complementary to existing investments, and which thus bring the total stock of capital nearer balance. We must thus distinguish between balance as the end result at which to aim, and balance as the method of approach. Where you start with imbalance, you need further imbalance in order to come closer to balance. It may be said that this still leaves the concept of the balanced-investment package valid, only stretching it over several investment periods. Thus, while we may be aiming at balance as an investment criterion, we achieve this objective by unbalanced investment.

We have now described six alternative approaches other than those singled out by the doctrine of "balanced growth." Each of these alternative approaches could conceivably, if successfully pursued, resolve the marketing deadlock which gave origin to the doctrine of balanced growth. Thus balanced growth should be judged not as a sole cure for the evil correctly diagnosed but as one of several possible cures. Which of the various cures will be the most appropriate will then depend on specific situations, and more particularly on the total volume of available resources. In this respect, the specific cure of the balanced-investment package does not compare well in the early stages of development because it requires large resources--in fact larger resources than most expositors of the doctrine seem to realize. The balanced-investment package cannot logically be confined to a group of projects which are self-supporting on the demand side; the package must include investment in agriculture and in the infrastructure. The cure is far from being the sole cure; in addition, it is an expensive cure and one which is most effective when taken as a mixture with other prescriptions.

But having thus defined the limitations of the doctrine, we are now perhaps in a better position also to appreciate its merits: the combination of self-supporting projects can serve to raise the productivity of investment. In particular, it can prevent the creation of "white elephants"--projects without a market--which dot the landscape in so many underdeveloped countries. As between alternative appropriations of given resources, the balanced-investment package has an inherent superiority--wherever the available resources are sufficient for such a package.

There is another lesson which we can learn from the doctrine of balanced growth. The inducement to invest will be greatly increased by expectation of expanding markets and expanding incomes. Inflationary expectations are one way of increasing the inducement to invest; an expectation of real growth would be just as effective--perhaps more effective. It is not sufficient that complementary investment which will provide markets actually go forward; it is necessary also that it be seen or known, or at least assumed, to go forward. For this reason, in any development program of an underdeveloped country it is crucially important to create a general sense of moving forward. The very formulation of development programs may be helpful in creating such a sense of moving forward--more specifically, I believe that this is also one of the most important effects of the community development movement in India. Balanced growth can play a part in improving what in trade cycle theory is perhaps rather vaguely called "the state of business confidence." A low-level deadlock of incomes and markets can be due to excessive self-justifying pessimism concerning future markets, particularly where there is a long history of stagnation or economic troubles. It is, however, not so easy for excessive optimism to be self-justifying--the inexorable limitation of resources stands in the way. Where the low-level equilibrium has been determined by excessive pessimism rather than by resource limitation, the doctrine of balanced growth acquires considerable theoretical as well as practical merit.

Finally, let us remember that the objections to the doctrine of balanced growth will be greatly reduced and finally vanish as the available resources increase in the course of economic growth. Thus interpreted, the doctrine should stimulate underdeveloped countries to undertake the necessary sacrifices in the early stages of development; it dangles before them a carrot--the hope that one day when resources have become big enough, balanced-investment packages will become possible. Having labored to the top, the balanced-investment package will help them to "slide down the other side of the roof," into the promised land of cumulative growth and compound interest.

Hans W. Singer

NOTES

[1]Allyn Young, "Increasing Returns and Economic Progress," Economic Journal, Vol. XXXVIII (December, 1928), pp. 527–542.

[2]"External Economies and the Doctrine of Balanced Growth," Economic Journal, Vol. LXV (June, 1955), p. 246. See also Fleming, "External Economies and the Doctrine of Balanced Growth: A Rejoinder to Prof. Nurkse," ibid., Vol. LXVI (September, 1956), pp. 537–539.

[3]Ragnar Nurkse, Problems of Capital Formation in Underdeveloped Countries (Oxford, 1957), pp. 30–31.

[4]Ragnar Nurkse, "Balanced Growth on Static Assumptions," Economic Journal, Vol. LXVI (June, 1956), p. 366.

[5]Nurkse, Problems of Capital Formation, p. 13.

[6]"Labor Productivity of the Cotton Textile Industry in Five Latin-American Countries" (Sales No. 1951.II.G.2.).

INFLATION IN ECONOMIC DEVELOPMENT

Geoffrey Maynard

University College of Wales, Cardiff

In discussions on problems and policies of underdeveloped countries, the issue of inflation takes a central place. Should inflation be permitted, even promoted, to stimulate growth? Is the alternative to some degree of inflation just stagnation? Can governments in fact pursue policies which, though keeping price stability, do not hinder growth? As in many, if not most, economic matters as crucial as this, opinions are divided and it is difficult to choose between them. In general the responsible international bodies--for example, the International Monetary Fund and the various economic sections of the United Nations--take a strong anti-inflationary line. To quote one United Nations Publication:

Inflation holds particular dangers for under-developed countries. In general their output is more rigid than that of industrialized countries and cannot easily be expanded to meet the pressure of rising monetary demand; the administrative and economic mechanisms required for keeping inflation in check are less developed; confidence in monetary stability and monetary institutions is less firmly established; while foreign exchange reactions are more closely watched and the danger of capital flight is greater. Inflation encourages the speculative and inessential transactions which are major obstacles to economic development; discourages domestic savings as well as foreign investment; disrupts foreign trade relations and lowers the general efficiency of production.[1]

Similar authoritative views have been expressed by various members of the staff of the International Monetary Fund and by other private economists. A more favorable, or at least a more tolerant, attitude is adopted by Professors Gunnar Myrdal and W. Arthur Lewis. Myrdal, while denying that he is a "theoretician of inflation" and not recommending it, argues that some inflation and development are better than stagnation; and, indeed, he affirms that those underdeveloped countries that have had most success in keeping financial stability have at the same time stagnated or at least have not developed as fast as they should.[2] He does not say, however, which countries he has in mind. Professor Lewis holds the view that "some inflation is helpful to economic development"[3] and he cites as examples Japan and Soviet Russia, in whose development inflation has played a prominent role.

It is clearly not easy to come to a view on this matter. The central issue is the effect of a rising price level, and the relative changes in prices that accompany it, on the volume and distribution of saving and investment; but a purely theoretical examination of this issue can hardly decide it one way or another. Theoretical models are invaluable, of course, for describing and emphasizing the crucial relationships which enter into such a problem, but depending on the values assigned to the variables and relationships incorporated in them, they yield widely varying solutions without giving a clue as to which of these solutions is most relevant. Suppose, for instance, a multiplier type model is set up to examine what will happen to prices when an increase in investment takes place in a situation of inelastic supply and when ex-ante saving does not increase correspondingly.[4] Assuming that prices are demand-determined, factors which are obviously important and have to be included in the model are: (1) the propensities of various income groups to save; (2) variations in these propensities during the course of inflation; (3) shifts in the distribution of income between income groups; (4) induced effects on investment; (5) the magnitude and nature of the yield from the initial increase in investment; and (6) the various time lags, including the gestation period of investment, which enter into the relationships.

Values can be assigned to these variables, relationships, and lags which would yield quite moderate rises in prices--for instance, if wages lag well behind prices, if the income groups which benefit from this lag have high propensities to save, if all income groups suffer from money illusion, and if there are no positive induced effects on investment. Alternatively, values can be assigned which would indicate a rapid and extreme inflation, and in some conditions, no price equilibrium at all. If the first group of values were relevant, we might conclude that inflation is an efficient process for raising saving; if the latter group were relevant, then we should regard it as highly dangerous. Unfortunately it is not possible to decide on a priori grounds which group in fact will be relevant, and it may even be difficult to determine this empirically. There can be little doubt that the crucial relationship is the reaction of wages to prices: if this can be minimized, then inflation will not be severe and saving can be more easily forced. It cannot be inferred, however, that strong labor organizations make inflation inevitable. In fact it has recently been argued that trade unions can play a vital moderating role, provided they are consulted concerning the means and ends of economic expansion.[5] Furthermore, as I shall stress later on, the pressure for compensating wage increases depends more on some prices than others, so if development is planned to minimize increases in these strategic prices then the danger of the inflationary spiral is so much the less. Certainly the outcome depends on a variety of political, economic, and social circumstances which differ from country to country and from time to time and which are hardly subject to generalization.

The effects of inflation on the volume and distribution of investment are equally indeterminate: both favorable and unfavorable effects can be expected. Rising prices, if it is anticipated with some degree of certainty that the trend will persist into the future, will raise the expected profitability of investment, and, depending on the horizon of expectations, will raise it in relation to long-term or short-term expectations. On the other hand, the suppliers of materials and productive services may also expect prices to rise, and by holding on to their supplies, bid up the current cost of investment projects, thereby reducing their profitability. Even if inflation induces the undertaking of more investment projects than would otherwise be the case, it does not follow that more investment will in fact be carried out: when resources are limited and cannot easily be directed or attracted away from other uses, more investment projects may be started than can be completed within a given period. For instance, two projects are started, with neither finished, instead of one's being started, with one finished. This tends to add to inflationary pressure since, in effect, the gestation period of investment is lengthened. Furthermore, as many writers have pointed out, there is considerable danger that investment and saving will be misallocated during the course of inflation. The possession of inventories, real estate, precious metals and stones, and foreign-exchange assets is a sure way of hedging against an internal and external fall in the value of money, but it is a form of investment that makes little contribution to future growth. In part, the attractiveness of this form of investment depends on the rate at which prices are expected to rise. The horizon of expectations that investors will attach to a slow rise in prices is no doubt much further into the future than the horizon they will attach to a rapid rise. Rapid price inflation cannot be expected to last for long, since in the end it will lead to disruption of the economic and social system, or will force the government to take prior anti-inflationary action. Hence, it will lead investors to prefer assets yielding quick, easily realizable capital gains. Slow inflation, on the other hand, particularly if the rate at which prices are rising is lower than the current money rate of interest, will encourage investors to look for longer-term income-yielding assets which are normally more favorable to growth. But if, on balance, inflation is considered to be prejudicial to growth-promoting investment, it must not be overlooked that, even in its absence, much personal saving in many underdeveloped countries does not go into agricultural or industrial investment. The absence of suitable financial intermediaries and a reluctance of savers to lose direct control over their capital cause saving to go into real estate and urban house building.[6] Two key factors seem to be the shortage of experienced entrepreneurs in underdeveloped countries and the absence of a capitalist class that thinks in terms of "re-investing its income productively"[7] for future income rather than capital gain. It is at least significant that, apart from wars, inflation in advanced countries is usually accompanied by considerable investment in fixed assets. We are told, for instance, that even in the hyperinflationary conditions of Germany in the 1920's, a considerable volume of fixed investment was carried out, and a marked improvement in Germany's industrial equipment took place.[8] It would appear, therefore, that a shortage of entrepreneurial talent, quite as much as the presence of inflation, explains the unproductive nature of saving in underdeveloped countries.[9]

Perhaps the most crucial and clear-cut objection to inflation, particularly if it is unilateral, is the pressure it places on the foreign-exchange market. For well-known reasons, inflation tends to cause a worsening in the balance of trade, so unless effective import controls can be imposed (which themselves might have an adverse effect on growth), the monetary authorities will be forced to bring inflation to an end or permit a continuous depreciation of the exchange rate which, however, only adds to the inflationary pressure. A healthy and reasonably stable foreign-exchange market is of considerable importance to most underdeveloped countries since they usually have to import a large proportion of their capital goods.[10] In the absence of sufficient foreign lending, their rate of investment, and therefore to a large extent their rate of growth, is dependent on their export receipts. In the words of the United Nations' Economic Survey, "Inflation cannot help to raise investment since this depends not only on saving, but also on foreign exchange required for the import of capital goods."[11] This objection, however, may be qualified in at least two respects: first, since most underdeveloped countries import a larger proportion of their total supply of capital goods than of their consumption goods, a shift from consumption to investment automatically puts pressure on the balance of payments, quite independently of inflation; and, second, if inflation and rising foreign-exchange receipts go hand in hand, the latter being the cause of the former, as would be the case when the demand for a country's exports is booming, then inflation may be the means whereby investment in the rest of the economy is stimulated to take advantage of the increased capacity for importing capital goods.

There are, no doubt, some very strong arguments which can be made against inflationary methods of promoting growth. Nevertheless, history presents us with two notable examples of effective inflation: the development of Japan from 1885 to 1914, and the development of Soviet Russia from 1930 to 1940. In each case a long period of inflation was accompanied by very rapid growth. Moreover, it is well known that the development of other present-day advanced countries was not accompanied by continuous monetary stability. Instead, growth has taken a cyclical form, capital being generally accumulated in the boom when prices were rising, and yielding its fruits in the subsequent depression. Ignoring the causes of cyclical fluctuations and looking at it from the narrow point of view of inflation and growth,

we can perhaps see the cyclical process as one of intermittent inflation during which the investment:income ratio has been alternately
forced above its "normal" level (that is, the level which can be sustained by voluntary saving), allowing a rapid accumulation of capital,
and alternately forced below its "normal" level, maintaining confidence
in the value of money. Whether the rate of capital accumulation would
have been even higher over the long period if monetary stability had
been the rule cannot of course be determined; and present-day advanced countries concerned with "ironing out" the cycle should not
necessarily be taken as examples for less developed areas. The
problem of advanced countries is, fundamentally, to maintain a rate
of investment that will absorb their high volume of saving and thus
prevent depressions. The problem of underdeveloped countries is to
force saving, not absorb it, and whether this can be achieved in a context of complete monetary stability can hardly be decided on a priori
grounds. At any rate, it is quite clear that it has not happened in the
past.

Inevitably, the general impression left by such an inexhaustive discussion as the foregoing is one of indefiniteness: neither an opposition of the conditions which favor the use of inflation as against those
which do not, nor a list of the pros and cons of inflationary methods
of financing can indicate where the balance of advantage lies. For
this reason it might be more profitable to look at the problem from a
somewhat different, though obviously related, point of view. What sort
of economic development will almost certainly be accompanied by
serious inflationary pressure? Can we isolate some factor which,
perhaps above all others, tends to produce inflation as growth proceeds? Can this pattern of development be avoided?

It is clear that during the over-all process of growth the yield of
investment should be in accordance with the distribution of consumer
demand, which itself will be changing during the course of development. Inflationary pressure arising from the diversion of resources
from the production of consumption goods to the production of investment goods will tend to be self-destructive if, in consequence of the
increase in investment, the output of consumption goods quickly rises
and its composition accords with the wishes of consumers. If, on the
other hand, to take an extreme example, the yield of investment takes
the form of further capital goods rather than consumption goods there
is no "let up" in inflationary pressure; indeed, unless the proportion
of income saved increases correspondingly, inflationary pressure will
intensify.

In a free-market economy, however, where the distribution of investment and resources takes place according to the criterion of
market profitability, it is unlikely that growth will take this "unbalanced" form. The profitability of investment-goods industries depends
on the profitability of consumption-goods industries, so that logically

the development of the latter should precede or at least keep pace with the development of the former. But at low levels of real income per head, both the proportion of consumers' income spent on food and the income elasticity of demand for food are high.[12] As a result, in very poor underdeveloped countries, at least in the early stages of their development, the scope for other, non-food consumption-goods industries is limited and the rate at which they can grow is determined by the rates at which population and agricultural output per head can grow. The conditions of agricultural supply, in other words, determine in large part the rate at which capacity in other consumer-goods industries, and therefore, at one remove, the rate at which capacity in investment-goods industries, can profitably grow. They therefore determine the rate at which the economy as a whole can grow. If the government of a particular underdeveloped country attempted to speed up the rate of growth by forced industrialization--that is, by moving labor out of agriculture at a faster rate than the growth of agricultural productivity will permit--it might result in considerable inflation and/or in unbalanced development.

The connection between lagging agricultural output, inflation, and unbalanced growth can easily be demonstrated. As industrialization proceeds, labor is being moved out of the agricultural sector into urban industrial occupations.

Make the favorable assumption that agricultural output does not fall; and in order to isolate the inflationary effect of lagging agricultural development, further assume that that part of the increase in industrial production which takes the form of capital goods--that is, investment--is matched by an equivalent rise in ex-ante or planned saving out of the marginal increase in income. It follows from our assumptions that total output and total real income will rise. But with a rise in real income the demand for food will also rise, depending on the income-elasticity of demand. Supply, however, is unchanged; hence there will be excess demand for food. On the other hand, given the assumption of balance between ex-ante saving and investment, the demand for consumption goods other than food will increase less than supply. Food prices will therefore tend to rise and other consumer-goods prices tend to fall, the relative rise in food prices being the greater, the lower the elasticity of substitution between the two. How far the relative price change will take the form of a fall in other consumer-goods prices rather than a rise in the price of food (ignoring the possibility of substitutability between these other goods, or of complementarity between any of these goods and food) depends on the cost-and-profit position of urban industries; some minimum level of profitability must be maintained in these industries if their expansion is to continue. On the other hand, the more food prices rise, the more difficult it becomes to keep labor in urban occupations, unless money wages are allowed to rise as well. This argument assumes that labor is more concerned with the rising cost of food than pleased by a fall in the prices of other commodities, an assumption which seems reasonable at low levels of per capita income. But if money wages do rise, a large proportion of the increase is again spent on food, putting further pressure on wages and prices while adding little or nothing to the profitability of urban industries. In brief, the government faces the dilemma of permitting an inflationary spiral of food prices and wages or of slowing down the expansion of urban industry.

This conclusion does not depend on an unchanged food output but only on the fact that supply per capita rises less fast than per capita demand. This can be illustrated by a simple arithmetical example. Suppose at given relative prices the initial level of output is divided between these items: food; non-food urban-produced consumption goods; and capital goods. Suppose further that the division occurs in the following proportions: food, 60 per cent; non-food consumption goods 30 per cent; capital goods 10 per cent. Writing $\underline{Y}$ for total output (and income), $\underline{F}$ for food, $\underline{C}$ for non-food consumption goods, and $\underline{I}$ for capital goods or investment, then

$$\underline{Y} = \underline{F} + \underline{C} + \underline{I}$$

Suppose the program of industrialization aims at increasing total output by 10 per cent in a given period, the increment being divided as follows: 20 per cent food, 60 per cent non-food industrial consumption goods, and 20 per cent capital goods, measured at unchanged relative prices. In effect, we have an ex-ante marginal supply equation (Δ representing the incremental factor):

$$\Delta\underline{Y} = \Delta\underline{F} + \Delta\underline{C} + \Delta\underline{I}$$
(or 100 = 20 + 60 + 20)

If the income elasticity of demand for food is 50 per cent, then the marginal propensity to consume food is 30 per cent; and if we assume that the increase in investment-goods output is balanced by an increase in savings out of marginal income, then the marginal propensity to consume non-food-consumption goods becomes 50 per cent. The ex-ante marginal demand equation becomes ($\underline{S}'$ representing savings):

$$\Delta\underline{Y} = \Delta\underline{F}' + \Delta\underline{C}' + \Delta\underline{S}'$$
(or 100 = 30 + 50 + 20)

the prime being used to distinguish this equation from the corresponding equation of supply. If these ex-ante aggregate demand and supply equations are opposed in the market, it is obvious there will be excess demand for food and excess supply of other consumption goods equal to 10 per cent of the marginal increase in output. Food prices must therefore rise relatively to industrial consumer-goods prices if the market is to be cleared. But if, owing to cost conditions in urban industries, this relative price change takes the form of an absolute rise in food prices, there arises the danger of a considerable inflationary spiral.

Suppose the government, anticipating the excess demand for food which will arise out of a 10 per cent rise in consumers' real income, tries to offset it by taxing incomes; that is to say, it aims at limiting the increase in consumers' disposable income so that, given the income elasticity of demand for food, the demand for food equals the supply. In our example, the increase in demand for food must be limited to 20 per cent of the increment; hence given an income elasticity of demand equal to 50 per cent (i.e., a marginal propensity to consume food equal to 30 per cent), the increase in disposable income must be limited to 66 2/3 per cent, that is, taxation must take one-third of the increase in real income. The ex-ante aggregate demand equation now becomes ($\underline{T}$ representing taxes):

$$\Delta\underline{Y} - \Delta\underline{T} = \Delta\underline{F}' + \Delta\underline{C}' + \Delta\underline{S}'$$

(or 100 - 33 1/3 = 20 + 33 1/3 + 13 1/3)

But although equilibrium in the food market has been achieved, the disequilibrium in the market for other consumer goods is much worse: there is an excess supply of 27 2/3 per cent, which implies the need for an even greater fall in prices than if taxation had not been imposed. In other words, in successfully combating an inflationary rise in food prices the government has at the same time reduced the scope for the profitable expansion of urban industrial production.

It is of course open to the government to use other methods to keep down food prices, for example, by subsidizing food to urban workers or by forcing the farm sector to sell its output at prices below those which would rule in a free market. But such remedies require a system of rationing and a firm control over black-market activities, both of which imply considerable administrative machinery and expertise. Price-fixing has the further disadvantage of perpetuating the crucial obstacle to industrial growth, since it offers no incentive to the farmer to increase his output.

An obvious escape from the dilemma, and one which densely populated countries eventually must take, is the development of an export trade in manufactures; food supplies can then be enhanced by imports, and a market is created for the newly-developing industries. If the government, however, finding this avenue of escape opening too slowly, nevertheless presses on with a rapid rate of industrialization, then it courts the risk of extreme inflation. Furthermore, because of the relative unprofitability of non-food consumption-goods production imposed by the high income-elasticity of demand for food, as well as perhaps by its own anti-inflationary policy, the product of this industrial growth must be increasingly directed into outlets other than the immediate satisfaction of consumer wants--for example, into the further expansion of investment-goods capacity or, if the political situation decrees, into the expansion of military strength. I do not want to suggest that the priority given by some governments, notably the government of the U.S.S.R., to the expansion of producer-goods capacity in preference to the production of consumer goods, stems directly from the factors I have mentioned; it may be, and usually is, the result of a conscious decision on the part of government, aimed at a more rapid rate of over-all growth of both investment and consumption in the longer run. My point is only that in conditions of lagging agricultural output, a high and expanding rate of investment-goods production may be a necessary condition for a currently high rate of industrial growth. Moreover, the chronic inflation which tends to accompany such a high rate of investment stems not so much from the failure to sufficiently restrict consumption, though this clearly does play a part, but more from the forcing of total consumption into a less desired pattern. It is not the excess of investment over saving which is so important, but rather the fact that investment is failing to produce yield in accordance with consumer demand.

Illustrations of the crucial part played by lagging agricultural output in inflationary development can be found in both past and very recent history, and it will be of interest to make brief reference to them. A familiar and classic example of unbalanced growth accompanied by extreme inflation is Soviet economic development in the 1930's. It appears that not even the most authoritarian control over the economy could contain the consequences of the failure of agriculture to keep pace with industry. It is well known that the Soviet government resorted to collectivization, and indeed devoted a large proportion of its annual investment potential to agriculture,[13] in order to ensure adequate food supplies for the growing industrial population. Despite the extreme pressure put on the farm sector, agricultural output barely kept pace with the rise in population: both rose by about 15 per cent from 1928 to 1939,[14] though output per farm worker rose by 28 per cent. The compulsory collection of the agricultural surplus at below "market" prices certainly succeeded in reducing the attractiveness of rural life, but it did not prevent an enormous rise in food prices to the urban worker. According to Jasny, food prices to urban workers rose by more than 900 per cent in the ten years 1927--1937,[15] and even at these high prices the demand for many necessities was not satisfied. The difference between the price paid by the urban worker and that received by the farmer was taken in the form of a turnover tax and used to finance capital accumulation in industry. Money wages rose by nearly 400 per cent,[16] and though heavily subsidized, prices of producer goods rose by 150 per cent.[17] Although the enormous priority given to the expansion of producer-goods capacity[18] was clearly the result of deliberate decision on the part of the Soviet government, nonetheless it seems quite possible that the failure of agricultural output to keep pace with the needs of a growing and industrializing population, and the reluctance or inability of the U.S.S.R. to take advantage of international trade, would have forced development into this pattern if industrialization had been the primary aim, quite apart from reasons of prestige and military necessity.

Coming to more recent times, it seems clear too that the extreme inflation that has characterized the development of many Latin-American countries in the postwar period has had much to do with the neglect of their agricultural sectors. I do not want to suggest that no other factors have contributed to inflation; fluctuations in the terms of trade and inadequate control over the money supply leading to exchange depreciation have also been of great importance. But two basic facts stand out: first, the wage-price spiral, with food prices taking the lead, has been the crucial factor in most countries, whether or not their labor has been extensively organized in trade unions; and second, in Latin America as a whole, and in many of its component countries, agricultural production per capita in recent postwar years has been running at about 8 per cent below its prewar level.[19] Although imports of agricultural products have risen and exports have fallen, it remains true that food supply per capita has lagged well behind the rise in per capita real income. It is of course to be expected that as real income rises, the demand for food will rise less than proportionately. The Economic Commission for Latin America has estimated that the income elasticity of demand for food in this region will be around 0.5 or 0.6;[20] and if this estimate is accepted it is easy to understand why food prices have risen so greatly, more than proportionately to all other prices. Whereas income per capita in the principal countries of the area has risen by about 40 per cent as compared with prewar income, food supply per capita has risen by no more than 8 per cent.[21] The income elasticity of demand for food would therefore have had to be less than 0.2 for pressure on food prices to be avoided.[22] An examination of the experience of individual Latin-American countries is also suggestive. Although there is no clear-cut correlation, the general impression emerges that inflation has tended to be most severe in those countries where food supply per capita has lagged farthest behind income per capita, yet whose over-all rates of growth, in the postwar period, at least, have been high. The table on page 97 gives comparable data for five Latin-American countries. Chile is an obvious exception. There food supply seems to have maintained a better relationship with income; yet inflation in Chile has been more severe than in any other of the Latin-American countries except Bolivia. The Economic Commission for Latin America indicates as major causes Chile's less favorable terms of trade and the powerful position of its trade unions.

	(a) Percentage rise in food supply per capita, 1937-1954	(b) Percentage rise in income per capita, 1937-1954	(c) (a) ÷ (b)	(d) Price change, 1937-1956	(e) Price change, 1948-1956	(f) Ann. av. percentage rate of growth per capita gross income, 1945-1955
Argentina	1	21	.05	9 fold	3 fold	1.7
Brazil	5	62	.08	12 fold	3 fold	3.8
Mexico*	14	80	.18	6 fold	+80%	2.5
Chile	13	37	.40	52 fold	12 fold	1.6
Colombia	34	49	.70	5 fold	+70%	4.5

*Agricultural output in Mexico has increased very rapidly during the last few years.
Sources: U.N. Economic Commission for Latin America, The Selective Expansion of Agricultural Production in Latin America and U.N. Economic Survey of Latin America, 1953.

The experience of Bolivia illustrates in exaggerated form the danger of a country's putting too much reliance on a favorable trend in its international terms of trade while neglecting its agriculture. Apart from agriculture, the output of Bolivia's extractive industries (mainly tin) makes the largest contribution to national output and provides the major source of its foreign-exchange earnings. Throughout the war and early postwar period, Bolivia benefited from a favorable trend in its terms of trade, and a considerable proportion of its foreign-exchange earnings was used to pay for food imports--45 per cent in 1955.

When the market for tin collapsed in 1952 there was an immediate and catastrophic effect on food supplies, and although Bolivia attempted to maintain its imports with U.S. aid and the running down of its foreign-exchange reserves, by 1956 the latter were exhausted and the former insufficient. The rate of inflation, which had been running at something like 150 per cent per annum since 1952, accelerated to almost 200 per cent in 1956. In the four years between 1952 and 1956 food prices rose 33 fold.[23] Again, it would be quite wrong to explain this enormous inflation solely in terms of food supplies: political and social troubles associated with revolution in 1952, perhaps unwise support given to active and aggressive trade unions, and the government's disastrous exchange-rate policy, which in effect made government budget deficits inevitable, were all of great importance.[24] Nonetheless the fact remains that between 1952 and 1956 agricultural output fell by 10 per cent, during which time population increased in like proportion.

No doubt the absolute decline in agricultural output during this period had much to do with the rate of inflation itself: farmers found it more profitable to engage in black-market, contraband, and speculative activities than to pursue their legitimate business of farming.[25] But the Economic Commission for Latin America dates the stagnation

of Bolivian agriculture from the 1930's, despite progress in other
sectors, explaining it by an inefficient system of land tenure, based
on semifeudal estates and absentee landlords, which gave no incentive
for the introduction of better methods or commercial crops.[26] A land
Reform Act introduced in 1953 failed to give results, at least up to
1956, mainly because by this time inflation had gotten completely out
of hand.

Fluctuations in the international terms of trade have very potent
effects on economic development, particularly for low-income countries relying on the export of a few strategic primary products for the
purchase of their capital equipment. A secular improvement allows
real income to rise at a faster rate than output while at the same time
acting as a spur to that output: the ability to save, the incentive to invest, and the capacity to buy capital goods from overseas are all increased at the same time.[27] A secular decline, of course, has opposite effects. Similarly, the terms of trade determine in large part
the behavior of the domestic price level.

A strong upward movement in export prices makes it difficult to
preserve price stability. Not only is the general price level directly
affected, but as multiplier effects impinge on the economy, all other
prices tend to rise as well. Furthermore, the expansion of export
receipts and the improvement in the balance of payments directly increase the money supply, thereby providing the leeway for inflation.
The impact of this inflation is hidden somewhat by the fact that real
income is rising: indeed, to a large extent the rise in the general
level of prices and wages is the means by which the benefits of improved terms of trade are distributed throughout the economy. Governments are prepared to put up with inflation since it is accompanied
by favorable effects on growth. But if the rate and character of
growth have been closely geared to the favorable trend in the terms
of trade--if, for instance, as appears to be the case in Latin America,
all the benefits have been channeled into industry to the complete ex-
clusion of agriculture--a break in the trend has serious consequences.
A sudden fall in export prices, instead of moderating inflation, may
sharply intensify it. At least three factors work in this direction.
First, worsening of the terms of trade implies a check to the growth
of real income and, in poor countries, even an absolute fall; but this
converts a rise in wages and prices which was formerly distributing
real income gains throughout the economy into a vicious spiral, as
all sections of the community attempt to maintain individual standards
of living which are no longer compatible. Second, since a large proportion of government revenue in underdeveloped countries is often
obtained by taxes on exports, a fall in export receipts automatically
creates a government deficit; governments cannot easily disengage
themselves from commitments entered into when receipts were high.
Finally, if the fall in export receipts provokes a balance-of-payments

crisis (and no reserves have been accumulated against this eventuality), the currency may have to be devalued, further increasing inflationary pressure on domestic prices. All these effects can be found in recent Latin-American history, and all are well documented in the various U.N. surveys of the area.

The development of Japan from 1880 is a striking contrast to the examples of extreme inflationary growth associated with lagging agricultural output and undue reliance on favorable terms of trade. A basic element in Japan's early development was the substantial rise in agricultural output which continued up to the First World War. Output per farm worker rose by more than 100 per cent, and although labor was moving off the land, total agricultural output rose by 80 per cent.[28] During the same period, population grew by 44 per cent, so agricultural output per head of the population rose by about 25 per cent. Real wages were rather stable up to 1900, but by 1914 they had risen by 20 per cent as compared with wages in 1885.[29] It is well known that the Japanese government resorted to heavy taxes on agriculture to siphon off the benefits of rising productivity and make them available for capital formation in industry but, at least up to 1900, the development of light consumer-goods industries which used up little capital and which could be integrated into rural life, was given priority,[30] forming "an extension of agriculture" rather than an alternative to it.

Japanese growth up to the First World War was of course accompanied by inflation, with the government and the banks willing to create credit rather than to see industry go short.[31] But in comparison with the Russian inflation, for example, the rise in prices was very moderate, averaging about 4 per cent per annum from 1885 to 1914, which in relation to the growth in income per head, also about 4 per cent per annum, can hardly be regarded as excessive.[32] The reason for the quantitative difference between the Russian and Japanese inflations evidently lies not in the difference between the respective governments' willingness to resort to inflationary financing or to force a rate of investment greater than voluntary saving, but rather in the more balanced development of Japan, based on a prior and simultaneous expansion of agricultural output. Significantly, and in clear contrast to Soviet and Latin-American inflations, agricultural prices rose at a slower rate than did prices of industrial goods.

The constriction that lagging agricultural development places on over-all growth is of course generally well recognized. At the same time, however, history shows that at a certain stage in their development, countries try to by-pass this constriction by taking advantage of the possibilities of international trade. Britain in the early part of the nineteenth century, and Japan in the twentieth, are prime examples of countries moving toward industrial specialization, exporting manufactures in exchange for food and primary products. That such specialization permits more industrialization and more growth can hardly be disputed; nonetheless it does not divorce industrial growth rates and the accompanying behavior of prices from the underlying supply conditions of food and primary products. The more a country specializes in either manufactures or primary products, the greater is the dependence of its rate of growth and the behavior of its price level on the international, as distinct from the domestic, terms of exchange between the two.

Basically, the international terms of trade of an industrial country improve, and those of primary-producer countries worsen, when the international trend of food and primary-product prices is downward, the opposite also being true. Hence it follows that industrial countries are likely to receive both the benefits of improved terms of trade on growth and of falling import prices on domestic price levels at the same time, whereas the benefits of improved terms of trade for primary-producer countries tend to be associated with rising export and domestic price levels. In other words, higher-than-average rates of growth are likely to be accompanied by falling price levels in industrial countries and by rising price levels in primary-producer countries. Evidence in favor of this contention can be found in Mr. Rostow's study of Britain in the nineteenth century and more recently in Professor Kuznets' quantitative analysis of variations in country rates of growth over time.[33] Thus, for instance, Britain's above-trend rates of growth are to be found during those periods when its domestic price level was falling, that is, 1815-1850, 1870-1895, and in the 1930's, when the world price level of food and primary products was falling. On the other hand, Sweden and Denmark, both more specialized in food and primary-product production, had above-trend rates of growth when the world price level of these products, and therefore their own domestic price levels, were rising. The United States' domestic price level also moved with world prices of food and primary products, but its rate of growth was not similarly affected. Total output being more evenly balanced between manufactures and primary products, fluctuations in the terms of exchange between the two resulted in purely domestic shifts in income rather than shifts across national frontiers as experienced by Britain, Denmark, and Sweden.

The general argument of this paper is that economic development will be accompanied by serious inflation if it takes an unbalanced form: that is, if the production of capital goods is given too great a priority over consumption goods, and if industrial development is given too great a priority over agriculture. Since in very poor countries, in the early stages of their development, total consumption largely coincides with that of food, the statement can perhaps be summarized by saying that chronic inflation will result if too great a proportion of a country's saving and resources is directed into industry and too small a proportion into agriculture. The conclusion can be carried over to more advanced countries and to the international sphere by saying that if the rate of industrialization throughout the world tends to be so fast in relation to the growth of food and primary-product output that the terms of exchange are moving in favor of the latter, the world economic climate is likely to be inflationary; conversely prices will tend to fall if primary-product production shows a relatively great expansion. In this case, of course, the danger lies in the possibility of a world slump. But how does this conclusion bear on the question with which we started--should inflationary methods of financing be used to promote growth?

In the course of a review of monetary developments, the Economic Commission for Latin America came to the conclusion that "countries which have experienced the sharpest degree of inflation and those which have experienced none at all show the least development."[34] The conclusion seems hardly surprising. It is generally agreed that the level of per capita income in most underdeveloped countries is so low, and the expansion of population, at least in absolute terms, so fast, that reliance on voluntary saving alone will imply at best stagnation, at worst an absolute decline in living standards. This points to the need for forced saving: it does not, of course, necessarily point to the need for inflationary financing, although given the administrative, political, and psychological difficulties in the way of an effective and equitable fiscal policy, some inflation seems to be inevitable. Whether inflation becomes self-defeating, in the sense that it does not give rise to additional real saving and/or distorts the distribution of investment, depends fundamentally on the reaction of wages to prices, that is, the wage-price spiral; and I have aimed at stressing in this paper that the key to the spiral is the behavior of food prices.

The inference is then obvious. Schemes of development, though explicitly based on the need for forced saving, are more likely to achieve their aim with the minimum of inflation if due priority is given to agricultural development and to industries complementary rather than competitive to it. The course of the terms of trade between agriculture and manufacturing must be prevented from moving in favor of agriculture, not, of course, by administrative subterfuges such as price control, but through the interaction of supply and demand. To allow the demand for food to outrun supply is to court the risk that the pressure of excess demand will quickly be replaced by cost inflation, that is, the wage-price spiral, a risk which is considerably less in the case of excess demand for other goods. The real danger occurs if governments pursue lax monetary policies from the very beginning without exercising some influence on the distribution of investment and resources; for if agriculture is neglected in the early stages, then forces are set up which will perpetuate this neglect.

Once the wage-price spiral starts in earnest, investment in agriculture, and in all basic long-term income-yielding sources, is at a disadvantage as compared with those prospects yielding speculative capital gains.

Emphasis on agricultural development does not conflict with the fact that the largest proportion of investment potential may still go into industry. As the Japanese experience shows, the introduction of modern farming techniques may yield substantial results without much investment; furthermore, in densely populated countries, drawing labor off the land may be an essential step toward raising agricultural output. But the substantial point remains: if growth is to take place with the minimum of inflation, food supply per head of the population must bear an appropriate relationship with income per head.

NOTES

[1] Methods of Financing Economic Development (United Nations, 1949), p. 19. See also various Economic Surveys prepared by the U.N. Economic Commission for Latin America, particularly that for 1955.

[2] Gunnar Myrdal, in R. Lekachman (ed.), National Policy for Economic Policy at Home and Abroad (Columbia University Bicentennial Conference Series, 1955), p. 291.

[3] W. Arthur Lewis, The Theory of Economic Growth (London, 1955), p. 404.

[4] For such a model, see S. P. Schatz, "Inflation in Underdeveloped Areas," American Economic Review (September, 1957), and further references cited therein.

[5] Asoka Mehta, "The Mediating Role of the Trade Union in Underdeveloped Countries," Economic Development and Cultural Change, Vol. VI, No. 1 (October, 1957).

[6] E. M. Bernstein, "Financing Growth in Underdeveloped Countries," Savings in the Modern Economy, ed. Heller, Boddy, and Nelson (Minneapolis, 1953).

[7] W. Arthur Lewis, op. cit., p. 232.

[8] F. D. Graham, Exchange, Prices and Production in Hyperinflation, Germany 1920–1923 (Princeton, 1930). For a somewhat different view, see Bresciani-Turroni, The Economics of Inflation (London, 1937).

[9] Of course, there is no point in using inflation to transfer income into the hands of people who will use it unproductively.

[10] Imported capital goods comprise about 35 per cent of total investment in Latin-American countries, and also the same proportion of their total imports.--U.N. Economic Survey of Latin America, 1951-1952, Tables 10, 11, pp. 20, 23.

[11] Ibid., p. 3.

[12] As high as 0.8 in India and 0.5 or 0.6 in Latin America.--See U.N. Commission for Latin America, The Selective Expansion of Agricultural Production in Latin America in 1957.

[13] Mr. Kaplan has estimated that about 19 per cent of Soviet gross investment went into agriculture in the 1930's.--N. M. Kaplan, "Capital Formation and Allocation," Table 27 in A. Bergson, Soviet Economic Growth (Evanston, Ill., Row, Peterson & Company, 1953).

[14] For estimates of population growth, see W. W. Eason, "Population and Labour Force," in Bergson, ibid. For estimates of agricultural output, see Naum Jasny, "The Socialized Agriculture of the U.S.S.R.," Stanford University Food Research Institute, Miscellaneous Publication 11 A (October, 1951).

[15] Naum Jasny, "The Soviet Economy During the Plan Era," Stanford University Food Research Institute, Miscellaneous Publication 11 A, Appendix, Table III, p. 111.

[16] Ibid., p. 69.

[17]Naum Jasny, "Soviet Prices of Producer Goods," Stanford University Food Research Institute, Miscellaneous Publication 11 A, p. 15.

[18]Kaplan, loc. cit.

[19]U.N. Economic Commission for Latin America, The Selective Expansion of Agricultural Production in Latin America, Chap. IV, Table 15.

[20]Ibid., p. 21.

[21]Argentina, Brazil, Chile, Colombia, Mexico, ibid., Chap. IV, Table 26.

[22]If meat and wheat are excluded from the foodstuffs, and Argentina and Brazil from the countries, then the over-all picture improves: the percentage rise in food supply per capita is then about 50 per cent of the percentage rise in per capita real income. But these items of food were of considerable importance in prewar Latin-American diet, and consumers could be induced to substitute other foods for them only by a large rise in price. Even in Mexico, a net exporter without serious supply problems, meat prices rose by about 60 per cent in 6 years, while in Brazil and Chile they rose by 100 per cent and 200 per cent, respectively.--Ibid., pp. 50-54.

[23]U.N. Economic Bulletin for Latin America, Vol. 11, No. 2 (October, 1957), p. 29 and Table 5.

[24]Ibid., p. 32.

[25]"Moreover, a considerable number of farmers came to the cities to form queues for the purchase of goods in official sales or at controlled prices in order to resell them in the black market, thereby earning more than they could in their agricultural pursuits."--Ibid., p. 34.

[26]Ibid., p. 55.

[27]For a detailed analysis of the effects of the terms of trade on Latin-American development, see the annual Economic Surveys produced by the Economic Commission for Latin America, particularly that for 1951-1952.

[28]Bruce F. Johnston, "Agricultural Productivity and Economic Development in Japan," Journal of Political Economy (December, 1951).

[29]Kazushi Ohkawa, The Growth Rate of the Japanese Economy since 1878, in collaboration with Miyohei Shinohara, M. Umemura, M. Ito, and T. Noda (Tokyo, 1957).

[30]Gustav Ranis, "Factor Proportions in Japanese Economic Development," American Economic Review (September, 1957).

[31]"In most underdeveloped countries, domestic voluntary savings are rather scarce, and if the amount of new investment is to be confined strictly to the amount of savings collected by the financial institutions, not much could be done. Throughout the course of economic development, Japan was always short of capital, and the government did not hesitate to take every possible means to augment the supply of credit."--Saburo Okita, "Savings and Economic Growth in Japan," Economic Development and Cultural Change, Vol. VI, No. 1 (October, 1957).

[32]Kazushi Ohkawa, op. cit.

[33]W. W. Rostow, The British Economy in the Nineteenth Century (Oxford, 1948). Simon Kuznets, "Quantitative Aspects of the Economic Growth of Nations," Economic Development and Cultural Change, Vol. V, No. 1 (October, 1956).

[34]U.N. Economic Commission for Latin America, Economic Survey of Latin America (1953), p. 73.

THE STRUCTURAL CRISIS IN ARGENTINA AND ITS PROSPECTS OF SOLUTION

Raúl Prebisch

The Economic Commission for Latin America

I. The Need for Industrialization

To the student of economic development, whether from the standpoint of theory or policy, the experience of Argentina offers an interesting object lesson. It shows, in the first place, that industrialization is an indispensable requisite for economic development in a country engaged in primary production, once such development has progressed beyond a certain stage. It also demonstrates how industrialization policy can be so seriously mistaken as to impose a heavy handicap on economic development itself and intensify the country's external vulnerability. Lastly, the case of Argentina presents a striking contrast between the ambitious scale on which development programs have been formulated and the singular lack of foresight with which the basic problems of the economy have been approached by the State.

It is not surprising, therefore, that programing and industrialization should have become two concepts which arouse opposition in certain sectors of Argentine public opinion. Their real significance has been falsified, and will have to be re-established, for without a positive industrialization effort and careful programing of the co-ordinated development of all sectors of the economy, the economic reconstruction of Argentina will, in my opinion, be indefinitely postponed.

The primary aim of this article is to discuss the foregoing aspects of the problem and sketch in broad outline the measures calculated to overcome the country's structural crisis. It is based on an analysis of the whole problem contained in a United Nations study now in course of completion.[1]

In Argentina, as in other countries in the process of development, there has been a gradual shift of the active population from agriculture to industry and services. But there is one fundamental difference. Whereas in the other Latin-American countries the land had been farmed for centuries by a population using primitive techniques, when Argentina was incorporated into the world market in the mid-nineteenth century, the fertile pampas were absolutely virgin soil and were very sparsely inhabited. Immigration from abroad is rapidly increasing their population as the railway network spreads over the interior of the country, and the immigrants bring with them farm practices from countries where agriculture is developed, although in Argentina, as land is so plentiful, extensive farming is the general rule. From the outset, therefore, the problem of rural overpopulation has been by-passed; the land absorbs only as many inhabitants as are needed to work it by extensive methods. Thus, at the beginning of the present century, no more than 40 per cent of the country's active population was employed in agricultural production, a figure comparable with that registered in the United States around 1890, and contrasting with the high proportion (50 per cent) recorded in the other Latin-American countries at the present time.

The growth of the population, together with the progress in the mechanization of farming which began in Argentina at the same time as in the United States and also developed rapidly until the thirties, gradually reduced the proportion of workers on the land. When Argentina's agricultural production attained its peak, in the period 1940–44, only 33 per cent of the active population was employed in farming.

Two other sources of manpower for industry and services were artisan activities and domestic service. In combination with agriculture, at the beginning of the century they were absorbing 67 per cent of the active population; this proportion had decreased to 50 per cent in the five-year period mentioned above (1940–44).

The quinquennium referred to has been chosen as a basis of comparison because up to that time economic policy had dictated no measure likely to hamper the development of agriculture, as was subsequently the case, although the incentives to production had been adversely affected first by the great depression of the thirties and later by the Second World War. Thanks to the technical progress achieved in agriculture, the same number of workers was no longer required to produce the same volume of commodities as before. While production expanded by 295 per cent in the forty years under review, the active population employed on the land increased by barely half that proportion. The employment of the manpower thus released from farming, artisan trades, and domestic service was not a matter of chance; it resulted from those changes in the composition of demand which accompany the growth of income and the development of State activities. Even during the phase characterized by an accelerated expansion of exports and, consequently, of imports likewise, the latter did not suffice to meet the demand of a rapidly growing population; this situation led to the gradual development of domestic manufactures and the absorption of a considerable share of the active population displaced from the other occupations listed above. Thus, between the two five-year periods 1900–04 and 1940–44, industrial production[2] increased by 470 per cent, and employment in industry--including artisan trades--by 211 per cent. The importance of the industrial sector's contribution to the aggregate product of the economy became progressively greater, so that while in 1900–04 it accounted for 21 per cent, by 1940–44 this proportion had risen to 28 per cent, the share of agricultural production having fallen during the same interval from 33 per cent to 25 per cent.

In those days, while there was not a superabundance of manpower available for agricultural production, except in transient periods like that of the world depression, there was no shortage, either, and the shift described was a normal phenomenon. It might be argued, however, that if industry had not developed, a larger number of the active population would have continued to work on the land, and agricultural production and the export trade would consequently have expanded. Had this been the case, the same line of reasoning might suggest, more manufactured goods could have been imported to meet the growth of demand, and there would have been no need for industrialization.

Rather than embarking upon a very controversial discussion about what might have happened in the past, a more interesting and more positive approach is to ask the same questions with respect to the future. As will be seen later, it is of vital importance for Argentina to increase its agricultural production and its exports, which have undergone a serious decline. According to projections in the United Nations report to which allusion has been made, by 1967 the country should be able to produce 65 per cent more agricultural commodities than in the five peak years from 1940 to 1944. This expansion would be achieved mainly by dint of improved yields, which, in combination with the mechanization of farming, would render it possible with a labor increment of barely 14 per cent. Consequently, the proportion of the active population employed in the agricultural sector, which amounted to 33 per cent in 1940–44, would drop to 21 per cent by 1967, given the fulfillment of the projections cited, which are by no means overoptimistic where the saving of manpower is concerned.

Herein, then, lies the crux of the problem from the point of view of industrialization. In agriculture, Argentina's technical progress has lagged behind that of other comparable countries. An effort to make up for lost time would mean that in the course of the next few years the experience of the United States might be repeated in Argentina; a considerable expansion of production would be possible with relatively little additional manpower.

The consequent increase in productivity per active person in the agricultural and livestock sector would lose its value for the economy as a whole if the population released from agriculture were not employed in other high-productivity occupations. This is precisely one of the dynamic roles that it will be incumbent upon industrialization to fill. In 1940–44 the proportion of the active population employed in trade, services, and public administration was already high--32 per cent--and it subsequently continued to rise unduly, reaching 39 per cent by 1955. Within a process of healthy economic recovery, by 1967 the corresponding figure could not be expected to be much more than 40 per cent. Consequently, it will once again fall to industry to contribute effectively to the absorption of the active population displaced from agricultural production; the proportion of the labor force employed in agriculture would seem to have been 33 per cent in 1940–44, as has already been noted, and should decrease to 24 per cent by 1967, while industry should enlarge its share from 28 per cent to 31 per cent.

This increase in the active population employed in industry, and the improvement of its productivity by virtue of an increment in per capita investment and a higher standard of technical training, would enable industrial production to expand by 238 per cent between the 1940–44 period and 1967, while agricultural production would expand by only 65 per cent. The disparity between these figures might give rise to anxiety lest the process of industrialization become too intensive. It is frequently asserted, in both Argentina and elsewhere, that this trend toward overindustrialization at the expense of agricultural production is the underlying cause of the country's difficulties. There is some confusion here which should be cleared up, and in view of the importance of this question not merely for the interpretation of the immediate past, but, in particular, for the planning of economic policy over the next ten years, this elucidation will now be attempted.

The industrialization of Argentina has most certainly not been carried too far. Not only should the country's present industrial output be larger than it actually is, but the per capita product should be much greater. Per capita product has not yet regained the peak levels attained in 1948, during the postwar years of rapid growth. It then amounted to 3,824 pesos at 1950 prices; during the last three years it has been about 3,640 pesos.[3] Argentina's development is seriously cramped by both external and internal factors, and industry in particular is adversely affected by the existing bottlenecks.

As regards external factors, Argentina's own resources are at present insufficient not only to import the capital goods that it urgently needs but even to cover essential imports of raw materials and intermediate products for industry and economic activities in general. Such is the nature of the external bottleneck which is constricting the expansion of the economy.

In Argentina the development of industry, like that of economic activities in general, has always depended, and will continue to depend, though not with the same intensity, on imports of essential goods. Demand for these and other imports tends to outgrow the aggregate product of the economy, and the latter to expand faster than exports. In view of these disparities, increased exports will not suffice to ensure the steady growth of the product; it is also essential that the expansion of demand for imports be restricted by means of a proper degree of import substitution.

The United Nations study discusses the possibilities of increasing the aggregate product in terms of the effort that could be made in these two fields--that of exports and that of import substitution policy. The conclusion is thus reached that the increment in the product could not exceed the 1955 figure by more than 40 per cent and 78 per cent in 1962 and 1967, respectively, unless a very favorable change were to take place in the external factors which condition Argentina's economic development.

These rates of growth of the product would imply increments of 70 per cent and 136 per cent, respectively, in demand for those goods which were imported in 1955. Exports, on the other hand, according to the projections in the study, could not expand by more than 58 per cent and 90 per cent in each of the two years cited. This patent disparity between exports and the growth of demand for imports calls for a vigorous import substitution policy, since otherwise the increase in the product assumed in the projections cannot be achieved.

The fact that Argentina has neither expanded its exports nor substituted domestic production for imports in the measure required to enable more essential goods to be imported, chiefly accounts for the external bottleneck affecting the economy. The annual average export quantum was 29 per cent lower in 1955–57 than in the five-year period preceding the Second World War (1935–39). Still sharper was the decline in the external purchasing power of exports, which dropped by 47 per cent, owing to the deterioration of the terms of trade. This circumstance aggravated the ill effects of the decrease in exports. In the postwar period the terms of trade had followed a trend very favorable to Argentina, reaching a level 34 per cent higher in 1947 than in the five years from 1935 to 1939. But a downward movement subsequently set in which, but for the interruption caused by the hostilities in Korea, has continued to the present day; in 1957 the terms of trade were 33 per cent lower than in 1935–39. It should be added that in this latter quinquennium they had already fallen 10 per cent below the figure registered during the three decades preceding the great depression of the thirties. This fact is of great significance for the economic development of Argentina in the period following the world depression.

II. Prospects for an Expansion of Exports

The decline in the export quantum which has just been described is attributable to the fact that while domestic consumption of agricultural commodities steadily increased, production contracted instead of expanding. Agricultural production for export, after reaching a maximum annual average value of 9,013 million pesos (at 1950 prices) in 1940–44, underwent a decline, since when it has increased again, but has never completely regained the earlier peak level. The annual average registered for 1955–57 was 8,058 million pesos.

This downward trend in production for export was determined mainly by the price policy followed during the postwar years up to 1952. The intensive improvement in the terms of trade after the war did not touch the producers of cereals and oil seeds, owing to the establishment of exchange rates which were overvalued in relation to the internal inflationary situation, and to the fixed prices deriving from the official purchasing monopoly. Internal relative prices were unfavorable to producers, and this circumstance, apart from depriving them of incentives to production, weakened their investment resources. The policy in question was modified in 1952, inasmuch as more favorable prices were established, but it was not long before the persistence of inflation led to a further deterioration in relative prices, until the devaluation at the end of 1955, and those which followed it,[4] once again turned the scale in favor of agriculture.

But it would be highly erroneous to suppose that a favorable price policy is all that is required for the development of Argentina's agricultural production. There is a much more fundamental problem. The land in the pampas area, which is the source of about 85 per cent of the country's agricultural exports, is now fully occupied. It is no longer possible to continue pushing forward the frontier of agriculture by bringing new land under annual crops, as was done in the past. The area sown to such crops amounted to 6 million hectares during the first five years of the century, and in 1940 reached a maximum of 21.1 million hectares, the peak figure that could be attained being 23 million. From then onward, stock farming developed at the expense of agriculture proper, though in recent years there have been signs of a reversal of this trend. But the development of the one activity at the cost of the other will not be sufficient in itself to bring about a steady increase in the total volume of production, once the level of former yields has been regained. What is essential is to improve these yields, and this will be impossible without the progressive introduction of more advanced farming techniques.

It has already been pointed out that Argentina has lagged behind other comparable countries with respect to technical improvements. In genetics, except that wheat yields have been increased, no appreciable progress has been made; and no increments in yields per hectare have been recorded for other cereals or for oil seeds, which, indeed, have shown a downward trend. Here the effects of soil impoverishment are also making themselves felt; the system of regular rotation of crops and stock which was formerly applied and which restored part of the depleted fertility of the soil largely fell into disuse when, instead of the introduction of a thorough and long-delayed land reform, from 1944 onward rents were frozen and the eviction of tenants and share-croppers was prohibited.[5] In any event, the use of fertilizers is unknown on the pampas in agricultural production for export, and no systematic experiments have been carried out in this connection.

Livestock yields in the pampas area are also low in relation to the very high quality of both the land and the animals themselves, especially the cattle. Of the 47 million hectares used for stock farming in the pampas, 67 per cent is natural grassland, producing much lower yields than artificial pastures. Furthermore, modern systems of pasture management, which have done so much toward increasing yields elsewhere, are very little known in Argentina. These and other technical weaknesses account for the fact that meat production per hectare falls far short of the level it might attain.

To all this must be added production losses due to weeds, which have become considerably heavier partly through the neglect of crop rotation and partly because the manpower shortage was not offset by an energetic mechanization campaign. These losses, together with others caused by the pests and diseases that attack both crops and livestock--pesticides are only just coming into more widespread use-- are estimated as ordinarily equivalent to 40 per cent of production, apart from the exceptional damage suffered from time to time.

Argentina has also fallen behind in the mechanization of farming. Tractors are available in the proportion of one to every 500 hectares, as against every 33 in the United States, and their average age, like that of other agricultural equipment, is very high. It is enough to mention that the capital invested in farm equipment in Argentina, which in 1930 had amounted to 5,612 million pesos at 1950 prices, dropped to a value of 3,360 million in 1955, according to approximate estimates.

The gradual correction of the technical defects referred to above will enable average land yields and the average per capita product to be progressively increased.

A brief review of these production possibilities in the pampas area will not be out of place here. By 1957 the area under annual crops had reached 18.7 million hectares, after attaining its maximum of 21.1 million hectares in 1940. As has already been stated, the area in question cannot exceed 23 million hectares, and the assumption in the projections is that by 1967 it will nearly reach this peak figure. According to estimates, in 1967 average cereal and oil-seed yields might be at least 31 per cent higher than the averages recorded for 1950–54.

The expansion of the area sown to annual crops will necessarily have to be achieved by encroachment on the 36.8 million hectares which in 1957 were under natural and permanent artificial pasture for livestock. By 1967 this grazing area should have decreased by 4 million hectares to make room for more annual crops. It is estimated, however, that on this reduced stock-farming area, production can be substantially increased. In the first place, the conversion of 3.9 million hectares of natural grassland into artificial pasture, together with improved pasture management, will permit a 29-per-cent increment in the number of animals per hectare. Second, pest and disease control, and the dissemination of more rational methods of feeding, will mean that the animals mature more quickly, so the proportion of meat produced will be greater in relation to existing stocks, and the yield of milk and wool will considerably improve; the expansion that can be achieved by these means is estimated at 36 per cent. Thus, if the foregoing percentages are combined, average production per hectare used for stock farming might be 75 per cent higher in 1967 than in 1950–54.

To sum up, if the average product of the land under annual crops is taken in conjunction with that of pasture land in the pampas, and to these are added further increments in farm produce (poultry, eggs, honey, etc.) and in the yields of minor crops, the estimated aggregate increase in mean production per hectare would average 90 per cent by 1967. For the rest of the country, where production is mainly for domestic consumption, a more moderate expansion is projected, deriving chiefly from the enlargement of the area utilized, for, although there is also plenty of margin for raising yields, it is felt that this will take longer.

Thus, estimates for the country as a whole place the value of agricultural production in 1967 at some 22,183 million pesos at 1950 prices, as contrasted with an average of 13,401 million in 1940–44 (the maximum period), which would represent a 66-per-cent increase.

Undoubtedly, if a more energetic effort than is projected were made to improve the techniques applied, it would mean that still larger production increments could be obtained by 1967 and, of course, in the intervening years. But conservative estimates were considered preferable. Furthermore, in view of current world-market prospects it was also thought unwise to calculate that the increase in agricultural exports would exceed $496 million by 1962 and $732 million by 1967, in relation to the $877 million registered in 1955.

According to projections, domestic consumption, in respect to both foodstuffs and over-all economic activity, should be 78 per cent higher in 1967 than in 1955–57. This increment is calculated on the basis of the average increase in per capita income estimated in the projections, and of somewhat low elasticity coefficients, which on an average would be only 0.5 for foodstuffs as a whole; nevertheless, despite these modest coefficients, by about 1962 the total increment in consumption would be equivalent to the present volume of agricultural exports.

III. Import Substitution through Industrialization and Petroleum

According to the projections, the increase in agricultural exports would amount to 55 per cent in 1962 in relation to 1955. Demand for those goods which were imported in 1955 would, on the other hand, expand by 70 per cent. This same disparity would continue in evidence in 1967, when the corresponding figures would be 84 per cent and 136 per cent, respectively.

These projections give a clearer idea of the nature of the external bottleneck which is constricting the growth of the Argentine economy. Even if the volume of current exports had been greater, this would not have been enough to avert the phenomenon in question; another requisite was import substitution on a larger scale than has as yet been undertaken, apart from the fact that the possibility of increasing industrial exports, especially to neighboring countries, has not been exploited sufficiently.

The substitution process has long been taking place within the Argentine economy, and what is necessary now is to direct it along more difficult and complex paths. There has been a gradual tendency to curtail imports of consumer goods and replace them by domestic production, so the capacity to import may be turned to better account for the purchase of raw materials, intermediate products, and capital goods; and the substitution process has in addition been extended to these same imports, some of them being restricted or eliminated altogether in order to permit the expansion of others.

This process has now for the first time reached a culminating point Imports of consumer goods have already been cut down too severely, and can be subjected to no further restriction, so henceforward new substitutions can be effected only for imports of production goods, that is, raw materials, intermediate products, and capital goods.

The immediate effects of substitution differ widely according to whether the imports to be replaced are consumer or production goods. When Argentina imported a substantial proportion of consumer goods, it was relatively easy to restrict such purchases abroad in order to facilitate the importation of other essential goods; certain consumer sectors were put to some inconvenience, while the lines of production concerned were not yet fully developed, but over-all economic activity did not suffer. Conversely, in the existing situation, where essential raw materials and intermediate products are involved, any contraction of such imports entails a corresponding degree of disemployment in the industries and other activities affected thereby; nor can imports of capital goods be reduced, not only because they are indispensable but also because they are being paid for with credits and foreign investment which are not available for imports of the materials in question.

The following figures confirm the statement just made: in 1955 only 1 per cent of end goods for current consumption was imported, whereas approximately 16 per cent of capital goods was purchased abroad. So much for finished goods; raw materials and intermediate products constituted about 5 per cent of the final value of all consumer and capital goods.

On reflection, this proportion of raw materials and intermediate products is seen to be relatively small, and, this being the case, it may occasion some surprise that its significance in the economy as a whole should be great enough for so modest a volume of imports to retard economic development in the manner already indicated. But they are essential ingredients in the economic process, and, slight as their relative importance may be, without them that process cannot take place. This is especially true of those sectors of the economy which are affected by the greatest pressure of demand--petroleum, iron and steel, productive machinery and equipment, pulp and paper, chemicals, building materials, and transport and electricity services. These sectors accounted for 25 per cent of total demand for goods and services in 1955, and for 72 per cent of total imports. Imports by this group of industries were equivalent to 22 per cent of the value of their production.

Meanwhile, this significant fact needs to be stressed: For the first time in its economic history Argentina is finding itself unable to make an immediate reduction in certain imports in order to increase others. The substitution of domestic production for imports of raw materials and intermediate products is economically possible, but it takes time and, in addition, requires heavy investment. Consequently, while at one time it was relatively easy to deal with a foreign-exchange short-age simply by restricting imports of consumer goods, this procedure is no longer applicable today, and substitution policy must be pro-gramed with timely foresight. The United Nations study includes a detailed analysis of substitution possibilities, beginning with petroleum.

Here the improvidence displayed in the past is striking. Domestic production formerly increased more rapidly than consumption, and during the five-year period 1940–44 came to account for 77 per cent of total consumption. This proportion subsequently declined, until by 1955 it had dwindled to 40 per cent. In 1955 12.7 million tons of pe-troleum equivalent and natural gas were consumed, and it is estimated that demand will have risen 56 per cent by 1962 and 89 per cent by 1967, thus reaching 19.8 million and 24.0 million tons, respectively.

Production in 1955 amounted to 5 million tons. Estimates suggest that it would not take long to double this figure, given adequate trans-port facilities. The want of these is the most serious obstacle at present, and it is expected that by 1961 the construction of oil and gas pipelines will have removed it. On the basis of official estimates for that year, it is considered that the output might reach 15.3 million tons by 1962 and 21.2 million by 1967.

According to the projections, production should expand at annual rates of 17.4 per cent between 1955 and 1962 and 6.8 per cent between 1962 and 1967. These rates are high, but comparable figures have already been registered within Argentina's experience. In fact, during the period 1934–43, the output of crude petroleum produced by the

State Petroleum Deposits (Yacimientos Petrolíferos Fiscales) increased by 13.6 per cent annually. Unfortunately, owing to the difficulty of obtaining equipment during the Second World War and the relatively modest resources subsequently invested in petroleum prospecting and exploitation, in 1943–55 the annual rate fell to 3.7 per cent. It may well be that in addition the relatively low petroleum prices determined by the external overvaluation of the currency adversely affected available investment resources in the case of petroleum, as in that of agricultural production.

Proven reserves of petroleum and natural gas are easily large enough to cover the projected increment in production. In 1955 they amounted to 160 million tons and by the end of 1957 to 420 million. These reserves are far in excess of the ratio normally assumed, representing seventy-five times this year's output. Clearly, it will now be necessary to press on intensively with the work of prospecting so that this ratio can be maintained or improved despite the expansion of production.

If the projections of consumption and production given above are fulfilled, the foreign-exchange savings achieved through import substitution will amount to $162 million in 1962 and $252 million in 1967, in relation to 1955. These figures will rise to $175 and $341 million, respectively, with the addition of the foreign-exchange savings obtained through the production of electric energy from hydraulic sources.

Other import substitution possibilities may now be reviewed. They relate mainly to iron and steel, non-ferrous metals, production equipment, pulp and paper, and chemicals, apart from other substitution processes on a smaller scale. With 1955 as a benchmark year, it is estimated that by 1962 and 1967 substitutions worth $662 million and $1,330 million, respectively, might be achieved.

Argentina's consumption of iron and steel is at present severely limited by the shortage of foreign exchange. In 1955, a high proportion of its value was represented by imports in the form of finished or intermediate goods, but, despite the substantial increments in the volume of consumption projected for 1962 and 1967, the growth of the iron and steel industry will permit import coefficient reductions that will imply a considerable saving in foreign exchange.

Given the external bottleneck affecting the Argentine economy, this saving alone would justify the development of the iron and steel industry. But, in addition, the size of the Argentine market is such that production could be effected on a sound economic basis, with costs differing little from those of imports. Moreover, Argentina has discovered iron and coal deposits on which it will be able to draw for a progressively larger proportion of the raw material and fuel needed for steel-making.

As regards non-ferrous metals, the country is in a position to expand its production of lead and zinc, hampered at present by transport and investment difficulties, but it will have to import other non-ferrous metals as raw materials or intermediate products. Even so, there are possibilities of reducing the import coefficient for this group of goods.

Great strides have been made in the manufacture of production equipment during the last ten years, and further steady progress must be achieved in the course of the next decade so that the heavy investment which will have to be effected may not entail a disproportionate expansion of imports. If import substitution projections are to be fulfilled, Argentina, which is already manufacturing a wide variety of production equipment, will have to expand its output considerably, embarking upon new lines of production which should include motor vehicles.

The pulp and paper industry is at present largely based on imports of the intermediate product. Argentina has great possibilities of developing plantations of salicaceae, other broad-leaved species, and coniferous trees, which it has begun to exploit; but, even if allowance is made for these potential resources, in view of the rapidity with which demand is expected to expand, on the one hand, and, on the other, the time it will take for the plantations to reach maturity and become susceptible of exploitation, substantial imports, especially of newsprint, will probably still be required in 1967. However, a moderate reduction of the import coefficient is projected.

The chemicals industry is only in its initial stage; but the need to economize in foreign exchange, and the growing size of the market, will lead to the satisfaction of an increasing proportion of consumer requirements and the development of certain lines of production in the petrochemical industry, with the consequent import substitutions.

As can be seen from Table 1, further import substitutions could be effected in other industries and activities, to values of $74 million and $218 million in 1962 and 1967.

The time has now come to envisage these industrial substitutions as a whole. Demand for imports (see Table 2) seems likely to be $897 million higher in 1962 than in 1955, but effective imports should increase by only $410 million, thanks to an increment of $4,826 million in domestic production, hence would derive a total import substitution of $487 million. By 1967--the point of comparison still being 1955--demand should expand by $2,450 million, effective imports by $455 million, and production by $9,367 million, so the aggregate import substitution would be $989 million.

Raúl Prebisch

Table 1

Projection of Import Substitution

(Millions of Dollars)[a]

Years	Total Supply	Net Domestic Production[b]	Imports[c]	Substitution of Imports with Respect to 1955[d]
		Production of goods and services and imports		
1955	13,452	12,280[e]	1,172	. . . .
1962	18,714	17,200[e]	1,514	662
1967	23,344	21,800[e]	1,544	1,330
		Petroleum		
1955	275	109	166	. . .
1962	430	332	98	175[f]
1967	521	458	63	341[f]
		Industrial products (total)		
1955	10,111	9,105[g]	1,006	. . .
1962	15,347	13,931[g]	1,416	487
1967	19,933	18,472[g]	1,461	989
		Iron and steel		
1955	231	30	201	. . .
1962	338	182	156	146
1967	457	273	184	235
		Non-Ferrous metals		
1955	53	11	42	. .
1962	75	18	57	3
1967	104	41	63	19
		Productive machinery and equipment (selected products)		
1955	600	297	303	. . .
1962	1,570	1,000	570	223
1967	2,045	1,420	625	408
		Pulp and paper		
1955	118	66	52	. .
1962	197	117	80	11
1967	270	169	101	23
		Chemicals (selected products)		
1955	745	666	79	. .
1962	1,060	936	124	30
1967	1,445	1,377	68	86
		Other products		
1955	8,364	8,035	329	. . .
1962	12,107	11,678	429	74[h]
1967	15,612	15,192	420	218[h]

[a]1955 prices.
[b]Net domestic production excludes imports of raw materials and intermediate products used in the production process.
[c]C.i.f. value; includes raw materials and intermediate product imports required for production as well as imports of finished goods.
[d]In each individual category of goods, substitution is calculated as the difference between actual imports projected after replacement by domestic production, and hypothetical import requirements, assuming that the coefficient of imports in relation to total supply existing in 1955 would continue in 1962 and 1967.
[e]Gross domestic production of goods and services valued at market prices.
[f]Includes an estimate of saving of foreign-exchange resources deriving from the expansion of the coefficient of hydraulic energy in substitution of imports of fuel.
[g]Value of manufacturing production at market prices, excluding imports of raw materials and intermediate products used in production.
[h]Includes some small amounts of substitution in other fields.

Table 2

Projection of Imports

Demand for Imports and Effective Import Capacity

(Millions of Dollars)[a]

Years	Agricultural Exports	Total exports of Goods and Services	Demand for Imports[b]	Effective Imports[c]
1955	878	948	1,172	1,172
1962	1,361	1,505	2,176	1,514
1967	1,592	1,790	2,874	1,544

[a]1955 prices.

[b]Based on an analysis of the elasticity of demand for imports implied in the projection of demand for consumption, investment, and exports, and the production and import requirements related to the satisfaction of this demand if there were no change in the structure of production in substitution of imports. The resulting coefficient of elasticity of demand for imports, in relation to total demand in the Argentine economy, is 1.76.

[c]Based on an analysis and projection of the balance of payments related to the projected export goals.

All these substitutions, together with those affecting petroleum and energy, will represent total values of $662 million in 1962 and $1,330 million in 1967, and will enable demand for imports to be brought into line with the increase in exports, estimated at $842 million, and with the country's financial commitments.

IV. The Internal Bottleneck

Apart from the determinants of the external bottleneck just described, other internal factors have existed which are seriously hindering the development of the Argentine economy, especially the transport and energy sectors.

As regards transport, the position is critical, particularly for the railways. Since 1930, and above all in the last twelve years, the renewal and upkeep of tracks, basic installations, and rolling-stock have been so irregular and inadequate that the capital required to bring the system properly up-to-date in the course of the next ten years is estimated, in the United Nations study, at about $875 million.

A similar situation prevails with respect to motorized transport. In fact, the present average age of the units composing the truck and passenger vehicles is fifteen and twenty years, respectively; it is

revealing to compare this state of affairs with the position in the
United States, where in 1956 the average age of trucks was under
seven and that of passenger cars under six years. The number of
passenger cars per thousand inhabitants was also 38 per cent lower
in 1955 than in 1930 (eighteen and twenty-eight units, respectively).

More than 80 per cent of the better- and more economically-sur-
faced roads, of which the aggregate length was somewhat more than
11,000 kilometres in 1954, were built during the ten years from 1932
to 1942. Subsequently there was a marked falling-off in the building
of new roads, and those already in existence deteriorated for want of
proper maintenance in keeping with traffic requirements.

Lastly, most of the boats used for coastal and inland waterway
transport are obsolescent, and the shortcomings of the river ports
are equally serious.

It is estimated that the growth of demand for transport in terms of
tons:kilometres will be more intensive than that of the aggregate
product. In 1962, to a 40-per-cent increase in the latter in relation
to 1955 would correspond an increment in the former of 70 per cent.
By 1967 the pertinent figures would be 77 per cent and 123 per cent,
respectively.

The electric-energy situation is also critical. The annual rate of
increase of installed kw, which was 2.5 per cent between 1935 and
1942, afterwards declined to practically 0.0 per cent between 1942
and 1948, and although a renewed expansion at a rate of 3.4 per cent
later took place, the time lost has not yet been made up. Moreover,
even these higher rates have not proved adequate. All this accounts
for the deficit of 700,000 kw in relation to existing demand which was
estimated for 1955, in which year the installed capacity was 2.1 million kw.

For this deficit to be gradually supplied, and installed potential to
be simultaneously increased at a rate commensurate with the growth
of the product, installed capacity will have to expand 108 per cent by
1962 and 209 per cent by 1967, rising to 4.3 million kw in the first of
these years and 6.4 million in the second.

The country possesses substantial water-power resources of which
very little advantage has been taken. In 1955 only 5 per cent of the
installed potential was of hydraulic origin. This proportion may increase to 14 per cent by 1962, and to 48 per cent by 1967, according
to the projections in the United Nations study.

V. Capital Investment

In the foregoing pages some idea has been given of the nature of
the structural crisis affecting the Argentine economy. It is not an
ordinary cyclical movement, but a deep-seated internal maladjustment
allied with an intensive deterioration of the terms of trade.

There have been maladjustments between industry, agriculture, and petroleum and within industry itself, because of the lack of a rational import substitution policy; and there have also been discrepancies between the growth potentialities of the economy and the development of transport and energy, as has just been pointed out.

The explanation lies mainly in the relative shortage of investment resources after the great world depression, and in the failure to turn such as were available to the best account.

During the three decades preceding the depression the average annual rate of growth of accumulated capital stood at 4.9 per cent; between 1930 and 1955 it was only 1.5 per cent. Among the several factors accounting for this contrast, two may be regarded as having been of decisive importance. These were the deterioration of the terms of trade, and foreign investment.

Between 1930 and 1957 the terms of trade were 19 per cent lower than between 1900 and 1930. In Argentina their fluctuations tend to set the pattern for the variations in the investment coefficient.

During the period beginning with the turn of the century, foreign investment expanded sharply in Argentina, rising from $2,020 million (at 1950 prices) in 1900 to $7,600 million in 1930, in which year it constituted 30 per cent of total capital, its share having reached a maximum of 48 per cent in 1913. From 1930 onward, the volume of foreign investment began to contract, until a minimum of $1,740 million was recorded in 1949, after which it resumed its upward trend, attaining $2,250 million by 1957. At present it represents barely 6 per cent of total investment.

The decrease in the volume of foreign investment is attributable to two factors. On the one hand, the changes brought about in the international capital market by the great world depression and the transformations of the Argentine economy to which the depression gave rise militated against the placing of further foreign investment, especially in the thirties. Second, it was during these years that the policy of repatriating investment was initiated, independently of the normal process of amortization of the public debt. The chief concern at that time was to relieve the balance of payments of the burden of financial services, which was undeniably heavy; in 1930 these services absorbed 41 per cent of the value of exports. Later, during the postwar years, such repatriation was greatly extended, partly under the influence of other than purely economic motives.

The reduction of foreign investment by $5,353 million between 1930 and 1957 indubitably alleviated the balance-of-payments situation. Nevertheless, in view of the serious external bottleneck affecting the economy, grave doubts arise as to the efficacy of this policy from that very point of view. The whole question is whether the more positive influence on the balance of payments can be exerted by using the country's limited investment resources for the repatriation of foreign capital or by devoting them to expanding exports and to substituting domestic production for imports, thus strengthening the country's economic structure.

The import substitution which was outlined earlier, and which, as will be recalled, amounted to $1,330 million in 1967 in relation to 1955, would require approximately $3,600 million worth of capital goods imports. In other words, in three years on an average, the foreign exchange saved would offset that expended.

To turn to consideration of the foreign-exchange economy effected by means of repatriation, in 1930, financial services represented 7 per cent of the capital invested, which means that the saving of foreign exchange achieved through repatriation would take fourteen years to compensate for the foreign-exchange expenditure deriving from such services.

Unquestionably, therefore, the foreign-exchange saving achieved through import substitution is the greater, and it becomes still more significant if the resources are used to expand exports, within certain limits. This does not mean that a repatriation policy may not be desirable in a country which is advancing toward economic maturity. It is all a matter of determining an order of priorities. If instead of resorting to premature repatriation Argentina had invested its foreign resources in petroleum, steel-making, production of machinery and equipment, and other substitution industries, as well as in the development of hydroelectric potential and the renewal of railway equipment, the strain on its balance of payments would have been eased sufficiently for it to adopt a policy of repatriating foreign investment at a later date. Failure to follow this course is now compelling it to turn to foreign investment once again, with no possibility of contemplating repatriation until after 1967.

Furthermore, the distribution of resources between the various forms of investment has been far from satisfactory. An exaggerated proportion of these resources has been channeled into non-productive investments.

The correction of these maladjustments calls for a substantial and carefully channeled effort. In the United Nations study the relevant capital requirements up to 1967 are analyzed and assessed. In 1955, import substitution industries, plus agriculture, transport, and electric energy, accounted for 34 per cent of the total stock of capital. It is estimated that within gross investment up to 1967 they will have to be accorded 68 per cent of the capital increment, in accordance with Table 3.

Aggregate gross investment up to 1967 should total some $44,300 million at 1955 prices. Out of this amount, foreign-capital requirements are estimated at $3,595 million, or 8.1 per cent; the remaining $30,705 million would correspond to gross investment from domestic sources. For the latter the annual average would be $3,070 million,

Table 3

Gross Investment Requirements in 1955–67

Activities	Proportion of Total Capital in 1955 (Percentage)	Gross Investment (Millions of Pesos at 1950 Prices)	Proportion of Total (Percentage)	Proportion in Foreign Exchange (Percentage)
Major investment sectors	33.9	143,414	58.0	11.4
Agriculture	14.7	46,861	19.0	0.1
Substitution industries	6.0	21,647	8.6	26.7
Petroleum	2.0	9,244	3.7	32.4
Electric energy	1.5	10,115	4.1	38.5
Transport	9.7	55,547	22.5	6.6
Minor investment sectors	66.1	103,702	42.0	3.6
Total (rounded)	100.0	247,116	100.0	8.1

which means that it would have to be increased by $360 million. To
judge from projections in the United Nations report, such an increment could be achieved without significantly raising the 1955-57 domestic investment coefficient, which was 23 per cent of the gross
product, largely on the basis of the latter's gradual expansion.

Hence the need for an energetic campaign against the factors determining internal and external bottlenecks, so that the gross product
may grow at a rapid pace and generate the increased savings that are
essential if its expansion is to continue. For this purpose foreign
capital is an indispensable requisite. Briefly, its temporary function
is to help the economy evolve the capacity to produce all the savings
it requires and convert part of them into imports of capital goods.

As already pointed out, this is not feasible at present because of
the unsatisfactory balance-of-payments situation. The cost of all
capital goods imported in 1957 had to be defrayed with foreign capital;
only 45 per cent will have to be paid for in this way in 1962, according
to the projections in the study, and by 1967 the need for further contributions of foreign capital will disappear altogether, as the expansion
of exports and the substitution of domestic production for imports--
capital-goods imports included--will have provided the country with
the margin of external resources required for importing those capital
goods which it could not produce economically.

VI. The Programing of Development

Never has economic planning been so strongly advocated in Argentina as in the years that witnessed the intensification of those structural maladjustments which had long been incipient in the Argentine
economy. As a matter of fact, the so-called "planning" consisted of
nothing but a succession of heterogeneous and totally unco-ordinated
projects, devoid of any attempt at a careful analysis of investment
needs, giving first attention to basic transport, petroleum, and electric-energy requirements.

It has now become essential that development be programed in accordance with a proper technique of analyses and projections whereby
capital requirements can be determined, together with the directions
in which investment must be channeled in order to fulfill certain specific aims, and the way in which the requirements in question can be
satisfied.

This last point is of the most vital importance. It has been shown
that Argentina has not been able to utilize its investment resources
efficiently or place them wisely, and if in the next ten years matters
do not improve in this respect the reconstruction of the economy may
be indefinitely postponed. The problem is in essence one of the distribution of the limited resources available, and unless a clear idea

is formed of requirements and priorities there will be a recurrence of the danger that these resources may be misapplied, as in the past.

Moreover, there must be compatibility between the investment effected, the aims of economic and social policy, and the instruments used for implementing that policy. The programing of development requires that the State become progressively more skillful in handling the instruments in question. This will be far from easy, for public administration, which formerly reached a reasonable, though not a high, standard of efficiency, has also strikingly deteriorated, and is one of the foremost victims of inflation. (The average income of the public employee in 1955 was barely 77 per cent of his income in 1935, while the average per capita product for the economy as a whole increased during the interval by 20 per cent.) The process of deterioration was accompanied by excessive State intervention in economic activity, resulting in the bureaucratic perversion of important aspects of the economic system. In Argentina, as in other Latin-American countries, the anachronistic concept still survives that if the State is to influence the economy, it must own not only certain public utilities-- which is understandable and justifiable in many cases--but also commercial and industrial undertakings in the case of which there is no reason to encroach upon the domain of private enterprise. This concept and the whole apparatus of intervention in private economic activity have created such complications that the high officials of the State, overwhelmed by the burden, have neglected to utilize those higher mechanisms of the economic system which are the very means whereby an efficacious influence can be exerted on the rate and direction of economic development and the progressive correction of outstanding defects in the distribution of the aggregate product. If these mechanisms are to be brought into play, targets and methods of attaining them must be clearly defined.

This is the role which, in my view, the programing of development in Argentina will have to enact over the next ten years, creating at one and the same time the requisites and the incentives for private enterprise to make its optimum contribution to the fulfillment of these aims.

NOTES

[1]Responsibility for this study is assumed by the Economic Commission for Latin America, and it was prepared in collaboration with the Technical Assistance Administration, the Food and Agriculture Organization, and other bodies. The author of the present article is the Executive Secretary of ECLA, but the views expressed herein are strictly my own.

[2]Industry includes manufacturing, mining, and construction activity.

[3]At 1950 prices, 5.5 pesos were equivalent to one U.S. dollar at 1957 prices. This is based on the estimated purchasing-power parity of the Argentine peso and the dollar in 1950, and takes into account the change in the price level in the United States between 1950 and 1957. All peso figures given in the present report have been calculated on this basis.

[4]By October, 1955, export exchange rates, which had stood on an average at 7 pesos to the dollar, had risen to a little more than 18 pesos, and thereafter, through the combination of rates, pursued an upward trend until a rate of more than 22 pesos was reached in the last quarter of 1957.

[5]This act was modified in 1956, when a system was introduced to facilitate the purchase of land by tenants and share-croppers, but it is too early as yet to judge the results.

Part III

Case Studies in Economic Development

Papers: Navarrete
Mayne
Bićanić
Hoselitz

MEXICO'S ECONOMIC GROWTH: PROSPECTS AND PROBLEMS

Alfredo Navarrete, Jr.

Nacional Financiera de México

I. Introduction

The present Constitution of Mexico establishes a democratic regime for regulating the life of the nation's thirty-two million inhabitants who live in an area of 764,000 square miles, approximately one-fourth the size of the continental United States. Drafted in 1917, it sets forth the legitimate aspirations of its people, arising from the profound social, political, and economic movement known as the Mexican Revolution--the first of similar twentieth-century movements in many parts of the world--initiated in 1910 against the dictatorship which ruled the country during thirty years. For Mexico, as a result, democracy means more than a legal structure and a political regime. It means essentially a system of life based on the constant economic, social, and cultural betterment of its people. Today, forty years after proclaiming Mexico's present Constitution, the Mexican people are broadly united on the objectives of its economic system: (1) to attain a rate of economic growth which exceeds its rate of population growth; (2) to attain that economic development with reasonable price stability and financial stability; and (3) to raise the standard of living of the great working majorities by increasing the social justice with which national income is distributed among the factors of production. It is therefore in the light of these Constitutional objectives that an attempt is made here to analyze the Mexican economy--the factors behind its recent growth as well as the prospects and problems it still must solve in order to attain further progress.

II. The Process of Mexico's Economic Growth: Some Institutional Aspects

After the armed phase of the Revolution, the country faced the problem of reconstruction and of setting the necessary basis for growth. Mexico lay in the apparently closed circle of poverty resulting from the narrowness of the local market, lack of fixed social capital, lack of savings, monopolistic advantages possessed by foreign enterprises exploiting local natural resources, and from many other hindrances to economic growth. This was the period of vital decisions for Mexico: the agrarian reform, large-scale public works, the expropriation of the railroads and oil properties, the enactment of labor laws, the reorganization of the University of Mexico and the establishment of the Polytechnical Institute, the strengthening of the financial system through a network of national banks to serve the agricultural, industrial, and commercial sectors of the Mexican economy, and the carrying out of many other important measures which created general conditions favorable to development. The principal pressure-groups were organized as sectors (workers, peasants, the middle class) under a powerful political party that backed the government's actions and policies.

Having been dormant for many decades, living on the basis of a settled peasant agriculture, the basic concern of Mexicans was to set the national economy into a self-sustaining growth process. Among the many socio-economic factors which explain Mexico's economic development, one must select a few for their strategic importance. Let's begin with the agrarian reform, which is one of the pillars of Mexico's economic growth. The agrarian reform broke up the feudal structure of land-holding and methods of production, and changed attitudes toward work. The pre-revolutionary pattern of self-contained, isolated units and absentee holdings provided little place for productive investment for increasing output on a commercial scale. When the land was redistributed, modernizing the techniques of production became an immediate social and political objective. Accomplishing this involved irrigation, education, the introduction of improved farming methods, and the use of agricultural machinery. These required large initial capital outlays and a system of production credits to the farmers.

For financing the necessary investments, the government established a network of financial institutions to provide the required funds. The Central Bank was established in 1925. Public works in irrigation and roads began in 1926, and the first national bank for agricultural credit was set up the same year. But not until the 1930's did agrarian reform take place on an extensive basis, along with the establishment in 1934 of the Nacional Financiera--the Mexican industrial bank, development corporation, and investment company aimed at accelerating the industrialization of the economy. Two other national banks, one for foreign trade and the other for public works, were also established in the mid-thirties.

During this initial "take-off" period, since voluntary savings from the moneylending classes (absentee landowners and merchants) were not available, the government resorted to forced savings exacted through central bank inflationary financing. Prices rose at a 14 per cent annual rate of inflation during the period 1934-46. However, contrary to some widely-held opinions, inflation in the Mexican case did not tend to feed on itself and grow into a generalized monetary bankruptcy. Actually, during the next decade (to 1956) the average rate of inflation decreased to 7.8 per cent, with a clear trend toward reasonable stability, which was attained in 1956, continued during 1957, and is holding currently in 1958.

Land reform and accompanying measures brought about increased productivity in agriculture, but they ultimately released additional manpower, swelling the reserves of underemployed--in some areas rural employment is limited to the three or four months of the year during planting and harvesting--many of whom migrated to the cities. This aggravated the employment problems arising from a rapidly increasing population. Mexico has one of the fastest-growing populations in the world. Its birth rate has been consistently increasing from 28.2 births per 1,000 in 1893 to 46.2 in 1956, while its death rate has steadily declined from 39.9 to 13.3, with a resulting present natural growth rate exceeding 3 per cent annually. Labor supplies were more than sufficient, but their skills needed improvement. The University of Mexico was reorganized in 1929 and the National Polytechnic Institute was established in 1936 in order to provide the technicians required for the economic development of the country. Biologists, textile experts, petroleum technicians, rural doctors, and business administrators received their training alongside the mechanical and electrical engineers. In 1935 the National School of Economics was created, and new courses in business administration, aimed at creating the managers for the new enterprises, were introduced at different schools.

The growing Mexican population started to acquire new technical knowledge, ranging from literacy--the sleepy villagers of the old peasant agricultural communities had little need for reading and writing--to modern science. Public and private education spread, illiteracy was reduced, and advanced technical and professional training and facilities, including research, were expanded and improved.

At the same time, labor laws were enacted, and the functioning of the labor market was smoothed through the creation of Boards of Arbitration and Conciliation.

These changes were accelerated by the expropriation of the oil and railroad properties in 1937–38. In the pre-revolutionary economy, foreign direct investments, concentrated in the great extractive industries such as oil and mining, served primarily the raw-materials needs of the originating countries and did little to increase the real income of the overwhelmingly rural Mexican population. The international boycott of Mexico that followed the expropriations forced a generalized drive for internal achievement. A hard-working type of new local manager for the railroad and oil industries, as well as national entrepreneurs interested in agricultural and industrial

investments in the home market, began to develop. The new generations have learned to advance on the basis of their own effort and not
to depend on fortuitous developments from without. The international
boycott united all Mexicans under the theme of "Work for Mexico in
order to survive now and later to grow." Paradoxically enough, this
vigorous domestic effort later induced complementary foreign capi-
tal--though under very different economic, political, and social condi-
tions--which has come in increasing volume to participate in the benefits of, and to strengthen, a rapidly expanding Mexican economy.

All these initial factors of political, governmental, and social in-
novations--land reform along with new production techniques, public
capital financing of infrastructure investments, the development of a
more skilled labor force and entrepreneurial groups, and, foremost,
the decision of the Mexican people themselves to advance--have led
to altered patterns of consumption and investment which are in keeping
with a progressive economy.

III.　Recent Growth of the Mexican Economy

The rise in national income has been the result both of shifting
labor from backward agriculture into modern industry, transportation,
and commerce, and of a higher output per man. Farming absorbed
70 per cent of the working force in 1930, 65 per cent in 1940, and 54
per cent in 1956. However, the rate of economic growth has not been
uniform.

The growth of the Mexican economy since 1939 (adequate statistical
data have been available only since then) has proceeded in two stages.
During the first stage--1939–45--output increased by as much as 8 per
cent per annum. Such rapid growth was achieved with investment not
exceeding 10 per cent of total gross product. Much of the increase in
production--geared to the Second World War--was made possible by
bringing into operation previously unused capacity which strengthened
the active capital resources of the economy. During the second
stage--1946–56--economic growth was slower, though investment was
higher than before. As the productive process became more capital-
ized, the ratio of capital to output began to rise, and the rate of growth
of output obtainable with a given savings-income ratio declined. However, a further decline in the rate of growth of per capita income did
not develop as more rapid accumulation of capital took place, that is,
the savings-income ratio rose. Investment averaged 14 per cent of
gross product and output increased by 5 per cent to 6 per cent per year.

The capital investment going to economic development in this
second period served both to increase the "capital depth" and to
broaden the employment base. However, the increase in employment
during 1946–56 was smaller than the growth in output. Hence the

over-all capital deepening in the economy was the primary factor responsible for the improved average productivity per man-hour. During 1946–56, while the index of national output increased 64.8 per cent, the volume of employment (man-hours) increased by only 46.2 per cent. These figures point to an increase of productivity of 12.7 per cent. The faster development of the more capital-intensive sectors of the Mexican economy, though partly due to technological factors, may have also been encouraged by rising wage-rates. Wages and salaries had been practically frozen during the war, thus depressing their share in net domestic product to an all-time low of 22 per cent in 1947. Considering the increased employment by sectors, employment in trade and services showed the greatest relative increase, but this reflected, partly, underemployment in the cities.

Mexico's four largest cities--Mexico City, Guadalajara, Monterrey, and Puebla--have grown more than 5 per cent a year since 1940. Mexico City has boomed to 4.5 million inhabitants and is now the second largest city in Latin America and fourth in the hemisphere. But this rapid urban growth has been accompanied by shortages of productive investment to absorb all the increased supplies of labor into average remunerative employment, with the end result that there are large numbers of underemployed, though their rate of increase has clearly diminished between 1939 and 1956. These pools of rural and urban underemployed have been the main source of migrant workers into the United States. Notwithstanding this spectacular urban growth Mexico continues to have a majority of rural population. Although the rate of increase of the urban population has been double that of the rural population, the rural segment represented 56 per cent of Mexico's total population in 1956.

Taking together the two periods from 1939 to 1956, in this brief span of less than twenty years, Mexico has attained a satisfactory annual rise in real national output averaging 7 per cent a year.

Mexico's economic growth has been achieved with a reasonable degree of balance between agriculture, industry, and services. Since 1939, agricultural production has grown two and one-half times as a result of new land brought into cultivation, which contributed about 40 per cent to the increment, shifts to more productive crops contributing around 35 per cent, and increased yields accounting for the remaining 25 per cent. Behind these results has been an intensive investment drive. Gross investment in agriculture increased faster than gross national investment in all fields--148 per cent and 130 per cent, respectively, from 1949 to 1955. Moreover, three-fourths of the total agricultural investment represented private investment. The increased use of fertilizers and agricultural mechanization in Mexico has proceeded rapidly--5,000 tractors in 1939 as compared with 60,000 in 1956. Other measures that have been helpful in expanding agricultural output are, of course, expanded credit facilities, the improved-seed programs, the provision of crop insurance, and the establishment of an extension service to furnish technical assistance, now operating in every state of the Republic. At present, 40 per cent of the agricultural output consists of raw materials for industry. Cotton production has expanded six fold since 1939, reaching a peak of 2.2 million bales in 1955. Mexico is the world's second-largest exporter of cotton. Coffee output has expanded from 54,000 metric tons in 1939 to 93,000 in 1955 and has become the second-ranking export product. The development of these money crops--coffee and cotton--has helped to diversify Mexico's export trade, which traditionally had been dependent on three principal mineral exports. These two crops accounted for 46 per cent of the value of total commodity exports in 1956. For the same year, imports of corn and wheat represented only 1 per cent of the value of total commodity imports. This sharp drop in food imports, which previously had accounted for more than 10 per cent of total imports, has been made possible, though per capita consumption of corn and wheat has been growing, by the tripling of wheat production to 1.2 million tons in 1956, as a steady shift from corn consumption to wheat has taken place alongside rising income levels. The corn crop is half-again as large as output in 1939. Thus, today Mexico itself produces more than 95 per cent of its basic foods.

Industrial growth has proceeded at an even faster rate. The annual volume of manufactures has grown by three and one-half times, along with a tripling of the output of electric energy and petroleum and petroleum products. Between 1938 and 1956 the nationalized petroleum industry has more than doubled its production of crude oil from 38.8 to 94.1 million barrels, tripled its refining capacity from 102,000 to 308,000 barrels a day, and nearly quadrupled its reserves from 763 to 2,900 million barrels. Natural-gas production quintupled from 24,000 to 125,000 million cubic feet. Petroleum supplies 85 per cent of the energy consumed in the country, and most of Mexico's output is used internally, at relatively low prices. Low-priced fuel and road and rail transportation have provided essential external economies for new private investment and the over-all economic development of the country. However, a recent process of gradual increase in the prices of these services is strengthening the financial position of the operating agencies and freeing budget funds used up until now by these entities.

Before the Second World War, manufacturing in Mexico was confined largely to the textile and food-processing industries, which did not make any appreciable contribution toward enhancing economic growth. Today Mexico has developed a diversified local industry. Manufactures include producer goods and a wide variety of consumer goods. The industrial profile includes steel and sugar mills, oil refineries, cement plants, chemical works, tire factories, machine shops, foundries, and all the hundreds of establishments that produce everything from steel pipe to refrigerators and washing machines and that indicate the existence of modern industrial complexes. And producer goods are growing even faster, spearheading the general industrial development as they provide increased purchasing power and hence additional demand for consumer goods. Manufacturing rose 62 per cent in volume from 1950 to 1956, while output of machinery grew 121 per cent, chemicals by 110 per cent, cement and glass production doubled, and transport equipment expanded by 78 per cent. The country's integrated and expanding iron and steel industry has in a few years doubled output to more than a million tons of steel ingots--with expansion plans presently being carried out to reach a million and a half tons by 1960--and has stimulated the establishment of many related metalworking industries. Heavy mass-production industries have been concentrated in a new industrial town, Irolo, and they are turning out Fiat diesel trucks, Toyoda textile machines, and freight cars for the Mexican railroads. Nacional Financiera has directly promoted this heavy-industry group as well as other basic enterprises such as steel, electrolytic copper, fertilizer, and recently pulp and paper plants. It has also provided about a third of the credit financing of the industrial enterprises of Mexico in recent years. However, the bulk of the funds for industrial investment originated in the undistributed profits of the business enterprises. The importance of the Mexican capital market as a source of funds is limited.

Mining is a sector which has advanced less, and its contribution to national output declined from 5 per cent in 1939 to 2.5 per cent in 1956. However, sulphur production during 1957 jumped to about one million tons, making Mexico the world's second producer. In the current year, sulphur may provide around $30 million of export income and by 1960 more than the earnings derived from exports of zinc or copper.

Agricultural progress and industrialization have required, and been facilitated by, adequate transportation and a host of financial and distributive services. From 1939 to 1956, the national highway system has quintupled to exceed 28,000 kilometers and today moves about half of the total freight volume--which has doubled in the meantime--handled by all types of carriers. The country has 39 public airports and 23,000 kilometers of railroads, with around 1,000 kilometers of new lines under construction. The combined assets of Mexico's credit and insurance institutions in 1956 amounted to 37 per cent of monetary national income, compared to 25 per cent in 1939; there are at present two securities exchanges--one in Mexico City, in the center of the Republic, and the other in Monterrey, in the north--and several investment companies.

The more or less balanced structure attained by the growth of the Mexican economy has been the result of directed policies which have

taken into consideration the interdependency of the principal sectors--
agriculture, providing food and raw materials; and a market for the
new industries, industry supplying the goods required to increase farm
productivity and relieving the population pressure in rural areas by
providing employment opportunities in the cities. The outcome is reflected by the percentage of total output originating in the different
sectors. In terms of the national product, agriculture, cattle raising,
fishing, and forestry in 1956 originated 24 per cent, industry 29 per
cent, trade 23 per cent, and other services the remaining 24 per cent.
With the development of the economy, farmers and workers have increased their shares in output. Wages, salaries, and supplementary
payments to workers accounted for 22 per cent of the net domestic
product in 1947 and had increased to 32 per cent by 1956. Earnings
of farmers also increased from 12 per cent of national income in 1947
to 18 per cent in 1956.

IV. Prospects and Problems for Further Growth

The concrete measures of progress in agriculture, industry, and
services just highlighted show that Mexico's economic growth has
been, on the whole, impressive. On the other hand, Mexico has had,
if the stimulus, also the burden of a rapidly-growing population. Its
rate of growth of 3.2 per cent a year means that by the mid-1980's
Mexico will have a population of more than sixty million inhabitants
to feed, clothe, and shelter, with the productive effort of only about
one-third of them--according to the average ratio of gainfully employed population from 1939 to date.

The past record, however, is comforting. Notwithstanding its high
rate of population growth relative to resources, real income per capita
has nearly doubled during this brief period since 1939. Yet, this remarkable achievement has to be tempered, considering that Mexico
had to start from a very low level of per capita income. The average
per capita product for Mexico in 1952–54 was $220, which, according
to a United Nations study of fifty-five countries, is about half the per
capita product in Europe, though well above that in Asia and Africa.
This average figure, moreover, conceals great differences in personal
income between the upper and lower classes.

The government has sought, therefore, to alter income distribution
in order to ameliorate the living conditions of the masses without dis-
couraging private investments necessary to economic growth. In the
case of the system of public finance, the taxes used to finance expenditure have relied increasingly on the income tax which, through
its seven schedules according to the origin of income, yielded 10 per
cent of total tax revenue in 1939 and more than 30 per cent in 1956,
while foreign-trade taxes declined from 47 per cent to 35 per cent,

and the remainder has been obtained from turnover and production taxes. On the expenditure side, though emphasis has been laid on development investment in highways, irrigation, railroads, electric energy, and oil, there has been some expansion in social-welfare benefits, in absolute and relative terms. During the period 1940–46 public investment in housing, schools, hospitals, and other rural and urban social services averaged 18 per cent of total public investment, and within the period 1950–56 this outlay had increased to 20 per cent.

The government has also intervened directly in the pricing system, establishing minimum-wage legislation and rent control on low-cost housing, and has tried to stabilize the supply and prices of popular basic foodstuffs. The government supports the farm price of wheat, corn, and beans and then sells them in the local market at relatively low prices, absorbing the losses as subsidies to bolster the purchasing power of farmers and the consumption of the lower-income urban groups. The outstanding fact about the government intervention is that, in the last decade, it has gone along with the firm expansion of private investment. As a result of a continuously expanding domestic market and a favorable environment to which the government has contributed significantly through its social overhead investments and diverse incentives for further private investment such as tax exemptions, fiscal subsidies, tariff protection, and a low tax burden, private investment has increased its share of total fixed investment from around half to presently two-thirds. The government tax intake has been below 10 per cent of national product through the whole period.

Thus, contrary to the assertion that once the government gets into business it tends to deter private enterprise, in the Mexican case, because the government has actively induced a process of development since 1934, acting in the absence of private initiative as an entrepreneur and financier, private domestic entrepreneurs and financiers have emerged and now account for the largest share of annual investment.

The steadily improving standard of living of farmers and industrial workers and the emergence of a rapidly expanding middle class--elements discernible through the increasing per capita consumption figures of basic foodstuffs, clothing, shelter, and consumer durables--point up the fact that the efforts of the Mexicans to attain their Constitutional economic goals have been fruitful. But while proud of their real and tangible achievements, Mexicans are aware that their principal task still is to reduce widespread poverty through relatively high rates of economic growth over sustained periods.

Fortunately, the Mexican economy has moved from dead center, and it bears the potential for continued growth. Internal policies and external developments will have, however, a decisive effect both on the rate of growth Mexico attains during the next decade and on whether the increases in physical output will be accompanied by proportionate increases in money incomes so that prices will be roughly stable or whether the increases will be such as to effect rapidly rising prices. In the early years, domestic inflationary financing reduced consumption and made resources available for productive investment. Later, expansion of the export sector and the establishment of export taxes yielded much of the necessary resources for domestic growth. However, the world-market outlook points to a gradual reduction of export tax income; hence new domestic sources of financing will have to be found.

As regards prospects, during 1957 the rate of growth slowed down from the 7 per cent average and in 1958 the retardation continues. But economic growth has proceeded in a cyclical pattern. The recessions of the years 1938/39, 1948/49 and 1953/54 were caused by stagnation in export industries and in domestic industries competing with imports, as well as by adverse weather conditions for agriculture. Mexico devalued the peso during the 1938/39 recession and again, like many other nations throughout the world, during the recession of 1948/49, with deteriorating terms of trade adding to the hardship involved in adjusting to postwar economic conditions. The 1953/54 recession again saw the devaluation of the peso. The basic external problem of Mexico and other raw-materials–producing countries is still that, relative to their economic capacity, an unduly disproportionate share of the burden of the world's market readjustments falls on their shoulders. The depressive effect is felt not so much in their employment levels as in their terms of trade, their volume of imports, and hence in their real income. Subsidized exports by economically more developed nations have added recently to the hardships of the poorer countries.

Devaluations in Mexico, however, have stimulated industrial production, and in a framework of growing world markets have also expanded exports. Although imports are restricted by permits covering about 20 per cent of total import value--and by differential import duties, this type of restrictiveness is aimed simply at limiting imports to Mexico's capacity to pay for them and to assure their highest possible contribution to domestic productivity and external purchasing power. Production goods make up 80 per cent of imports in comparison with 34 per cent in 1939. Thus, in Mexico, devaluations and import restrictions have helped to balance external payments at rising levels of output, income, and foreign trade.

Income from international transactions on current account has grown seven fold in dollar terms since 1939 to its present level--near $1,500 million. Considering both income and expenditure, Mexico's international transactions amount annually to a $3,000 million two-way business, 80 per cent of it with the United States. Mexico's share in world trade also is higher than it was before the war. This impressive expansion of the international account has taken place under complete convertibility of the peso, and free exchange.

In the two decades from 1938 to 1958, Mexico's booming imports and other foreign-exchange needs have been financed principally by growing exports of goods and services. The net inflow of direct private investment and development loans from abroad have contributed, on the average, around 10 per cent to the annual fixed capital investment of the period.

Up to now--April, 1958--the economic recession which began in 1957, unlike previous recessions, has not meant unbearable pressure on the peso. This is an indication of the soundness of the Mexican economy. Central-bank policy has kept credit expansion within bounds. The government has shown great restraint in spending and accumulated budget surpluses during 1955 and 1956. The total public debt has declined relatively from a level representing 14 per cent of national income in 1939 to 8 per cent in 1956. Prices have been relatively stable during 1956, 1957, and 1958. And the monetary reserves have doubled from $200 million in April, 1954, to more than $400 million at present--a level sufficient to finance imports over a four-month period and one which also covers more than 50 per cent of Mexico's money supply. This, in spite of the drop in prices and the demand for coffee, cotton, and metals, and a severe drought which compelled us to import large quantities of corn in 1957.

The outlook for economic growth in the years beyond 1958 will be much influenced by the success in maintaining domestic financial stability and by the avoidance of a much deeper world economic recession. Assuming both conditions are met, it would seem likely that between now and 1965 the Mexican economy will grow at an average rate of about 5 per cent per annum, that is, not much below the average rate for the past decade. However, if balance-of-payments equilibrium is to be maintained, a progressively smaller portion of the growing level of consumption and investment will have to be supplied from abroad. At present, imports represent about 14 per cent of the total annual supply of goods and services. While gross product is expected to increase by some 5 per cent per annum from 1957 to 1965, real foreign-exchange earnings on current account are not likely to rise by more than 3 per cent per annum, according to present trends. Imports would have to be limited on the average to this 3 per cent annual increase--a higher increase in any one year would have to be offset by a lower increase in another year--unless present trends change both in the income and the capital accounts of Mexico's balance of payments. Tourist income might be the item which could lift the current account upwards; in a few years' time it has rapidly increased to a level of more than $500 million annual gross income, and there is a general feeling that a wider promotion of tourist attractions could yield significant increases.

Furthermore, the 5 per cent rate of economic growth will require total fixed investment at close to 15 per cent of gross product, since some decline is likely in investment yields. Experience in the past decade suggests that the level of voluntary savings which can be expected is somewhere between 12 per cent and 13 per cent of gross product. During the period 1951–56 the net inflow of long-term official capital and direct foreign investment averaged $100 million per year, or 1.7 per cent of gross product. If the same average percentage level of foreign-capital inflow is maintained in the future, voluntary savings, supplemented by foreign-capital inflows, would sustain a volume of investment of about 14 per cent of gross product.

The gap between investments required to maintain this rate of economic growth and the available domestic voluntary savings and long-term external capital is thus of the order of magnitude of 1 per cent of gross national product, or 1 to 1.5 billion pesos. This is a relatively small gap which should not be too difficult to bridge over a period of time, chiefly through increased domestic savings. The maintenance of domestic financial stability would in turn attract a growing inflow of foreign capital, and the latter would facilitate the former.

The economic progress of the Mexican people is thus tied to the skill and ingenuity which they can develop to raise increasing volumes of internal and external savings for business and government investment operations. As long as the government continues to be pressed at the same time for higher social-welfare benefits, the share of the national product which is used in collective consumption through the State will have to be carefully balanced with the public-development investments needed by the required growth of the Mexican economy. This task has been entrusted since 1954 to the Investment Commission, established in the Office of the President, whose duty is to formulate an annual co-ordinated program of investments by the public sector-- which includes government, decentralized agencies, and State enterprises--with determined priorities. At the same time, a Special Commission on External Financing was set up in Nacional Financiera, the co-ordinating agency for long-term financing from abroad for use by the public sector. The commission's task has been to assure prudent use of external credits as an important supplementary source of financing productive investments, always within the economy's capacity to pay.

Long-term credits amounting to $570 million have been supplied to Mexico since 1942, when this type of operation was initiated, principally by the Export-Import Bank, the International Bank for Reconstruction and Development, and during recent years by a growing number of private banks and suppliers in the United States and Europe. Of this amount, $256 million has been repaid and $58 million has been expended in interest charges. The servicing of these strategic credits has been modest, averaging a little more than 3 per cent of the country's foreign-exchange income on current account, or only slightly higher than the servicing of the old public debt--2 per cent--which has had no counterpart in current investment during this period. As the old debt is paid off, the capacity to service new active development credits will increase.

The servicing of direct private investments has been somewhat heavier, averaging about 7 per cent of income on current account since 1939. New investments amounting to approximately $680 million have flowed into the economy in this period, most of it from the United States, and profit and other remittances have totaled $890 million. The dynamic quality of these investments has had a profound impact on Mexico's development, bringing production and employment in new fields and generating new income and exports.

As regards foreign financing, the problem ahead is to strike a satisfactory balance between direct foreign investments which in joint participation with Mexican capital sink their roots more deeply into the Mexican community, and a more flexible type of foreign develop- ment loans for use by the public sector in order to provide widened basic facilities for private investment.

For the last four years the Mexican Government has been setting the annual target of the convenient level of public investment and its internal and external financing according to a satisfactory rate of growth of the national economy and the likely level of investment originating in the private and international sectors.

Considering the key role to be played by domestic financial policy, the future economic progress in Mexico will depend on:

a) an increase in private savings through greater use of domestic currency securities which protect the purchasing power of national savings. To meet this growing demand the Nacional Financiera has recently issued the Certificate of Industrial Co-proprietorship in a common fund of securities, half of which consists of shares to protect the value of the investment, and the other half of bonds to assure a minimum yield; these certificates are paying 8.5 per cent in compari- son with 8 per cent on mortgage bonds and 5 per cent on the partici- pation certificates with a repurchase-at-par clause. Securities with varying features as to their liquidity, yield, and capital protection are being offered to meet the preferences of different groups of savers; in this connection index-tied securities are under study as well as the issuance of low-denomination common shares.

b) An increase in public savings through expanded government revenues by means of improved tax collections and new selectively higher tax rates. The introduction of an additional tax schedule for personal global income or a progressive expenditure tax has been discussed at length in government circles. A fiscal reform has long been overdue and when put into effect by the government it will have the co-operation of all the private sectors involved.

Mexico, on the basis of its record, can view with satisfaction the advancement achieved thus far in its secular struggle against illness, ignorance, and poverty--which history and geography combine to make at once urgent and difficult. In a world so lacking of freedom and economic welfare, Mexico has furthered both at a surprisingly high rate, despite the many problems which have harassed its economy. Certainly there is no room for complacency, and every Mexican is keenly aware of it. Based on its present work in progress, Mexico looks with confidence into the future.

PROGRESS, PLANNING, AND POLICY IN PUERTO RICO

Alvin Mayne

Director, Puerto Rico Planning Board

Governmental policies are forged in the process of choosing among alternative plans designed to achieve a variety of, and frequently conflicting, objectives. It is primarily through an analysis of the rate of progress toward objectives that new plans are developed and old ones modified. These, in turn, call forth policy decisions regarding the speed with which particular objectives will be sought. An analysis of progress in the economic development of Puerto Rico since 1940 provides not only a record of the transformation of an economy but also insight into the change in plans, techniques, and policies designed to achieve rapid economic and social development.

I. Progress

The Economic and Political Setting of the Puerto Rican Economy

Before discussing the development of the Puerto Rican economy during the last few years, it is important that the unique characteristics of the relationship between the Commonwealth of Puerto Rico and the United States be noted. The special political relationship with the United States results in: (1) access of Puerto Rican products to United States markets on a duty-free basis; (2) the refund of United States excise taxes and customs duties to the Commonwealth government; (3) exemption of all Puerto Rican residents from federal taxes; (4) substantial expenditures by the federal government in the Island, including direct operational disbursements, contributions to joint projects with the Commonwealth government, and transfer payments to individuals and businesses; (5) common citizenship with the United States, which has made possible large-scale migration to the mainland; (6) inclusion in the United States monetary system, which makes possible the free flow of abundant capital resources.

The economic development of Puerto Rico has been retarded by a lack of natural resources. Many of the underdeveloped areas of the world have mineral or other resources that can be developed. Thus, Venezuela is exploiting large petroleum reserves, and India's second five-year program rests on rich iron ore and coal deposits.

Alvin Mayne

Except for a possible million tons of iron, and some marble, lime-
stone, and clay, Puerto Rico has no mineral wealth. Despite its heavy
agrarian employment, the amount of land available for cultivation is
only 0.4 acre per capita compared with 2.7 acres per capita in the
United States.[1] The inability of Puerto Rico to look to agriculture as
the dominant sector of development is revealed by another comparison,
namely, the acreage available per individual employed in agriculture.
In 1954, the Puerto Rican ratio was 5.1 acres per agricultural worker
as compared with 50 acres in the United States.

The importance of economic integration with the United States industrial complex can most readily be seen if the meager possibilities
of a self-contained program of economic development are analyzed.
The local market for consumer goods, for instance, consisted of only
2,270,000 persons as of April, 1956. Their incomes are relatively low.
Production limited to a level of output consumable by only the local
market would generally be inefficient and would therefore yield a relatively low real income for the ultimate consumer and probably for the
producer. The market for producers' goods would be even narrower
and therefore plant capacity would be even more costly.

Despite these higher costs, a developing country may deem that the
long-run growth of these high-cost industries would be beneficial and
may adopt a protective tariff to keep out lower-cost imports. But this
is not a feasible approach for Puerto Rico, since it is impossible to
isolate the Puerto Rican market from the efficient United States producer in order to assist infant industries designed for home consumption. The only competitive advantage that a Puerto Rican producer has
in the local market is lower transportation costs or the existence of
imperfect competition derived from the preference of the local consumer for Puerto Rican brands. But more than offsetting the inability
to shut mainland products out of the Puerto Rican markets through the
use of tariffs is the free access that Puerto Rican products have to the
wealthy and vast United States market. The possession of this freedom
of access is the envy of every developing and every fully developed
country of the world.

The lack of a skilled labor force is a factor that tends to hold back
development, since the low level of productivity may offset a significant proportion of the wage differential that exists between Puerto Rico
and the continental United States. Only in the very near past has on-
the-job training in industry become a possibility. As recently as 1940,
45 per cent of total employment was in agriculture, and an additional
21 per cent was in relatively inefficient trade and service activities.
The skills created in manufacturing operations were practically nonexistent. Handicraft industries, which some underdeveloped economies utilize for training workers in manual dexterity, were also virtually absent. The population, largely of Spanish origin, was heavily

dependent on the mother country for goods. The atmosphere of a strong native culture which tends to foster handicrafts has been lacking.

Demographic Developments

From 1940 to 1950 the population of Puerto Rico increased by more than 400,000 persons, or 21 per cent, owing to a dramatically falling death rate coupled with the birth rate, which increased until 1947 and then began to drop. Since 1947 the population has been approximately stable. Gross birth rates are dropping now by about the same amount as death rates, as the first signs of a decrease in the fertility of women in the younger age groups is being observed. The rate of natural increase is still very high but migration can be depended upon to keep the population at about its present size, as it has since 1950. Recessions in the United States may temporarily lower or interrupt migration, but such interruptions will undoubtedly be followed by higher subsequent rates of migration. The dependability of migration as a factor in keeping population size stable rests essentially on the very large number of Puerto Rican families already residing in the United States.

The growth of population from 1940 to 1947 was accompanied by a gradual lowering in the average age of the population. Now that population size has stabilized, the average age of the population is increasing rapidly. The median age is expected to increase from nineteen years to twenty-eight years within the next decade. The proportion of persons under twenty may be expected to drop sharply during the 1960's, the population between the ages of twenty and forty-five will remain relatively constant, while the number of persons over forty-five will increase from 17 per cent to 30 per cent of the total. This rapid shift in the age of the population, due principally to heavy migration, means that the Puerto Rican labor force will grow substantially in the next twenty years even though the total population remains stable. Migration has also caused some shift in the sex ratio, especially between the age of twenty to thirty-five. The excess of females over males in this age bracket is now somewhat over 50,000.

Until 1940 the rural and urban population of Puerto Rico were both on the increase, but between 1940 and 1950 the rural population increased by only 1 per cent, whereas the urban population grew by almost 60 per cent. Since 1950, with the total population remaining stable and the urban population continuing to increase, the rural population has undoubtedly declined in absolute numbers. This rural-urban population shift would probably have been even greater except that many people have continued to live in rural sectors while working in urban areas. In the shift from rural to urban residence the metropolitan area of San Juan has had, by far, the largest growth. The largest population movement of all has been, of course, the change of residence from Puerto Rico to New York City and the rest of the United States.

Economic Developments

While the Puerto Rican economy has achieved a rapid rate of growth since 1940, the foundations for an acceleration of the growth was laid down primarily during the last ten years. From 1940 to 1947 real gross product per capita rose by 2.5 per cent, while during the last ten years the rate of increase has been 5.4 per cent per annum, with per capita personal income reaching $470 per year.

This rapid improvement in levels of income and in the standard of living of the people of Puerto Rico was accomplished by increased productivity in the individual sectors of the economy and by changing the structure of the economy from a preponderance of output and employment in the low-wage sectors of the economy, such as agriculture, home needlework industries, and domestic services, to the high-wage sectors, such as manufacturing, public services, and trade. In 1940, 60 per cent of employment was concentrated in sectors which as late as 1957 could yield only $671 compensation per annum in contrast to annual compensation of $2,116 in the high-wage sector. By 1950, employment in the two sectors was approximately equal, with the increases in the labor force being absorbed by the high-wage sector. The most striking shift occurred during the past seven years, with a 33 per cent decline in employment in agriculture, home needlework, and domestic service as contrast with a 20 per cent increase in employment in the higher-income sectors. It is estimated that the shift in structure has accounted for 40 per cent of the increased output and the remainder either increases in productivity or shifts within the sectors themselves.

Industrial development.--The possibility that Puerto Rico's economy could be shifted from an agricultural economy to that of a diversified manufacturing economy was realized less than ten years ago. The first steps taken toward industrialization developed largely from specific problems which arose, first as the result of the great depression, and then as the result of the Second World War. In order to supply cement to public-works programs of the 1930's, a cement mill was constructed by the government, and to provide bottles and cartons for greatly expanded rum shipments to the United States during the war, glass, paper, and box factories were constructed and operated by the government. Until that time the program for development had been concentrated in agriculture.

When the funds invested by the government were compared with the employment generated, it became clear that a program of industrialization owned and operated by the government and designed primarily for the home market would be insufficient to absorb sizeable quantities of manpower. The government had neither the industrial know-how nor the funds to launch an industrialization program aimed at the United States market. It was then decided that the role of the government would be that of a catalyst, utilizing its funds as an incentive together with other incentives to induce entrepreneurs with production know-how, capital, and markets to locate in Puerto Rico. In a sense the present industrialization program may be considered to have been initiated in 1950, just ten years ago.

During this period, there has been a conscious effort to adapt the tools available to the Commonwealth government to the problem of rapid industrial development. Promotional programs in the mainland were developed which are equivalent in intensity and quality to those utilized by automobile companies to sell their merchandise. Plants were constructed by the government at low rentals--amortization and interest charges. When it became clear that industrialists were not being attracted to Puerto Rico because of the lack of vacant factories, the Puerto Rico Industrial Development Company initiated a program of construction which provided an inventory of vacant standard buildings. Funds for equipment and inventory loans which could not be made through the commercial banking system were provided by the Government Development Bank, which today has assets of $70 million. If an industry is deemed to be a core industry, necessary for a balanced development of the economy, special incentives, such as free rent for a year, transportation costs of machinery, and training costs, may be provided. When geographic data revealed that the industrial development was being heavily concentrated in the San Juan area, rent differentials favoring the less urbanized areas were created and the grants of special incentives were stepped up for these areas.

From the very beginning, it was recognized that the lack of a skilled labor force might become a barrier to rapid progress. Vocational education for adults was initiated as well as on-the-job training assisted by government funds. Scholarships for professional and foreman training in the United States were provided.

As the industrial complex broadened and as incomes rose, the possibilities for vertical integration became greater. Economic studies of the feasibility of particular industries were begun. The development of a small marble quarry, a kraft board facility from bagasse, (the crushed, juiceless sugar cane as it comes from the mill), a hard board plant from bagasse, an improved furniture industry, and a synthetic fiber plant from petroleum by-products was deemed feasible.

At the end of 1957, approximately five hundred manufacturing plants employing 40,000, or half of the present manufacturing employment, had been established under the industrial-development program. The impact of these new plants was to diversify the manufacturing sector. Concentration shifted from agriculturally-based or small home-market industries to export industries based upon imported raw materials and components. In 1950 sugar mills and refineries accounted for

34 per cent of net income originating in manufacturing. By 1957 they accounted for only 10 per cent.

Table 1

Relative Importance of Selected Manufacturing Industries,
Fiscal Years 1949/50 and 1956/57

Industry	Percentage of Manufacturing Income	
	1950	1957
Total	100.0	100.0
Sugar mills and refineries	33.7	10.5
Beverages	4.9	5.1
Other food products	8.2	6.5
Tobacco products	5.6	4.5
Textiles	1.2	4.5
Apparel	19.6	22.1
Wood products	4.7	5.2
Chemical products	6.2	4.1
Stone, clay, and glass	5.4	6.3
Machinery and metals	3.0	13.6
Others, not specified	7.5	17.5

Exports of new kinds of manufactured products have risen from about $30 million in 1950 to $216 million in 1957 and now account for 46 per cent of total exports as compared with 13 per cent seven years ago.

Agricultural development.--In the 1930's Puerto Rican agriculture was dominated by a small number of large corporations, growers and processors of sugar cane, many of whose principal stockholders did not live on the Island. The land reform of the 1940's broke up a number of these corporations, reduced the size and power of those that survived, and brought about a transfer of ownership to local residents.

The break-up of these corporations was accompanied by an increase in the number and acreage of owner-operated farms of medium size. The land reform also brought into being the public corporation as a large holder and operator of farm land.

Apart from increases in number and acreage, the medium-sized farm has made little progress. In fact, the commercial family farm,

with some exceptions, finds itself in a progressively worsening cost-price squeeze. The remaining agricultural corporations, public and private, though similarly squeezed between rising costs and stable prices, are in a relatively better position to do something about it than their smaller competitors. With few exceptions only the larger operators of farm land have been able to improve the efficiency of production and marketing techniques rapidly enough to pay higher wages and also meet competition.

The development of co-operative associations has helped some medium-sized farmers to solve some of their marketing, credit, and production problems, but only to a limited extent. Similarly, the development of agricultural markets, schools, credit institutions, and organizations that provide machinery, chemicals, feeds, and improved plants and animals has not progressed enough since the 1930's and frequently not in the right direction, to solve the problems of the small and medium-sized farmer.

Physical output of the agricultural sector has varied little since 1950, with net income reflecting in large measure the changes in prices and such events as drought and hurricanes. The unique role which sugar plays tends to make expansion of the agricultural sector extremely difficult. Because the sugar crop has a guaranteed market at a subsidized price, it is difficult to shift land resources, except of the more marginal character, to other types of commodities. Because the sugar quota puts a virtual ceiling on the output which can be marketed, there is no incentive to expand the productivity of the land unless the alternative crops will provide additional net income from the land which is freed. As long as labor is abundant at a low wage, there is no incentive to introduce labor-saving devices or shift to crops which will yield a greater income per worker.

In a sense the important developments which have occurred in the agricultural sector have resulted from the operation of such outside forces as the shortage of agricultural workers in the United States and the expansion of the manufacturing and allied sectors of the economy. Employment has fallen from 214,000 to 150,000. The importance of this drop for agricultural development is that the calculus of agricultural investment will shift from concentration on efforts to improve output per acre to output per worker. The implication of this for government policy will be discussed in a later section.

Construction.--As might be expected in an economy that is growing rapidly and changing its structure, the construction industry has shown considerable expansion. Value put-in-place has expanded from an annual rate of $79 million to $168 million during the last seven years. The greatest increase was in the construction of plants, which rose from a rate of $34 million a year to $90 million. During the last two years, largely owing to the availability of external mortgage capital under provisions of the FHA and the creation of large-scale housing developments, dwelling construction has reached an annual rate of almost $50 million a year.

Government sector.--The federal government plays five roles in Puerto Rican economy: (1) as a purchaser of goods and services, primarily for defense reasons; (2) as a supplier of funds in the form of grants-in-aid for programs such as roads, school lunches, and public welfare; (3) as a guarantor of certain types of credit utilized by the private and public sectors of the economy, such as public housing bonds and FHA mortgages; (4) as a source of transfer payments to individuals and businesses; and (5) as a provider of laws governing interstate affairs, such as the federal Fair Labor Standards Act.

The federal government as purchaser of goods and services played an important role in the development of Puerto Rico immediately after the outbreak of hostilities in Korea. Net income generated by the federal government sector rose from $42 million, or 7.5 per cent of total Commonwealth net income, to $134 million, or 15 per cent. Subsequently, it has been reduced to $75 million, or 7.5 per cent of the total. In effect, the Puerto Rican economy has weathered a major reduction in activity of the federal government during the last four years without serious repercussions.

The grants-in-aid to the Commonwealth treasury are provided essentially under the same formulas utilized for making grants to a state. The only exception is with respect to public welfare, in which the grant is much less than the formula, owing to a Congressional limit of $5.2 million per annum. The total grants-in-aid in 1957 amounted to $24 million, or about 12 per cent of the total revenues available to the Commonwealth government. To a large extent matching funds are required.

As of 1955, the total of federal government agencies loans amounted to $65 million outstanding and about $60 million FHA mortgages under guarantee. Offsetting this were the holding of $112 million of United States government securities by the Commonwealth government and $45 million of such securities by the banking system, making a total of $157 million of loans to federal government by the Puerto Rican economy.

Transfer payments largely due to veteran benefits amounted to $78 million in 1957 and accounts for approximately 50 per cent of the merchandise trade deficit. It is expected that this will decline during the next three years as veteran benefits are reduced.

The contribution of the Commonwealth government has advanced from 10 per cent of the total net income to $133 million a year, or 15 per cent. This growth has been largely dependent upon increased revenues which have expanded, with no major change in tax structure except for the addition of the "pay-as-you-go" plan in 1956, from $95 million in 1947 to $200 million, including federal grants-in-aid. In addition, a small amount of borrowing takes place for capital improvements. Education accounts for 27 per cent; health, 15 per cent; general administration, 10 per cent; protection, 9 per cent; and public welfare, 8 per cent.

Supporting sectors.--The expansion in the supporting sectors of trade, finance, and utility services has roughly corresponded to growth in the primary sectors of the economy--from $253 million to $466 million in ten years. Structural changes which may be expected to develop in a rapidly changing economy have occurred. In distribution, for example, the chain food-store has been introduced with astounding success. The distribution trades are about to enter a period of rapidly increasing productivity, with the result that the number of persons engaged will decline. It is unlikely that the transformation will have as serious an impact on employment as it did on agriculture, for higher incomes will expand the need for the supporting industries.

Capital formation.--The economic progress that has been made can probably be best summarized in terms of the rate of capital formation that has been taking place. During the last ten years gross investment has amounted to $1,600 million, with the rate climbing each year until in 1957 some $261 million, or 21 per cent of the gross product, was invested in fixed assets. The major share--$83 million--was in the form of plants and equipment. This amounted to 17 per cent of private gross product. The private sector accounted for two-thirds of plant and equipment expenditures, mainly in the form of machinery. Government business enterprises, primarily the government-owned public utility, accounted for the remainder. Power requirements have been expanding at the rate of 18 per cent per year during the last several years.

In recent years investment funds have been supplied equally by external and local sources. Thus, local savings, generated primarily by the government, and business depreciation and retained profits amounted to $155 million in 1957. Individual savings were negative by $17 million. Nearly 50 per cent of the external funds was in the form of direct investment, primarily in equity capital.

Utilization of Human Resources

Rapid economic growth which involves major structural changes has a serious impact upon the ability to fully utilize the labor force of an economy. Despite a decline in the total labor force due primarily to reduced labor-force participation and despite a 5.4 per cent rise in gross output per year, the level of unemployment has remained virtually the same--85,000 to 90,000, or 13 per cent of the labor force. The inability to reduce the size of unemployment is the result of either increased productivity per man by the introduction of labor-saving devices, the dropping of marginal units of operation, the longer workweek and the longer seasonal employment, or of the virtual disappearance of marginal industries such as tobacco-stemming and home needlework. The effect in the improvement of quality of jobs through either longer work-weeks or more steady work throughout the year can be seen in Tables 2 and 3.

Table 2

Steadiness of Employment by Industry and the Number and
Percentage of Wage and Salary Workers Reporting
"Steady" Employment during Year

Industry	Number of Workers (Thousands)		Percentage of Total	
	1953	1956	1953	1956
Total	245	292	47	56
Agriculture	53	55	31	39
Manufacturing (excluding home needlework)	39	56	48	55
Trade	28	38	65	72
Government	43	50	81	39
Construction	19	24	50	56
Other	63	69	46	39

Table 3

Wage and Salary Employees Working Thirty-five Hours or More
Per Week, by Industry, Fiscal Years 1952/53 and 1956/57

Industry	Number of Workers (Thousands)		Percentage of Total	
	1953	1957	1953	1957
Total	238	277	62	70
Agriculture	40	42	40	48
Manufacturing (excluding home needlework)	41	58	72	81
Trade	34	40	89	91
Government	36	40	78	77
Construction	22	28	63	72
Other	87	95	83	94

The disappearance of some 115,000 jobs, or 20 per cent of the total, within a period of seven years points to one of the major problems facing a rapidly developing economy. The inability to compete with lower-wage economies of the world was clearly the downfall of the home-needlework industry. Even though home needlework was the lowest-paying industry in Puerto Rico--25 cents per hour--it could not survive unless the hourly wage was reduced to 10 cents or 15 cents an hour. Tobacco-stemming unemployment results from the introduction of a technical development which replaces hand labor by mechanical means. At the docks similar developments are occurring. The sugar-growing industry is on the verge of even greater increases in productivity with corresponding reductions in employment. What makes it so difficult for a developing economy to absorb these technological advances is that they frequently affect a major segment of the employed population. In a developed economy with a full complement of industries and with virtually full employment, the introduction of technological improvements has little impact on the total economy, and the transfer of released labor to another sector can be accomplished more efficiently.

Partly as an effort to make sure that the fruits of the external capital investment are made available to the Puerto Rican economy in an equitable share and partly because of the need to achieve the same minimum-wage standards in Puerto Rico as in the United States, wages under federal and Commonwealth government auspices have been rising rapidly. The greatest drive is in industries engaged in interstate commerce, but agriculture, retail trade, and other local industries are included. Manufacturing hourly-earnings are roughly one-third those of the United States. In the last two years they have risen 14.5 per cent and 18.5 per cent, respectively. Since this is three times faster than the rate of increase in the United States, the absolute differential remains the same--$1.35 per hour. If wage increases and, in turn, income increases are to be sustained in the Puerto Rican economy, the utilization of labor-saving devices must be expanded, and the shift to more heavily capitalized industries must be continued. To a government embarked on the task of achieving rapid economic development, the problem of achieving increased income under the threat of the loss of jobs in the less productive but generally politically important sectors of the economy, is one of the most difficult to solve. In a later section of this paper the beginnings of a policy designed to cope with this problem in Puerto Rico will be discussed.

It should be noted that the impact of rapid increases in wages in Puerto Rico is somewhat different from that in most developing economies. Since there are no trade barriers between Puerto Rico and the United States other than transportation costs, wage increases at rates which are greater than productivity increases cannot be passed on to the consumers, except to a limited extent in the home market. Instead, the industry must strive to absorb the increases or disappear.

II. Planning

The Framework for Planning

The progress report given in the first section of this paper points
to an extremely rapid rate of growth during the last seven years.
There are clear indications that, unless a natural calamity visits
Puerto Rico or extremely adverse political decisions are made by
either Puerto Rico or the United States, there is reason to expect a
continuation of this rapid rate of growth. In light of the growing importance of the most dynamic sector, manufacturing, there is even
considerable likelihood that the rate of growth may be stepped up. It
is true that cyclical movements in the United States economy will
mean that the course of advance will not be smooth, but there is no
reason to believe that the funds generated by the local economy and
those invested from the United States economy will not continue to
expand if the favorable climate continues. In light of this belief in the
future growth, one of the prime objectives of economic planning is to
examine government programs necessary to make such growth feasible. On the assumption that rapid growth will continue, what steps
should the government undertake to ensure that such growth will take
place?

In addition to determining the government's actions which should
be undertaken to support rapid economic growth, the planning technique is designed to ensure that the ultimate goals of an improved
level of living, not only in the economic sense but also in the social
and spiritual sense, will be reached. In fact, the techniques for planning which are now being formulated will require that budgetary and
legislative actions be made explicit with respect to choosing between
the rate of attainment of social, spiritual, and economic objectives if
the schedules are in conflict.

The first step has been to provide a scaffolding of basic economic
and demographic projections.[2] These have been in terms of the national income accounts, population by sex and age, labor force by sex
and age, productivity, and the resultant employment and unemployment. Depending upon the program being investigated, these projections can be refined for a particular sector. Thus, for tax purposes,
forecasts of estimates of family income by source can be made.

Implication Studies

A series of implication studies are being made which utilize the
basic projections to formulate concrete government programs. The
first of such studies which has been completed deals with the manpower
problem.[3] The study revealed that the existing educational program
will fall short of supplying a labor force with sufficient training to
achieve the man-year productivity called for by the projections of

economic development. As a result, the Department of Education has been given the responsibility of expanding its retention program, of increasing its teacher-training program, of stepping up its search for new forms of educational devices, and of expanding its adult-education program. The possibility of developing programs aimed at altering the net migration flow so as to reduce the movement of the more skilled workers to the United States is also being investigated by the Department of Labor.

The long-range port program is being studied, utilizing estimates of cargo movement which can be made from the basic projections. Consideration is being given to the impact of the latest techniques, such as trailer ships and the bulk loading of grains and sugar. The vital role that the internal transportation system must play in economic development is under study. With family-income projections now available, it is no longer necessary to make trend projections of the number of passenger vehicles which will probably be on the road during future years; it is now possible to relate them to family-consumption patterns.

Housing needs are being investigated in light of the projections of income and family formation, based upon a sample survey of housing conditions made a year ago. The social objectives as revealed by the various laws dealing with housing and slum clearance become the controlling factors in the forecasts. The extent that housing conditions can be improved by the private sector can also be estimated. Similar studies are being carried out with respect to changes in the client population for public welfare, medical assistance, and other social programs being conducted by the government, not only in light of current conditions but also of future economic conditions. The possibility of changing the service and selection standards under which these programs operate is under review to determine the costs of more quickly reaching the objectives desired. Part of the computation will involve an estimate of the burden on the Commonwealth budget, including administration costs.

Since there has been a tendency for industrialization programs to concentrate in the San Juan area, the spread of economic growth has been uneven. Another group of studies involves the creation of regional development plans. These plans will be based upon the potential rates of growth in the various regions of Puerto Rico, subject to the restraints of natural resources which cannot be altered by the government within the planning period.

Concurrently with the investigation of programs, financial studies are being conducted which will reveal the availability of funds to meet the budgetary needs of the various programs. Because it is likely that these funds will be insufficient, proposals to increase revenues by altering the tax base will be made. However, the climate necessary

for continued economic growth and social equity will be kept in mind
in the development of new revenue proposals.

It is through the endeavor of balancing need with respect to financial resources, both as to magnitude and in time, that policy decisions
are generated. It is not possible, merely from a government-expendi-
ture standpoint, to do all the things one wishes to do. Certain programs must be allocated less than they need. At the same time the
desire to increase financial resources also involves conflicts with
social and economic objectives.

III. Policy

Shifts in policy are frequently subtle and not consciously made.
They may come as the result of a review of the past development,
either successes or failures, or they may come about through pressures created by segments of the economy or population or by the
frame of reference--political, economic, or social--in which the
economy must work. It might be well to review some of the policies
which have been in force in Puerto Rico or which are being currently
evolved in relationship to the record of progress cited in Part I and
the planning in Part II of this paper.

In 1940 the policy emphasized agrarian reform, since about 35 per
cent of the net income was generated in the agricultural or agriculturally-based manufacturing sectors. Industrialization was embarked
upon only as the result of the war. A review of the rate of progress
in the late 1940's caused the policy of development to shift from publicly-owned enterprises to privately-owned ones. From an analysis
of the potential of the local market and local funds available, it became clear that it would be necessary to adopt a policy of attracting
export industries with external capital, markets, and know-how. Appropriations enabling a large promotion program were made. The
publicly-owned industries were sold to gain capital and the Government Development Bank was strengthened. Tax laws were revised to
make investment in Puerto Rico more attractive.

When industrial concentration in the San Juan area became heavy,
the policy of decentralization was introduced by giving positive incentives to companies willing to locate out in the Island. The concept
of regional planning was initiated.

As the impact of rapid economic development on the employment
of the labor force became apparent--namely, the continuation of
unemployment at a high level--a shift in objectives regarding economic
development had to be made. It became clear that rapid economic
growth and the wiping out of unemployment are not identical objectives,
especially in the short run. If the greatest rate of economic growth
feasible is to be achieved, it would appear that reaching the objective

of wiping out unemployment will be delayed. In fact, the decision to pursue rapid economic growth has necessitated creating a series of tools and policies to take care of the transitory unemployment which will last for about twenty years; a small program of public works and the use of severance pay where definite technological developments have thrown workers out of employment are examples. Since it appeared that owing to chronic large-scale unemployment, migration would probably continue for some time, the policy of teaching English in the public school was altered. The program has been intensified by lengthening the study period and by sending English teachers to the mainland.

The analysis of the potential rate of income growth in the various sectors of the economy is gradually leading to a revolution of the policies regarding the nature of the shifts in employment which must take place among the older industries in Puerto Rico, particularly agriculture. As yet current policy has not fully accepted the implication of these evaluations. For example, in the case of agriculture it is difficult for a government dedicated to the welfare of its people to accept the disappearance of a marginal sector of agriculture such as coffee. Strong efforts are being made to improve the productivity of coffee acreage through new plantings, price-support programs, fertilizer loans, etc. The government has not as yet faced up to the question of whether these sectors can pay the income per worker which is to be expected by the employees of the expanding sectors of the economy.

The continued attempt to subsidize the inefficient units of production so that they remain in operation after their economic justification has ceased, will delay the ultimate adjustment in the structure of the economy. If the government decides, because of welfare or political reasons, to subsidize units of production in a given industry, it can generally do so only by taxing the rest of the economy. The maladjustment is likely to grow and become more burdensome as the gap increases between the high-wage and low-wage sectors of the economy. The existence of a subsidy will also discourage the development of efficient production by the nonmarginal units of production.

From the standpoint of welfare, therefore, the government must seek other methods of giving aid to those individuals who are losing their employment either because they are themselves inefficient or because they are employed in inefficient units of production. If the demand for human services is great in the new high-wage sectors of the economy, some assistance might be given in the form of training for new skills. However, if the unemployed are not readily absorbable, then the government on its own account should utilize them to increase the output of the economy; it is recognized that the government may be forced to carry out its functions by utilizing an inefficient combination of tools and human resources in order to transfer income to those

families caught under the wheels of economic development. It is be-
lieved that in the long run a stronger economy will result if the government uses direct employment instead of trying to subsidize the inefficient use of tools and human resources by industries which must either
compete abroad or increase the real income of consumers by lowering
local-market prices.

The challenge, then, to a welfare government is to discover means
for shifting the preponderance of employment from the low-wage sector to the high-wage sector with the least hardship to individuals.
This shift must be accomplished in such a way that the economy will
be left free, and in fact encouraged, to add tools and equipment and
corresponding skills to its human resources and thereby increase the
payment to workers for their services.

IV. <u>Summary</u>

What lessons can be learned from Puerto Rico's experience that may
be of help to the developing countries? There are several. First,
there is the technique of administration, particularly the planning apparatus set up by the Commonwealth government which attempts to
assure that conscious decisions are made by the government several
years in advance regarding the allocation of financial resources among
the various development schemes.

The second group of lessons deals with the method of creating the
capital formation on which the economic growth will be based. It has
been demonstrated in Puerto Rico that capital formation can be generated through the use of incentives. While it might be argued that
many elements in the Puerto Rican–United States relationship cannot
be duplicated in other countries of the world, it can be demonstrated
that the exploitation of this relationship so as to generate capital flows
on a large scale has required specific organization and a concerted
drive by the Puerto Rican government. Its experience with United
States capital investment also demonstrates that foreign private capital need not be exploitive. There are methods of containing it so that
sufficient benefits may filter through the economy and raise the standard of living.

The government must also make positive contributions to capital
formation. It must improve communication systems, whether by
highway, railroad, telephone, or telegraph. Power developments must
be accelerated. Certainly at an early stage there is good reason for
establishing basic industries, such as cement, paper, and glass bottles,
aimed primarily at supplying the local market and supported directly
by the government, at least until private capital can be found. Above
all, investment in human resources in the form of mass education and
health must be expanded. Budget allocations for such investments

should not be regarded as competitive with funds spent on fixed capital but complementary to them.

The third group of lessons deals with problems resulting from changes in economic structure. The ability of the old low-wage sectors to disgorge unemployment in an almost never-ending stream is far greater than is generally recognized, and there is danger that at mid-stream a sense of frustration and failure may be felt with regard to the development program. What has been learned in Puerto Rico is that the goals set by the development program should not be in terms of jobs or reduced unemployment. Development plans should not be hampered through the desire to achieve a spreading of employment except in thos fields of public works where the additional costs can be treated as an unemployment subsidy. On the whole, productive capacity should be designed to provide the lowest cost per unit of output so that payment for services can be increased, the price in the local market be reduced, or the product can be competitive in a foreign market.

Finally, the government in its efforts to improve the welfare of the less productive families must concentrate on specialized programs to assist them. It is not possible to rely on the creation of new jobs alone, because many of the families have no potential workers. In addition, the persons who become unemployed in agriculture and the old sectors generally cannot be transferred to the new sectors because they do not possess the new skills required. The government must act as a reservoir to create income for those members of the labor force who, in effect, have been left behind in the development of the economy with its requirement for efficiency.

NOTES

[1] Twenty-eight per cent of the labor force is employed in agriculture as compared with only 10 per cent in the United States. Of the 3,148,000 cuerdas of total land area (a cuerda is slightly less than an acre), only 422,000 are suitable for mechanized cultivation (flat), and 653,000 can be cultivated only by hand because of the slope. The remaining 978,000 cuerdas are suitable for low-value cover crops such as forests.

[2] See "Proyecciones del Desarrollo Económico de Puerto Rico," published by Junta de Planificación, Estado Libre Asociado de Puerto Rico. These forecasts are for five-year periods from 1955 to 1975.

[3] See Puerto Rico's Manpower Needs and Supplies, a joint publication of the Committee on Human Resources, Department of Labor, and the Planning Board.

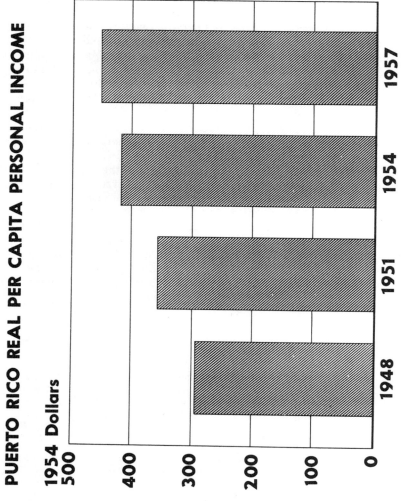

PUERTO RICO REAL PER CAPITA PERSONAL INCOME

1954 Dollars

Fiscal Year

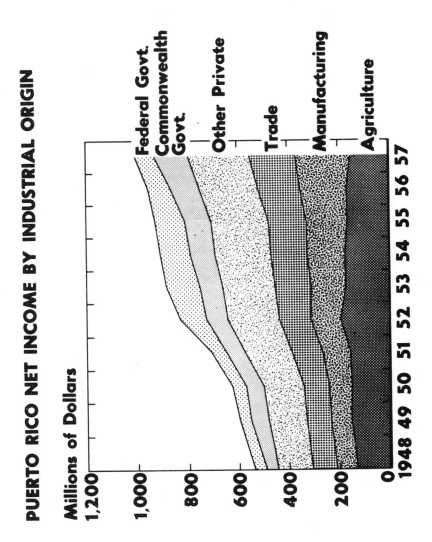

PUERTO RICO NET INCOME BY INDUSTRIAL ORIGIN

Millions of Dollars

Federal Govt.
Commonwealth Govt.

Other Private

Trade

Manufacturing

Agriculture

1,200

1,000

800

600

400

200

0

1948 49 50 51 52 53 54 55 56 57

Fiscal Year

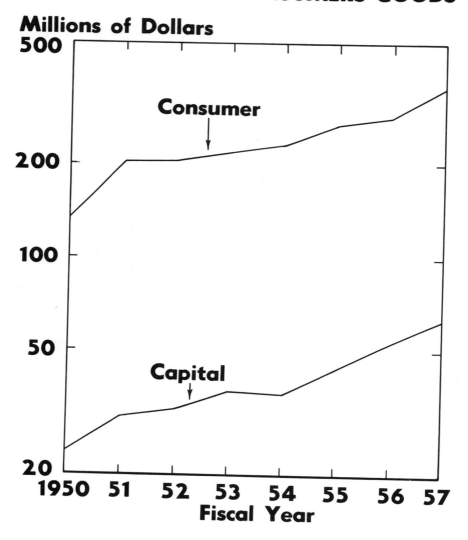

RATES OF GROWTH OF IMPORTS OF CAPITAL AND CONSUMERS GOODS

Millions of Dollars

Consumer

Capital

Fiscal Year

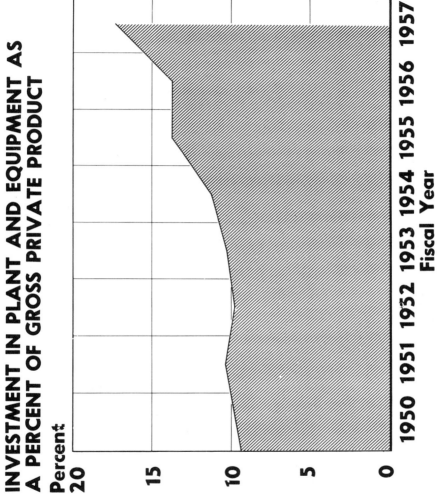

INVESTMENT IN PLANT AND EQUIPMENT AS
A PERCENT OF GROSS PRIVATE PRODUCT

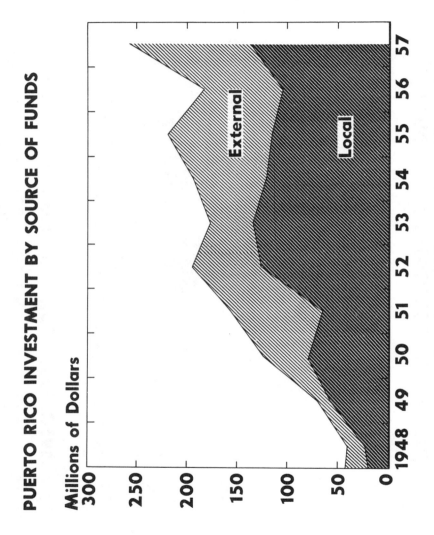

PUERTO RICO INVESTMENT BY SOURCE OF FUNDS

PUERTO RICO LOCAL SAVINGS BY SOURCE
(Millions of Dollars)

Item	1948	1951	1954	1957
Total	23	64	120	136
Business	31	64	81	103
Depreciation	26	42	57	82
Undistributed Profits	5	22	24	21
Government	18	35	45	50
Individuals	-26	-35	-6	-17

Alvin Mayne

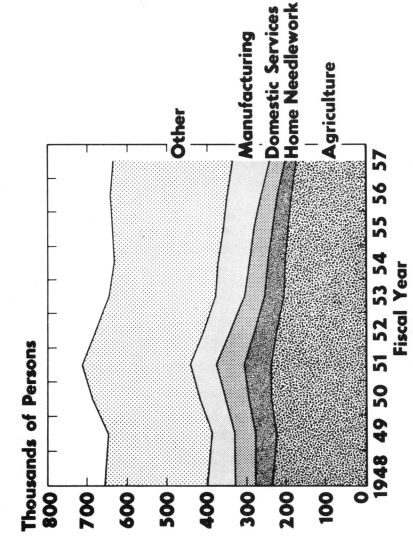

PUERTO RICO LABOR FORCE BY SELECTED INDUSTRIES

Thousands of Persons

Other

Manufacturing
Domestic Services
Home Needlework
Agriculture

800
700
600
500
400
300
200
100
0

1948 49 50 51 52 53 54 55 56 57

Fiscal Year

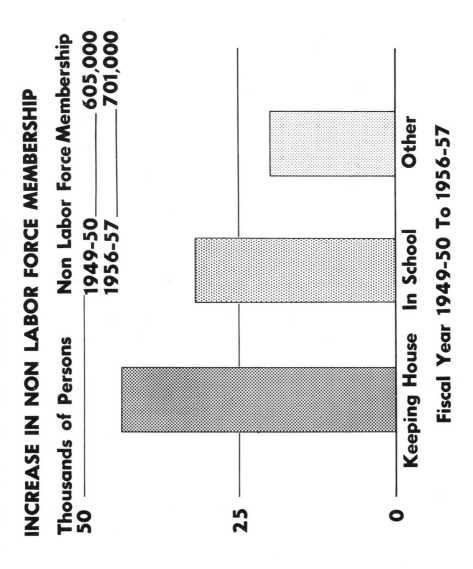

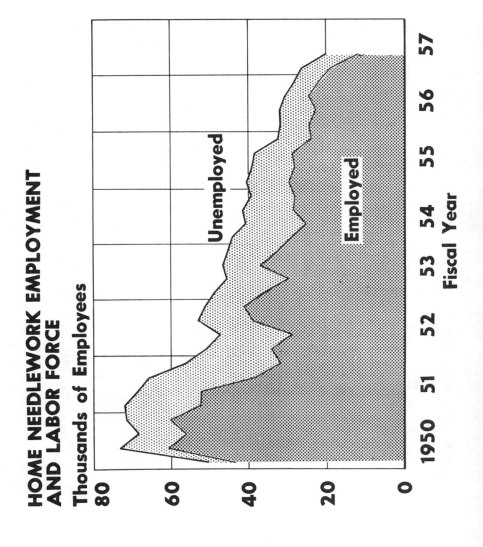

STEADINESS OF EMPLOYMENT

Industry	Number of Wage Earners (Thousands)		Percentage of Total	
	1953	1956	1953	1956
Total	245	292	47	56
Agriculture	53	55	31	39
Mfg. Excl. Home Needlework	39	56	48	55
Trade	28	38	65	72
Government	43	50	81	83
Construction	19	24	50	56
Other	63	69	46	56

EMPLOYEES WORKING
35 HOURS OR MORE PER WEEK
(Annual Averages)

Industry	Number of Wage Earners (Thousands)		Percentage of Total	
	1953	1957	1953	1957
Total	238	277	62	70
Agriculture	40	42	40	48
Mfg. Excl. Home Needlework	41	58	72	81
Trade	34	40	89	91
Government	36	40	78	77
Construction	22	28	63	72
Other	87	95	83	94

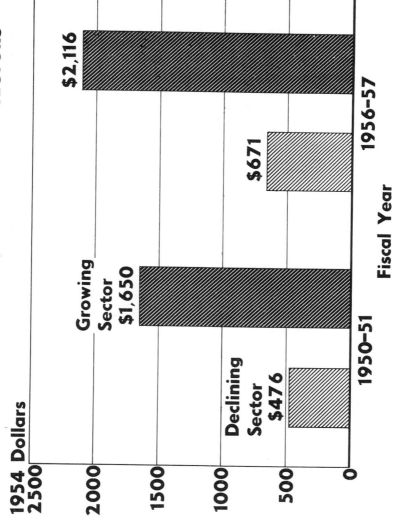

PUERTO RICO COMPENSATION PER PAID EMPLOYEE IN DECLINING AND GROWING EMPLOYMENT SECTORS

1954 Dollars

Growing Sector $1,650

$2,116

Declining Sector $476

$671

1950–51

1956–57

Fiscal Year

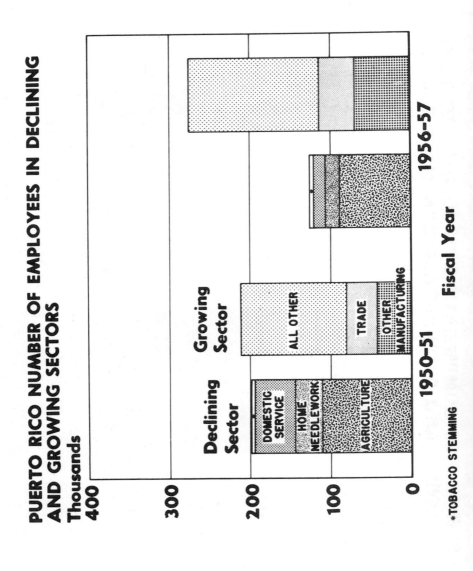

PUERTO RICO NUMBER OF EMPLOYEES IN DECLINING AND GROWING SECTORS

*TOBACCO STEMMING

ECONOMIC GROWTH, DEVELOPMENT, AND PLANNING IN SOCIALIST COUNTRIES

Rudolf Bićanić

University of Zagreb, Yugoslavia

(The University of Texas)

I. Definitions

Most authors make no distinction between "economic growth" and "economic development." Sometimes the distinction between "economic development" and "economic planning" is blurred. By differentiating between these and similar terms we may help to clarify the concept of economic change and sharpen some tools for macroeconomic analysis.

"Economic growth" is usually defined as the increase of real output, or real income, aggregate or per head, over an indefinite period of time.

"Economic development" is economic growth resulting from the conscious action of decision-makers, directed from one level of equilibrium (or quasi-equilibrium) to a higher one by autonomous means, introduced from outside.

"Economic planning" is institutionalized--previously quantified by rational means and conscious action--economic development over a definite period of time.

"Economic progress" is economic growth measured against a previously determined goal; progress is a teleological concept.

"Economic program" is a more or less consistent set of economic policy measures, with no timing and no a priori quantification of targets.

Economic growth.--Most economists understand the term "economic growth" to mean an increase of physical production or of real income.[1] They measure the growth of the national economy by the increase in the flow of goods and services within the territory of a political nation. The differentiation of growth under different institutional sectors brings the theory of growth closer to the reality of many heterogeneous economies, particularly those in transition from one socio-economic system to another.[2]

This definition is based on the assumption of unidimensional growth with purely operational limits as to its magnitude and to time. It is a

quantitative measurement, with no regard for possible qualitative
changes involved. The ends of economic growth are not questioned,
as growth is, by definition, a process whose ends are not examined,
and it is not considered to be the task of economists to pass value
judgments at the initial measurement stage as to the complex ends of
this process. So for some economists it is an end in itself. Left at
such a stage, the concept of economic growth becomes a de-humanized,
de-personalized, and de-institutionalized approach to growth.

This approach should not be underestimated as a statement of fact
in a prima facie analysis, for it prepares the ground for further and
more refined analytical devices. The time over which growth is
measured is neutral, chronological time, with no historical meaning
or economic or statistical significance.

But the term "growth" has been borrowed from biological science,
where it implies certain stages of growing from youth to maturity,
and aging. Logically it should retain some of its original meaning,
but this would not imply accepting an organic theory of growth. The
theory of economic growth ought to give some guidance in answering
such questions as which nation is growing and which is in decline;
what, economically speaking, is a young or an old nation, a developed,
underdeveloped, or a lesser developed country. What is economic
stagnation and what is growth? Plain statements of facts of growth
in arithmetical terms are not satisfactory. And has not Marx given
political economy the ambitious task of discovering the laws of the
rise, development, and downfall of societies?

The approach to economic growth from the point of view of stages
of growing brings up the problem of qualitative changes.

Measuring economic growth by the flow of goods and services
gives ground for further consideration. To say that economic growth
is constant is to say that the productive apparatus of our society has
grown, and also that our flow of consumption goods has grown. This
implies a concept of growth of the national wealth measured by increase of production. In other words, we measure the increase of
stock by the increase of flow. This method, although convenient for
practical purposes, opens many problems, because the interrelation
between the increase in stock and that in flow is not always proportional. In spite of the problems and inconsistencies which such a
method must ignore or gloss over, it is necessary to take a decision
and hew to it. For purposes of this paper economic growth is defined
as increase of national wealth over longer time periods, and growth
is measured by increase of the national wealth. One of the reasons
for optimism at mid-twentieth century is the increasing number of
studies measuring national wealth.[3]

Economic development.--"Economic development" has been defined
as economic growth by conscious action of decision-makers, moving
an economy from one level of equilibrium (or quasi equilibrium) to

another, by means of autonomous, exogenous variables. Each economic development is a particular case of economic growth.

Regarding the actors of developmental economic growth, there must always be somebody to decide about the ends and means of the development. This actor is an identifiable person, or body of persons, private or public. Economic development is always a deliberate and purposeful action of organized men, by definition not a spontaneous process. The term "economic development" is usually applied to schemes of action by public bodies, whereas "economic growth" is a term of general economics.

A part of the total national economy may be the object of developmental policy. In the first case we talk about the developmental and nondevelopmental growth of the economy. This nondevelopmental growth also can be either directed, spontaneous, or automatic.

By "spontaneous growth" is meant growth that develops from an internal cause within the economic system itself.[4]

Economic development cannot be spontaneous, nor can it be automatic, as automatic action implies not only growth from an internal cause (which makes it similar to spontaneous growth), but also adds to it certain regularity and reversibility (which is incompatible with the definition of spontaneous growth).

Not all deliberate measures of economic policy are developmental.[5]

Economic development represents an economic activity which has its clearly distinguishable beginning (an established equilibrium or quasi-equilibrium for that variable). It also has a definite end--the raising of the national economy to the higher-level equilibrium of self-sustained growth. The development is finished when this aim has been achieved.

Economic development is always linked with some strain on the economy--not only on that part of the economy which is under developmental pressure, but also with a definite positive and/or negative effect on the spontaneous part.

The distinction between economic development and economic growth raises the question of their mutual interrelations and interactions. We also ought to distinguish between the tempo of economic development and that of spontaneous growth. In general, the purpose of activity is to speed up the growth of a national economy. But not infrequently the spontaneous, undevelopmental growth has shown a faster rate of increment than the developmental one. This can occur even in centrally planned, state-controlled economies, as we shall see later.

The distinction between the respective directions of growth and development is important. They can be parallel, in the same general trajectory. Development can strengthen growth and vice versa. But it can happen also that development and spontaneous growth may move in opposite directions. Indeed, most developmental schemes have been set up with the purpose of redirecting economic growth.

Situations in which two or more developmental programs take place
in one and the same national economy (a not-so-infrequent case as
may appear at first glance) bear many similarities within duopolistic
competition.

Economic development always takes place under the influence of
autonomous forces. The concept of development used here is based
on autonomous factors introduced into the economic process to influence economic growth toward definite ends. This independent variable
does not consist only of autonomous investments but also of many other
developmental factors, economic and extraeconomic.

Economic development presupposes a previously determined objective: to achieve sustained growth with independent effort from
within the system. These autonomous forces can be economic in a
narrower sense, or political, psychological, institutional--with a less
direct effect on economic growth.

Economic planning. --"Economic planning" is defined here as an
institutionalized, previously quantified, rationalized process of economic development, over a definite period of time.

Planning is not only the drawing of plans; it is also operating the
economic process following the pattern of the plan. Planning is institutionalized action, with specific organs created for the planning
functions.

The role which the actor performs in the more simple economic
decisions is, in planning, extended to all the functions of preparation:
decision-making, execution, and control of the plans. There is a great
variety of methods in which these organs can be constituted and in
which they perform their function. Naturally, institutionalization does
not mean that all planning must necessarily be State planning and that
by police force.

Planning means that men take conscious action to achieve developmental growth, as against spontaneous growth. It does not mean that
all economic activity is planned. There is no national economy in the
world which could be totally or integrally planned in this sense, and
there is a lower and an upper limit circumscribing the utility of planning.

The limitations of planning open another question: How free are
men to plan their decisions? This involves a great many problems
as to the planability of different economic activities (e.g., agriculture
is less planable than manufacturing, production less than financial
operations, current production less than investment).[6]

Not every decision affecting future action based on forecasting is
planning. In planning, the ends of economic action are expressed as
previously quantified targets, be it in physical or in value terms. Not
all products produced, exchanged, or allocated are expressed in such
quantities, only the main ones. Their choice depends on the methods
and aims of planning, and there are a great many different methods.

In some economies, as many as sixteen thousand groups of articles are planned in detail; in others only some four hundred critical ones suffice for planning purposes.

Rational method is essential for planning. Any method of forecasting or directing economic action in the future, based on the traditional or routine experiences of the past, could not be considered as planning. The rationality of this leads to the problem of expressing planning targets by mathematical method. It goes so far as to result in some planners' abandoning any more refined statistical methods of quantitative analysis, and satisfying themselves with empirical methods of trial and error, "as the system of equations in such complex matter as planning a national economy may be just a system of undetermined equations with too great a number of unknowns, not giving real solutions."[7]

The essential of the economic plan is its consistency. The way in which means are allocated to achieve planned targets in a specific time requires an internally balanced system of equations.

Finally, planning is generally linked to definite time periods. The continuous economic process is ideally divided into periods of time to which plans refer, and targets are set in accordance with these periods. This time is neutral calendar time--chronological units--and is only partially adapted for measuring economic processes.[8] A plan differs from a developmental scheme to the extent that the latter is linked to the historical time necessary for qualitative changes in economics to take place, which may or may not be possible to forecast exactly. In planning, the time period is determined with little direct regard to its economic meaning. Thus one developmental scheme can consist of several planning periods. Yearly and quarterly periods certainly have economic (seasonal) meaning. The Soviet medium-period plans (e.g., five-year plans) are explained as being determined in an objective way by Marx's industrial-production cycles, and subjectively as being short enough to mobilize the workers for an attainable target in the future. To these arguments Bobrowski added: enough room for planners to maneuver; and sufficient time to develop a succession of priorities and effect structural changes. On the other hand, this period is short enough to avoid most revolutionary changes in technique.[9]

II. Economic Growth, Development, and Planning in Socialist Countries

Marx formulated his theory many times, but perhaps most succinctly in this brief passage from a contribution to "The Critique of Political Economy":

In the social production of the means of life human beings enter into definite and necessary relations which are independent of their will, production relations which correspond to a definite stage of the development of their productive forces. . . . At a certain stage of their development, the material productive forces of society come into conflict with the existing production relationships, or, what is but a legal expression for the same thing, with the property relationships within which they have hitherto moved. From forms of development of the productive forces these relationships turn into their fetters. A period of social revolutions then begins. With the change in the economic foundations, the whole gigantic superstructure is more or less rapidly transformed. In considering such transformations we must always distinguish between the material changes in the economic conditions of production, changes which can be determined with the precision of natural science, and the legal, political, religious, aesthetic or philosophical, in short, ideological forms, in which human beings become conscious of this conflict and fight it out to an issue.[10]

Marx's theory has all the characteristics of a theory of economic growth. It refers to the increase of productive forces over a long time. The actors in this process of growth are the social classes, who are at the same time the product of the growth of the production forces. In fact, Marx's theory is more than a theory of economic growth: it is a theory of the growth of societies, based on economic growth. Marx's formula of growth could be put in the following way:

$$r = f(p).$$

Production relations (r) are a function of the growth of production forces; (p), the end of this process of growth, is also a dialectical outcome of its economic growth. Marx summed it up rather well as follows:

Self-earned private property is supplemented by capitalist private property. . . . What has now to be exploited is not the capitalist who works many labourers. This expropriation is brought about by the operation of the immanent laws of capitalist production, by the centralisation of capital. . . . Capitalist monopoly production becomes a fetter upon the method of production which has flourished with it and under it. The centralisation of the means of production and the socialisation of labour reach the point where they prove incompatible with their capitalist husk.[11]

Lenin started from Marx's basic principle that socialist production relations can be successfully established only when the production forces have grown to an adequately high level. But Lenin's idea was that, when the State is taken over by the proletariat, they can use the State power to develop the productive forces much faster than the capitalist class could and thus create conditions which can serve as the basis for the whole superstructure of the socialist society. After the successful revolution of 1917, Lenin repeatedly warned that the advanced political structure must imperatively develop a corresponding economic basis, by industrializing the country, thus creating the proletariat. If this is not done, the whole political superstructure would crumble. Lenin stated it as follows:

The result of the revolution has been that the political system of Russia has in a few months caught up with that of the advanced countries. But that is not enough. It puts the alternative with ruthless severity: either perish or overtake and outstrip the advanced countries economically as well.[12]

So Lenin turned the theory of growth into a theory of development. The formerly dependent variable of growth--the production relations--was inverted into an independent variable of development, as the State power became the autonomous actor in development and the function of investment was made the main task of the State. On the other hand, Marx's independent variable (the growth of the production forces) was turned into a dependent of the State action, wherein

$$p = f(r).$$

This developmental activity had a beginning in the quasi-equilibrium of the slow growth of the Russian economy before the revolution. The end of this development was not so easy to determine, for it was difficult for anyone to say when the changes in the production forces would be sufficiently developed to maintain the socialist superstructure.

As there were no cases from which a generalization could be drawn and an absolute standard established, relative measurement was used, i.e., to overtake and outstrip the most advanced capitalist countries, not only in absolute output but also in output per head.

Stalin followed Lenin's theory of economic development and forged for it the tools of economic planning. In the beginning of the planning era, the struggle in the Soviet Union between the geneticists (Bazarov, Groman) and the teleologists (Strumilin et al.) over what character the plans should have, was to a great extent that the geneticists wanted to build the economic plan on the basis of objective economic growth, with as little government decisions as possible (e.g., in-built stable proportions derived from historical observations of economic laws and the assumption of a dynamic equilibrium). The teleological school wanted to value the objectives of the plan on their own merits outside the economic system, and considered the role of the planners to be that of finding the right means and roads toward these ends. In other words, they based their concept of economic planning on a development theory in harmony with Leninism.

Stalin put the State power at the pinnacle of economic law, making it the only independent variable of economic growth. During his time even the existence of economic laws which lead to voluntaristic subjective definitions of economic development was questioned, such as: "New economic laws, economic laws of socialist development, cannot operate automatically; they materialize by means of the planning activity of the Soviet State, and of the working population, led by the Communist Party."[13]

In 1936 Stalin proclaimed with the new Soviet constitution that socialism had been achieved in the U.S.S.R., but he continued to press

for outstripping the most advanced capitalist countries by economic
relations, i.e., by volume of production per head, and this has continued to be the aim of socialist economic development. The main
method of achieving it was through economic planning in the form of
a series of five-year plans.

In this planning, the institutionalization was very strongly emphasized by the introduction of an integral centralized monocratic method
of State and business administration. The economic growth was interpreted as resulting only from policy directives, while the possibility
of spontaneous economic growth was ignored. The quantum targets
became government orders, not just forecast magnitudes. The total
rational method of planning was meant to be a strictly scientific
process, and its very empirical application in practice, with hardly
any theoretical refinement, was not mentioned at all.

When, after the Second World War, the new states had to be supplied
with a theory of socialist economic growth as the basis for economic
development and for long-term planning, such theory was called the
basic law of socialism. This law was stated by Stalin as "securing
the maximum satisfaction of the constantly rising material and cultural requirements of the whole of society through the continuous expansion and perfection of socialist production on the basis of highest
technique."[14]

We shall examine this law from the point of view of economic
growth under the following aspects:
    1. Planned versus spontaneous growth
    2. The autonomous variable (authoritarian normative planning)
    3. The rational (scientific) character of planned proportions
    4. The basic law of socialism
    5. The economic proportion
    6. The system of priorities

    1. Planned development versus spontaneous growth.--The first
point regarding this theory of economic growth is the problem of
planned development versus spontaneous growth. Is spontaneous
growth made possible in socialist planning?

Stalin's basic law of socialism has first a negative developmental
decision: Continuous expansion of socialist production excludes all
production which is outside the socialist sector. Thus this law does
not operate under the assumption of maximization of total production,
but only of production in the socialist sector established by law. By
the constitutional laws of all socialist countries and by other laws on
nationalization, land reforms, etc. the growth of the capitalist forms
is restrained or prohibited, and a small private sector is tolerated
temporarily. However, all spontaneous growth is also considered as
nonsocialist and is constantly discouraged even in the socialist sector.
Spontaneous growth is considered obnoxious, and is prohibited as being
damaging for socialist economic growth. It is considered to be led by

a reactionary force, rotten liberalism turning against the scientific guidance and the political leadership of the socialist State.

At the same time the theory was developed that "the socialist forms of economy cannot emerge and develop spontaneously, of their own accord. They arise and develop as the result of the planned activity of the proletarian state and the creative activity of the working masses."[15] Here the exogenous character of the activity of the State is clearly stated. In the late thirties this was expressed even more emphatically in the statement already cited from the Soviet encyclopedia: "New economic laws, economic laws of socialist development, cannot operate automatically; they materialize by means of the planning activity of the Soviet state and the working population led by the Communist Party."

This position raises several questions: What is "socialist production"? Does socialist production include only that in the socialist sector as defined by administrative or legal measures? Is the term one of objective meaning, or should it be left to subjective and changeable decisions of authorities to determine it? Does socialist production include only those hitherto recognized forms? When, how, and by whose decision can new productive forces become a part of the socialist sector? Why is it that there can be no spontaneous growth of socialist forms (even after the revolution)? And is socialism limited to only the constant support and approval of the coercive power of the State?

Thus this theory of socialist economic growth anticipates an actor who will perform the function of securing that growth, and this is "the socialist or proletarian State and the working population led by the Communist Party."[16]

2. The State power.--The institutionalization of growth was built around the introduction of an autonomous factor: the State power, operating through a whole system of planning organs, and establishing administrative planning patterns and redistributing the greatest part (two-thirds) of the national income. The method of authoritarian coercive planning prevailed; planning by orders of higher political authorities to lower ones, without mechanisms for questioning the wisdom of their decisions, merging all public and business administration into one system for transmitting such decisions from the top to the bottom operational unit. Not even a limited autonomy of planning was left to direct producers. The main incentives to those carrying out the plans were administrative incentives, predominantly negative ones, based on fear. To keep the operators in line, a whole set of "disciplines" was introduced.[17]

They transformed the economic process as if it were a procedural matter of administrative law. The authoritarian decision-making assumed that the system of stochastic equations was changed into a deterministic system of equations, with no random elements in it.

The whole process was strictly centralized, as if the whole enormous State and its economy was "one enterprise and one office, uniting the will of hundreds of millions of people." Thus the macroeconomic decisions were transformed almost into microeconomic decisions and the macroeconomic planning into huge microeconomic planning with one single chief.

3. The scientific method.--It was assumed that centralized planning was the most rational method of securing the maximum growth. The advantages of this system were great in so far as it could have the benefit of choice over a wide area of activities, and could give its chosen objectives a high degree of priority at the expense of other objectives. It did not take into account the interests and the autonomy of the operators carrying out the plans, and a centralized State budget enabled the planners to carry out the plans at all costs, and all results merged into one huge profit-and-loss account. Although the struggle against technically unlimited centralization of productive forces started in the early 1930's (the struggle against gigantomania), the limitations of centralized management were not taken into account.

The second assumption was that of the unlimited advantage of planning and of no limitations to planning decisions. Gradually the whole economic activity had to be embraced in one totally integrated plan, and if there were some parts of the economy not yet fully enclosed, the only reason was that it was a technical impossibility. The consequence of this axiom was the planning of the maximum and a complete disregard for any concept of planning the optimum.[18] The economists calculating the costs were forced to give first place to the politicians and the technologists.

Authoritarian, administrative, and centralized planning implied the evasion of the problem of costs. There was no use to pretend that only general social cost counted and that the individual costs of the enterprises--the "affair of small shopkeepers' mentality" (Stalin)-- did not count. So the losses were hidden in the lump sums of centralized averages. The individual costs of enterprises are not an accepted measurement of social utility, and the measurement of such complicated and complex magnitude as social costs is not calculated at all, so little remained to give a measurement of the socially necessary work attributed to the individual products.[19]

The authoritarian and coercive character of the plan does not mean that the plan was not changeable. On the contrary, there was no limit to the changes required by the decision-making authorities which the planners had to incorporate into the over-all revised plan to "eliminate disproportions." Thus the planning discipline so strictly imposed applied only to those carrying out the plans. Constant revisions through the introduction of even higher priorities and super priorities led to uncertainty in the lower-priority groups, and finally threatened to destroy the consistency and the unity of the plan. This practice introduced into the plan an element of strained belligerence which had certain temporary advantages as a mobilizing factor but which in the long run damaged the methodical work of achieving planned growth.

The Soviet Textbook on political economy said that planning in the U.S.S.R. is done on a strictly scientific basis. But Strumilin, emphasizing the importance of solving many practical problems which in theory look insoluble to the scholastic theorists, says that the demand for exactness should not be exaggerated.

The driving force behind these changes was the political decision. I cannot better describe their effect on planning than by quoting a Polish economist, specialist on planning, who called this system planning by empirical macroeconomic choices:

> Truly speaking, in such setup the object of realization of the plan is not the written official plan, but an unwritten plan implicitly contained in the choice of basic decisions. . . . One of the most fundamental characteristics of the Soviet system of planning is not to treat the official plan as a supreme law setting up intransgressible principles (except for explicit modifications) of the allocation of factors of production and of distribution of the national income, but as an approximation susceptible to changes at any moment if the non-written plan requires so. This is particularly confusing to those who wish the planned economy to be an organized system, free from oscillations. . . . Finally as the non-written plan is reduced to a certain number of macroeconomic choices, its supremacy means a defeat of all attempts at giving importance to economic calculations.[20]

4. The basic law of socialism.--The economic decisions directly concerning economic growth, in the basic law of socialism, are those which refer to the optimum balance in the satisfaction of the rising needs of the society through the constant expansion of production. To achieve this is one of the main tasks of the planners, whose choice is limited by the requirements of this basic law. Expressed a different way, their activity is preponderantly negative: to eliminate disproportions in economic growth.[21]

The analysis of this basic law of socialism brings forward the following seven points:[22]

The real consumable income of the population was to be increased.

Potential productive forces aiming at the increase of potential wages had to be provided for in future investments.

The proportion of saving to consumption is not decided. Only one guiding principle has been laid down: that the satisfaction of needs depends on the expansion of production.

No ratio was set as to the current potential consumption level and the potential consumption increase in the near future.

The question of maximum or optimum growth was decided in favor of the maximum, which meant the continuous use of marginal production units.

No mention of costs of growth was made, and no estimate of the ratio of maximum growth to maximum consumption was set.

The time dimension, usually a constituent part of such statements ("the fastest possible"), was entirely missing, giving the impression that the urgency of growth is not so great as before.

5. Economic proportions.--A particular law of planned (proportional) development is the second law concerning the Soviet developmental theory. It is considered to be the "regulator of socialist industry," and the distributor of means of production and labor power among the various branches of the socialist economy. The assumption for the functioning of this law is the planned conduct of the national economy; a proportional development of all branches of socialist economy; and the fullest and most effective use of the country's material, labor, and financial resources. It is a law without "a purpose," dealing with methodology, and its "tasks" are determined by the basic law of socialism. This law says that correct proportions must be preserved and a rational allocation of resources established.

The principals in the operation of this law are the Communist Party and the socialist State, who by their decisions set what have to be considered the right proportions. In practice it appears impossible to prevent the occurrence of disproportions.[23]

The main task of the planners is then reduced to the task of regulating production and distribution so as to eliminate disproportions hampering this law in its operation.[24] This again is a negative developmental activity for three reasons: the right proportions are fixed in advance by the decision-making authorities; they are constantly disturbed by growth; and they have constantly to be returned to the proportions prescribed by the State power.

This, combined with the point already made (that the socialist economy cannot grow by itself), leads to the conclusion that we have here to deal with an economy in labile equilibrium. According to this theory, the socialist economic process can be neither an automatic nor a self-sustained process. It is a constant upswing movement, which operates under a persistent strain and has constantly to be propped by the action of the extraeconomic State power.

6. The system of priorities.--Some economists think that the right proportions are established by technological coefficients; others stick to economic ratios. No objective principle of right proportions is discernible.

The great strain imposed on the economy by the range of priorities in the economic plans, and on the task of the planning organs, does not justify the reversal of priorities. These priorities have, in the course of time, grown from tendencies in the policy to sacred principles of an ideology. There are four of them:

Fixed priorities of investment: economic growth depends on the growth of industry, which depends on the growth of basic industry, which depends on the growth of machine-building industry. Agriculture yields precedence to industry, and consumption to production.

This priority of investment makes consumption of residual magnitude, dependent on the ratio of compulsory saving.

Fixed priorities in production relations: the socialist sector comes before the nonsocialist sector, and in the socialist sector the State property forms before the co-operative forms. The growth of the nonsocialist sector is considered obnoxious, though it is sometimes tolerated. The growth of capitalistic production relations is prohibited.

Fixed priorities on different levels of centralization: The central government (federal agencies) has an established priority, the republics come next, and the local interests are the last to be considered.

The decisions of the Communist Party organs have priority over those of State organs, which in turn, have priority over any decisions of the working collectives.

III. The Experience

A. Planned Development and Actual Growth

The system of administrative, authoritarian, centralized planning has not succeeded in stopping spontaneous growth despite all measures of coercion. The planned economies of socialist countries have grown at a very high rate, but not always as directed by plan.[25] All of this nonplanned growth can be considered as spontaneous or as obnoxious to the socialist sector. The phenomena of such nonplanned growth are varied and their existence is only occasionally registered in statistics. Various aspects of nonplanned growth are here considered:

Spontaneous growth.--In many cases the disproportions in the national economy became greater than before the planning period. Not all disproportions in planned growth are derived through interference of the superior authorities. Most of these were incorporated into the plan, or at least the plan is adjusted to them. Many other disproportions resulted from unequal fulfillment of the plans: overfulfillments on one side, and shortages on the other.[26]

Growth from fear of planning discipline.--It is an established practice of socialist enterprises to hide accumulated reserves of raw materials, fuel, spare parts, and even machines, from planning authorities, and to keep them for production outside the plan or for assuring current production in an easier way. Much of this production is not reported as planned production. Reserves in labor and credits and finished goods are treated in a similar way.

The very extended practice of two plans.--To have one plan for "those upstairs" and another for actual use in the factory is a more rationalized practice of extraplanned growth.[27] The extent of this practice is demonstrated by the continuous and constant struggle of the authorities to maintain planning discipline and protect State property from "spontaneous activities."

Often such activity has been carried on in good faith to "improve upon the judgment of the planners" and with the intention of having the extraplan growth legalized later. Some of these practices were even tolerated and supported by higher, if not by the highest, authorities. For instance the practice of setting planned output below the actual capacity to produce in order to be able to achieve the planning target more easily, and to obtain the rewards for the overfulfillment of the plan, or to engage in investments which the central planning authority would not permit, has been an established practice, from ministers of central governments down to the managers of factories and workers. The general reaction of the planning authorities to this practice was to impose a linear increase on all plans, which did not improve the situation. There are no estimates of such unauthorized spontaneous growth, but some figures showing the amount of circulating capital invested as fixed capital for building and buying of machines in Yugoslavia turned into billions of dinars.

Centralized planning.--This enabled the central Ministries to develop departmental isolationism and autarchy, which made it possible for a minister to run the whole production process according to his "own plan" with no regard for additional costs.[28]

Localism and nationalism.--Allocation of means because of local and national preferences, and because of loyalty to local interests above central plans, is a logical consequence of centralized planning. This has at times enabled the local economy to grow at a faster rate than central planning would have permitted.

The cost of nonplanned growth.--All this nonplanned growth and other expenses found their place finally in the account of raw material, fuel, and energy, which amounted to more than 70 per cent of the cost of production.[29] (In Yugoslavia the material costs amounted to 53 per cent of the total value of the output.)[30]

The kolkhoz markets.--In agriculture the most striking appearance of spontaneous growth is the increase of the marketable production from the kolkhozniks' plots.[31] These plots were left to the peasant families to help feed them, but the peasants have used them to increase their production and enlarge their sales, at a rate higher than the rate of growth of planned agriculture. This was finally legalized by the authorities and taxed accordingly. A more-than-proportional part of the total sales of agricultural produce came from these sources.

The difference between the official harvest and the harvest in the barns of the kolkhozes and State farms amounted on an average to 20 per cent. This form of spontaneous growth of peasant income was a counterpart to "socialist primitive accumulation" and the unequivalent exchange practice of the State.

Workers' allotments.--Twenty million allotments covering 1.6 million hectares of land is another example of unplanned growth. Such plots developed very intensive agriculture, with the greatest density of cattle per hectare of all forms of property (480, as compared to kolkhoznik plots [400] and the socialist sector [25]).

Extra work.--The workers' off-factory work on their own account or for private handicrafts, on repair jobs, cottage industry, etc. increased their incomes faster than normal wages in factories.[32]

Insecurity.--The great number of prescriptions, rules, and laws put every enterprise in a position of insecurity. The choice was between the anvil and the hammer: to break the laws and rules or not to fulfill the plan. Under such pressure many skilled men used their skill to pull wires, to serve as intermediaries, and develop a widespread system of contacts based on family ties, protection, friendship, and personal influence to achieve what the plan could not secure.

The black market.--Finally the confusion of moral standards created by unlimited use of coercion led to black- and gray-market activities in raw materials, spare parts, imported goods, foreign currency, and even in labor and services. As a corollary to it, "white-collar" crimes, bribery, forgery, theft, and other "economic" crimes developed to such an extent that they represented a problem not only of legal but of economic policy.

The result.--The discrepancy between planned development and real growth grew greater and greater and increased the tension between the production forces and production relations. One could almost speak of two economies, the normative one and the real one.

B. Obstacles to Development

The other of the most important facts was that centralized planning began to cause serious obstacles to further development of production forces, for the reasons listed below.

Its administrative costs were increasing, and the share of labor used in nonproductive occupations was increasingly out of proportion.

In several countries forced collectivization led agriculture into such crises of underproduction that the policy had to be reversed and the kolkhozes allowed to disband. (Yugoslavia, Poland, partly Hungary.)

The system of centralized authoritarian planning prevented agricultural and industrial production from growing according to their objective possibilities.

There was an increase of the labor force and at the same time a delay in the increase of productivity of labor.

No proper method for assessing the profitability of investment was found, and many losses were due to improper location, overhead costs, and oversized or failed investments, allowing even a parasitic growth of costly, uneconomic, and unnecessary building of factories because of ignorance in central offices, local prestige, departmental jealousies, and personal ambitions of influential leaders--all of which could be maintained only by subsidies from the centralized State funds. The best proof that the practice of authoritarian centralized planning had a retarding effect on economic growth is the increase of the rates of growth when some of these obstacles were removed.

C. Changes in the System of Planning

Difficulties in the planning system made changes in the planning methods necessary. The authoritarian centralized system of planning was first abandoned in Yugoslavia in 1952. Tendencies toward major changes have taken place in economic planning of socialist countries as follows:

Administrative incentives are being replaced by economic incentives (higher wages for workers, high prices for agricultural goods, etc.).

Planning is being decentralized, i.e., important decisions are no longer all made in one place, but in many centers. This decentralization is more an accommodation to space than to function.

The administrative role of State organs is being reduced or replaced by a more or less autonomous organization of socialist enterprises.

The enterprises are becoming more independent; their provisions for self-financing have facilitated growth and proportioned it to need and function.

In some countries democratization of planning has taken the form of workers' management, e.g., in Yugoslavia and Poland.

The rigid system of priorities in economic development has been discontinued, the development of consumer-goods industries strengthened, and agriculture given a somewhat higher priority than before.

The rigid priority of State forms over other (co-operative, private) forms of organization has given way to a more flexible approach, e.g., transferring agricultural machines from State ownership to co-operative ownership; or disbanding collective co-operatives and returning them to peasant-family holdings.

Spontaneous growth has been sometimes liberalized and treated as a legitimate form of economic growth. For the first time in the history of planning, these changes were not explained as having the purpose of changing the production relations but as being the consequence of the growth of the production forces.

This opens the field to two possible explanations: (1) Were these changes due to qualitative changes in the national economies, meaning that a sharp decline in the usefulness of State power has taken place? (2) Is this change due to the economic growth which makes the changes inevitable? The explanation to the first question has been formulated best by Oscar Lange.[33] He says that the development of socialist countries must necessarily pass through two historical stages. The first is characterized by extraeconomic, administrative guidance and management, and also by noneconomic incentives (patriotism, class consciousness, etc.). The second stage is due to economic incentives, which make people automatically react in the way desired by the planner.

Socialist revolution was an extraeconomic force guiding the economy by means of "war communism" and organizing rapid development of underdeveloped countries by breaking the vicious circle of backwardness. But such guidance has its limitations. Political and moral appeals work only under exceptional circumstances. Administrative allocation of resources has proved to be wasteful and inflexible. A bureaucratic group has developed conservatism based on vested interests in the method of State management.

One view is that the need arose to introduce economic incentives in response to changes in the forces of production resulting from planned and guided development by the conscious will of the organized society, that social ownership gives the society the degree of freedom to establish incentives designed to achieve desired results. To this theory the following can be objected:

The change of planning methods took place in socialist countries of different levels of economic development, sometimes later in those more advanced than in those less developed. The pace of these changes is very different. Therefore, the historically objective character of these changes has to be proved.

The inefficiency of centralized, normative, authoritarian planning methods has manifested itself in more advanced as well as in less technically developed economic activities. A situation developed in which the rate of growth of agriculture, using most primitive means on very limited kolkhozniks' plots and peasant-family holdings, happened to be greater than on collective and State-farm fields, armed with the most advanced machines.

The changes were not planned but were forced by events; therefore they had a more elemental character than that of planned, conscious change.

It is worth while to examine the oversimplified assumptions under which the Soviet system has operated. They include: an unlimited demand for capital goods, in a definite order of priorities; an unlimited demand for consumer goods, in a population purposely kept at low levels of consumption; unlimited efficiency of administrative incentives; an unlimited role of State power in economic planning. These assumptions are open to question for the following reasons:

Once an economy achieves the level where for various reasons-- economic, technological, and strategic--demand for capital goods (or of a certain type of capital goods) is no longer unlimited, various causes start to work, and decelerators appear to redress the balance, such as increased foreign trade, foreign aid, etc. Another range of priorities is established.

Once the supply of consumer goods surpasses the minimum level for satisfying the need of the people in quantity and in quality, the demand for certain shoddy consumer goods may turn out to be quite inelastic. Newly published Soviet studies on market research indicate such a trend.

Once the administrative incentives begin to lose their efficacy for various reasons--economic, political, financial--the efficiency of the State power as the infallible planner decreases, and other more effective economic incentives have to be applied.

Once the system of authoritarian, centralized planning is outmatched by the extraplanned spontaneous growth at higher rates and lower costs, and once this planning system gets more and more split into a normative economy and an empirical one, the strength of spontaneous production forces becomes more evident. In this stage the spontaneous growth of socialist forms may increase more and more and develop self-sustained growth in an economy in which the use of force has become an obvious impediment to economic growth.

Thus new changes in the planning policy of socialist countries may not be changes caused by economic development but by total <u>economic growth</u>.

NOTES

[1]There are many criticisms of this definition of growth. See particularly a very systematic one of F. Perroux in his "La théorie de progrès economique," <u>Cahiers de l'Institut de Science Economique Appliquée</u>, Serie I, No. 1.

[2]See my paper "Some Problems of Sectors in the Social Accounting of Different Economic Systems," presented before the Third Conference of the International Association for Research in Income and Wealth, 1953. (Mimeographed.)

[3]At the fifth meeting of the International Association for Research in Income and Wealth in 1957, thirteen estimates of national wealth were listed, including countries such as the United States, France, West Germany, Canada, South Africa, Sweden, Argentina, as well as India and Yugoslavia.

[4]The idea has been advanced that development should include only those economic activities which the automatic activity of the price system would not perform. See J. J. Spengler, "Economic Factors in Economic Development," <u>American Economic Review</u> (1956), Suppl., p. 431.

[5]What was meant by "<u>dirigisme</u>" in France or by "interventionism" in Germany is not development. This type of planning acts to introduce changes in the spontaneous economic growth, but not necessarily to achieve an equilibrium at a higher level. It merely set some particular parameters for action to direct economic activity. It did not set qualitative change. <u>Dirigisme</u> may have had a greater degree of consistency than interventionism, and some more clearly expressed goals, but it aimed more at re-establishing the threatened old equilibrium than at lifting the national economy to a new level. Within these determined ends it had to choose means to maintain these social and economic ends. The freedom of choice was reserved to the means but not to the choice of ends.

[6]See my paper "Economic Growth under Centralized and Decentralized Planning--Yugoslavia--A Case Study," Economic Development and Cultural Change, Vol. VI, No. 1 (1957), pp. 63–71.

[7]S. G. Strumilin, Planirovannie v. SSSR, p. 19.

[8]On this aspect, see the very interesting reflections of F. Perroux, loc. cit.

[9]C. Bobrowski, Formation du système Sovietique de planification (Paris, 1957), p. 37.

[10]Extracted by Emile Burns in A Handbook of Marxism (New York, 1935), pp. 371–372.

[11]Ibid., p. 554.

[12]Lenin, Collected Works, Vol. XXI, Book I, p. 216, as quoted by Stalin, Leninism, pp. 242–243.

[13]Bolshaya Sovyetskaya Enciklopedia, 1932, Bk. SSSR, p. 769.

[14]Stalin, Economic Problems of Socialism in the USSR (Moscow, Foreign Languages Publishing House, 1952), p. 45.

[15]Political Economy: A Textbook (Moscow, 1957), p. 419.

[16]There was a time when even the existence of objective economic laws was questioned in the U.S.S.R., and the expressed will of the Communist Party (led by Stalin) was considered as economic law; so, according to the theory, the merger of the political decisions and the economic laws was complete.

[17]There were quite a few of them: socialist discipline, State discipline, planning discipline, production discipline, technological discipline, labor discipline (including also the financial discipline), and, last but not least, Party discipline controlling all controllers.

[18]Only in 1957 did Strumilin, as an exception, introduce the concept of optimum in his definition of the task of the national economic plan, which he defined as "the optimal utilisation without crises, and the expansion of the reproduction of socialist relations and productive forces of the country, at the possibly fastest rate and with the goal to achieve maximum satisfaction of the need (of the population) with the minimum of costs."--Strumilin, op. cit., p. 18.

[19]Stalin in Economic Problems of Socialism in the USSR maintained that such calculation of individual costs is important. But Soviet economists still complain that there are no methods in the U.S.S.R. by which to assess the quantitative effects of the law of value. See, e.g., M.B. Breev, Obshchie Voprosi Teoriji Narodnohozjajstvenogo Planirovannia (Moscow, 1957).

[20]C. Bobrowski, op. cit., p. 91.

[21]To avoid any doubt about which maximum was the dependent variable, the Textbook on political economy added: "The basic economic law of socialism is inseparably linked with the law of the priority development of industries producing means of production, that is to say, their relatively more rapid development compared with that of industries producing consumer goods."

[22]See the analysis of this definition in the Economic Survey of Europe for 1955 (p. 198), from which many points were taken.

[23]Stalin, op. cit., p. 46.

[24]It is interesting to note what are considered to be the main proportions in planning practice: (1) Proportion between production, distribution, and the consumption of material goods (in physical terms) for interregional and intraregional distributions. (2) The grand proportions between production and general consumption: manufacturing industry and agriculture; production of the means of production and the means of consumption; between production and transport; between building industries and financial investments. (3) The national-income proportions (consumption and accumulation), the personal, general, and government consumption; the balance of labor power; the foreign trade between socialist-bloc countries.

[25]For the critical approach to Soviet-type developmental planning, see among the more recent publications: Braginski-Koval, Organizacia Planirovania Narodnogo Hozyaystva SSSR (Moscow, 1954), pp. 77–92; M. B. Breev, Obshchie Voprosi Teoriji Narodnohozjajstvenogo Planirovania (Moscow, 1957), pp. 96–104; I. A. Gladkov, Ot Plana Goelro k Planu Shestoy Pyatiletke (Moscow, 1956); C. Bobrowski, Formation du

système Sovietique de Planification (Paris, 1957), passim; Dyskusya o Polskim Modelu Gospodarczm (Warszawa, 1957), particularly the articles of E. Lipinski, Fabierkiewicz, S. J. Kurowski, M. Mieszcankowski, C. Bobrowski, J. Pajestka, and S. Jenrichowski; Jiri Reznicek, Organizace Planirovani v CSR (Prague, 1956).

[26]" Hidden" price increases, adding to the cost of living but not reflected in the price-index numbers, seem to have been common last year (1957) in most Eastern European countries, and prices of scarce secondhand goods are frequently above their legal retail prices. In Hungary the Statistical Office has estimated that "hidden" price increases have tended to raise the cost of living from 1 per cent to 2 per cent each year since 1949. The intensified shortages produced a new spate of complaints about such long-standing abuses as under-the-counter sales, illegal price increases, and cheating in weights--as well as growing irritation at the ease with which large incomes could be made by "speculators" in private trade or operating illegally within the state trading system.--Economic Survey of Europe for 1957, pp. 1, 26.

[27]The Soviet General Statistical Office complained that two sets of figures are supplied: one by Ministries, another by Directorates of statistics.--Pravda, July 4, 1957.

[28]See the mention of many instances of such plain departmental abuses in Khrushchev's speech of April 8, 1957. "Every ministry draws up plans for production and construction . . . without taking into consideration what is being done by other ministries."--Khrushchev, Theses, March 30, 1957.

[29]Gladkov, op. cit., p. 294.

[30]Statisticki Godisnyak, FNRS, 1957, p. 130.

[31]The kolkhozniks' plots occupied 4.3 per cent of the total sown area, and contributed to the state deliveries 19 per cent of meat, 16 per cent of milk, and 11 per cent of wool. In 1957, dividends and money income of the kolkhozniks from the common land brought them 43 billion rubles, and the kolkhoz market, 36.5 billion rubles.

The retail trade in government shops increased between 1940 and 1955 from 100 to 120, and in the kolkhoz market from 100 to 168 in total turnover. The prices increased in the former to 137 and in the latter to 111 index.--Statistical Yearbook, U.S.S.R. for 1956, Sec. 1, pp. 25-26; and Economic Survey of Europe for 1957, Chap. I, p. 10.

There are eight thousand kolkhoz markets, handling about 17 per cent of all the retail food trade, and supplying some towns and cities (e.g., Odessa) up to 60 per cent of their requirements.

[32]In industry, occasional work and black-market work is particularly profitable for workers who can manage to use tools or materials from their factories. Skilled workers in the building trades can frequently earn more in a few days of private work than during a month of normal employment.--Economic Survey of Europe for 1957, pp. 1-18.

[33]Notes from his lecture in Zagreb in 1957.

THE PROSPECTS OF INDIAN ECONOMIC GROWTH

Bert Hoselitz

University of Chicago

India is, after China, the largest underdeveloped country in the world. It has the second-highest population of any country in the world, and its area is large enough to be referred to sometimes as a subcontinent. It has varied and rich natural resources, it has able and well-trained leaders, and it has a skillful, adaptable population. Yet with all these assets it has remained a poor country, and up to the present its efforts at economic development have not produced very impressive results. Although the total national income of India has hovered around 100 billion rupees, or more than $20 billion, its per capita national income has been one of the lowest in Asia and has shown very little increase in the last decade. Between 1948 and 1956 per capita net real output increased by only 10.2 per cent, and this increment occurred for all practical purposes in two spurts within the period 1951 to 1954. Since 1954 per capita real output has grown by only 1.4 per cent, and the recent discussions on the economic crisis in India, although centering around the lack of foreign exchange and the consequent difficulty in fully implementing the Second Five-Year Plan, have, in truth, a much more fundamental aspect--the general poor prospects of economic growth in India.[1]

I. Prospective Growth of Population and Resources

An analysis of this problem must start by taking account of the basic framework in which economic growth in India is to occur. This framework is determined by the prospective development of population, resources, and economic policies. Economic policies will be discussed somewhat more in detail later in this essay; it is the growth of population and resources that will be of principal interest at this point. Now, as has already been noted, India is the second most populous country in the world. But this fact does not fully convey India's population problem. According to the census of 1951, India--without Jammu and Kashmir--had a population of almost 357 million. More than 82 per cent of the population was rural and only slightly more than 17 per cent urban. In other words, if there is overcrowding in India at present, it is due not to the high incidence of urbanization but

to the density of population in agriculture. And although in India, as
in other countries of Asia, there is today a noticeable growth of cities,
the bulk of the future population increase will occur among the rural
population.

What is the magnitude of prospective population growth? On this
point there exist numerous conflicting opinions and estimates. In the
absence of adequate procedures of birth and death registration, and
hence of reliable data on birth and death rates, the projection of India's
population has been a favorite field of speculation. In the Second Five-
Year Plan, the Planning Commission has estimated that India's population by 1976 would be 499 million; Professors Coale and Hoover
have arrived at substantially higher figures on the basis of better
methods of demographic analysis.[2] The latest estimate, which was
made by T. Chellaswami of the Planning Commission and is as yet
unpublished, is based on the component method of population projection, using cohorts of five-year groups. On the basis of different assumptions concerning future fertility and mortality rates, Chellaswami
arrives at estimates of India's population in 1976 ranging from 486.5
million to 521.4 million. In view of the fragmentary evidence on current birth and death rates, the higher rather than the lower estimate
of Chellaswami appears to be more likely.[3]

It is difficult to estimate from these figures what would be the
likely labor force of India in 1976. On the basis of the 1951 census,
the labor force was slightly below 40 per cent of total population.
This figure seems very low, especially if it is compared with corresponding proportions in more advanced countries. The Planning
Commission has since made further studies of the labor force and
has concluded that 44 per cent is apparently a more accurate figure.[4]
If it is assumed there will be a population of 521.4 million in 1976 and
a labor-force ratio of 44 per cent, there will be a prospective labor
force of India in 1976 of close to 230 million.

Let us now look at the quantity of natural resources available to
India and the prospects of increasing this quantity. Here any predic-
tions are even more tenuous than those of population, since technological developments, the kinds of development programs, and the over-
all effects of planning must be taken into account. Rather than attempting to predict how much agricultural land and other nonhuman
resources will be available in 1976, the kinds of problems encountered
in augmenting these resources will be emphasized and the directions
in which the most likely developments are going to take place will be
indicated.

In a country with such a high density of rural population, agricul-
turally usable land is one of the strategic factors. There is no doubt
that the effective land area of India could be increased and that much
land which is presently providing only low yields could be made more
fertile. The main requirements are water and fertilizer. But the

difficulties of progress in agriculture are illustrated in the record of the achievements of the First Five-Year Plan during which special efforts were undertaken to improve India's agricultural output. It may suffice to cite just two figures, those relating to cropped area, in general, and those to irrigated land. From 1950/51 to 1955/56 the total net area sown in India increased from 293.4 million acres to 319.8 million acres, and the net irrigated area from 51.5 million acres to 56.3 million acres. In each case the increase was about 9 per cent. The total increase in farm production in this period was 13 per cent, a figure which shows that much of the added production was achieved by increase in cropped area rather than by increase in yield per acre.

Additions to the cropped area are becoming more and more difficult to make. To be sure, there exist still some excellent opportunities for irrigation projects, but these are also becoming increasingly more expensive. And any intensification of agricultural production in India depends to a large extent on the availability of water, for, in spite of the impressive annual rainfall in many parts of the country, the high seasonal concentration of rain during the monsoon is often a menace rather than a blessing to greater productivity in agriculture.

To sum up, we may confidently expect that further extension of the cropped area and the irrigated area in India will meet with increasing obstacles and that, therefore, the addition to the number of farms by internal "colonization" is strictly limited. Any increase of agricultural output must be met, in the future, mainly by improved methods of production, and, as will be seen later, this is one of the most strategic vulnerabilities of India's economic prospects.

The limitations of natural resources for industrial development are much less severe in India than those of agricultural resources. India is not rich in petroleum deposits, but there are ample deposits of iron ore, coal, and most of the other chief industrial minerals. In fact, in view of the relative facility with which some of these deposits can be exploited--provided the required capital can be made available--and in view of the fact that India has an abundant labor force, part of which is endowed with considerable industrial skills, it seems likely that in the future India will have a comparative advantage in industrial rather than agricultural production. In other words, the development of industry, particularly metal industries, holds out considerable promise, and it is not surprising that in current economic planning in India substantial emphasis is placed on industrial development in general, and on the heavy industries in particular.

II. Growth of Indian Industry

This brings us to one of the central points of Indian economic development in the next two or three Five-Year Plan periods: the growth of Indian industry. In developing current economic plans, some attention has been paid to long-run growth patterns of the Indian economy. The Planning Commission has worked out a developmental "model" in which some forecasts of national income, investment, and other variables are made. Although these data are highly tentative and their actual attainment is contingent upon actual implementation of each successive plan, we will consider, for the time being, the investment figures presented in the Planning Commission's model as fairly reliable forecasts of India's investment activity. In terms of 1952/53 prices, total combined public and private investment is to rise from 31 billion rupees during the First Five-Year Plan to 148 billion rupees in the Fourth Plan. In other words, investment is to be somewhat more than quadrupled between the First and the Fourth Five-Year Plans. To attain a smooth transition to the higher investment level, the model of the Planning Commission anticipates that investment during the Second Plan period will be approximately double that of the First Plan and that investment during the Third Plan period will be somewhat more than three times that made in the First Plan. This would bring total investment during the Third Plan period to almost 100 billion rupees, or 20 billion rupees per year. Since national income (expressed in 1952/53 prices) is expected to rise to 172.6 billion rupees per year by the end of the Third Five-Year Plan period, an investment of the size indicated would represent a savings ratio of 13.7 per cent, and during the Fourth Plan period this ratio would be further increased to 16 per cent of national income. Whether or not these targets can be met depends upon several factors, chief among which is the program of industrial development.

It has already been seen that increases in agricultural output will require sizeable investment not only in irrigation and land-reclamation projects but, above all, in procedures designed to improve agricultural productivity. Clearly the ambitious targets of doubling national income and quadrupling investment cannot be achieved if industry of various kinds is not fostered. Hence the determining how realistic are the targets set by the Planning Commission depends upon a further spelling out of the process of industrial growth in India during the next fifteen years.

In analyzing the industrial growth in India it is useful to make several distinctions. First and foremost is the distinction between modern large-scale factory industry and small-scale, or cottage, industry. Only the first group will be discussed at this point, though a few brief comments on the letter will be made later in this paper. Factory industries which are relatively well established in India may be further distinguished from those which are in the process of establishment and have received, therefore, special attention under the Second Five-Year Plan, and from those which either are as yet unknown in India or show an output of only insignificant proportions. Among the established types of industries are cotton textiles, sugar milling, and some other consumer-goods industries; among those in process of establishment are basic steel, cement, fertilizers, and heavy chemicals; and among the third group are various types of special machinery, implements, and some of the more complex chemicals and drugs.

In the Second Five-Year Plan, targets expressed in physical quantities have been established for most of these products. Though it is uncertain whether in view of the difficulties in which the Indian economy finds itself at present the targets will actually be met, there is good reason to assume that the main industrial objectives of the Second Five-Year Plan are regarded as being of crucial importance. Hence the government is likely to use all means at its disposal to push investment in such industries as steel production, coal mining, electric-power production, and cement production to a level which will permit the physical targets set for the Second Five-Year Plan to be met and perhaps even to be slightly exceeded.

A forecast of industrial growth in India may, therefore, fairly safely be based upon the assumption that by the end of the present Plan steel production will amount to some 6 million tons annually, coal production to some 60 million tons, and cement production to some 15 million tons. These targets (for 1960/61) constitute in themselves substantial increases over current production. Compared with 1955/56, steel output at the end of the Second Plan is to be increased fourfold, cement production threefold, and coal output by 50 per cent. But since these products are commonly acknowledged to be the basic ingredients of further industrial development in India, the most serious efforts are being made to bring these industries to a level of production where they can effectively form the starting point of further and more diversified industrial development.

If it is granted that the assumptions on the success of the industrialization program of the Second Plan are correct, it becomes a fascinating game to set up an input-output matrix for Indian industry stipulating certain major targets to be met by the end of the Third and Fourth Plans. Although I have tried my hand at such a matrix, it would not be suitable to present it here in detail. It must suffice to indicate some of the main results and some of the problems encountered in this attempt.

One of these problems is the question of the speed of growth to be assumed for different industries, and the second is the selection among alternative technologies of one which under Indian conditions would seem to be most suitable. This last problem is not very complex for most of the heavy industries, since the technologies applied in the advanced countries are so superior that they can be used without substantial change in India also. In fact, the simultaneous establishment of three different steel mills--one with German aid at Rourkela, another with Russian aid at Bhilai, and a third with British

aid at Durgapur--suggests very small variations in technological coefficients as between these mills. The matter is different in light
engineering and many consumer-goods industries, and there the relatively labor-saving, capital-intensive technologies of some advanced
countries may not be optimal in a country in which the relative scarci-
ties of labor and capital differ so widely from the supplies of the corresponding factors in economically advanced countries. In these industries new techniques may need to be worked out which are especially suited to Indian conditions, i.e., to the relative prices of factors
prevailing in India. But since these industries require, under any
conditions, relatively small quantities of capital, as compared with
steel production, mining, petroleum refining, the production of cement,
fertilizers, and other heavy chemicals, any errors which may arise
from the selection of a "wrong" technology are not likely to affect the
end result greatly.

As concerns the speed of growth of different industries, a common
experience of countries which have passed through a lengthy industrialization process was assumed to apply to India also. I refer to
the observation that, other things being equal, the younger an industry
is, the faster it will grow, and the better established it is, the slower
it will expand.[5] Bearing these distinctions in mind, it was assumed
that the older industries, i.e., those already well-established in India
at the inception of the First Five-Year Plan, will at most double their
output by the end of the Fourth Five-Year Plan, that the industries
which have been established since the attainment of independence and
which are now entering a period of consolidation and reinforcement
will somewhat more than triple their present output; and that the
newest industries, those which have been established only in the last
one or two years, will increase their output at least tenfold and possibly more. It was concerning this last group that the most daring
assumptions had to be made, but, as already pointed out, this class of
industries customarily uses less capital-intensive techniques than
the main heavy industries, and the proportion of investment which
must be allocated to these industries does not vary a great deal even
if relatively great variations in output are stipulated.

To illustrate some assumptions of the speed of growth of different
industries, I cite the following examples. In the first class of industries, in which less than a doubling of output was assumed, it is suggested that output of cotton textiles will rise from 5,500 million yards
by the end of the Second Plan to 8,000 million yards by the end of the
Fourth Plan. Similarly the output of sugar is to rise in the same
period from 2.5 million tons to 4 million tons. In the second class of
industries, where a tripling of output was assumed, fall some of the
main branches of industrial production. Steel output, which by the
end of the Second Plan is assumed to amount to 6 million tons, is
stipulated to rise to 20 million tons by 1971; coal output is to increase

in the same period from 60 million tons to 200 million tons; cement production from 15 million tons to 35 million tons; and nitrogen fertilizer from slightly below 400,000 tons to 1,200,000 tons (in terms of fixed N_2). Finally in the third class there are such industries as those producing machine tools, electric motors, and ball bearings, in which present output is very small and in which increases to ten times or more the present production is estimated for the end of the Fourth Five-Year Plan.

In an input-output matrix composed of some fifty entries, it now becomes possible to calculate whether these objectives are mutually consistent. It goes without saying that such an exercise also requires the determining of labor inputs, especially of skilled labor, and there is reason to assume that the present supply of technically-trained personnel, particularly of university-trained specialists, is too small to permit these outputs. Thus, a condition upon which the realization of this program is contingent is the availability of sufficient training posts for chemists, engineers, and other technically-qualified personnel. In view of the abundant present and prospective supply of unskilled and semiskilled labor, it is not likely that a bottleneck will develop for lack of this type of labor.

Table 1 presents a rough picture of the industrialization program outlined in this paper. I have computed approximate investment requirements, based mainly upon current technology in India, and assumed stable prices. The year 1952/53 was used as a base year.

As can be seen from Table 1, the amount of industrial investment required would remain below a quarter of total outlays proposed by the Planning Commission for the Third and Fourth Plans. In view of the fact that in the Second Five-Year Plan provision was made to allocate close to 7 billion rupees from public funds for industry and that an additional 6 billion rupees of private industrial investment is likely to be forthcoming during the Plan period, the investment requirements during the Third and Fourth Plans will remain, percentagewise, within the same order of magnitude. The remaining three-quarters of outlays proposed for the Third and Fourth Five-Year Plans can then be allocated to such projects as the development of electric power, transportation facilities, agricultural development, housing, education, health, social services, and other objectives.

III. Crucial Aspects of Future Indian Economic Development

To estimate prospective industrial development is the easiest portion of tracing the possible future course of the Indian economy. The actual implementation of this program is contingent upon a number of factors whose future trends are predictable with only a much smaller degree of probability than the investment needs of large-scale

Table 1

Production Targets and Investment Requirements in Indian Industry, 1961–71

Area of Production	Unit	Production Targets		Investment in Mill Rs.	
		3d Plan 1961–66	4th Plan 1966–71	3d Plan 1961–66	4th Plan 1966–71
Steel ingots	mill t	12	20	5,000	13,500
Coal	mill t	120	200	2,000	3,000
Cement	mill t	25	35	700	750
Crude oil	mill t	12	16	4,000	3,000
Sugar	mill t	3	4	300	600
Cotton textiles	mill yds	6,500	8,000	550	800
Fertilizer (fixed N_2)	thous t	800	1,200	1,200	1,200
Heavy chemicals				550	750
Paper & pulp	thous t	1,100	1,800	1,000	1,250
Aluminum	thous t	60	120	250	550
Miscellaneous*				7,500	10,000
Total investment				23,050	35,400

Table 1 (Cont.)

Production Targets and Investment Requirements in Indian Industry, 1961–71

Area of Production	Unit	Production Targets		Investment in Mill Rs.	
		3d Plan 1961–66	4th Plan 1966–71	3d Plan 1961–66	4th Plan 1966–71
Total Investment				23,050	35,400
Total Plan investment 2d Five-Year-Plan projection**				99,000	148,000
Percentage of industrial investment				23.2	23.6

*Includes mechanical and electrical machines, prime movers, transportation equipment, containers, structural materials, and miscellaneous consumer-goods.
**See Government of India, Planning Commission, <u>Second Five-Year Plan</u> (New Delhi, 1956), Table on p. 11.

industry. I shall not dwell long on some of these factors--as, for example, the availability of foreign exchange or the establishment of
sufficient training facilities for skilled workers and management per-
sonnel--for they depend either on world conditions, largely beyond the
control of India, or involve such complex policy decisions that an adequate analysis of them would lead us too far beyond the limits of this
paper.

Rather I should like to concentrate in the remaining space at my
disposal upon three main aspects of future economic development of
India which appear crucial, not only as conditions for the realization
of the industrialization program outlined earlier but perhaps for the
survival of a viable economy in India altogether.

These three factors are the problem of increasing food output in
India; of increasing the savings ratio from the present low level to
one consistent with the higher capital requirements needed for laying
the basis of an economy capable of self-sustained growth; and of providing employment opportunities for the growing number of persons
of working age.

The food problem is doubtless the most crucial. It appears to me
to be the major economic problem which India faces today. Unfortunately, it is not easy to offer very specific suggestions as to how
higher food output can be attained. A number of very general policies
have, of course, been proposed. Some place their chief hope in land
reforms, others have argued that increased food output could be attained only if more and cheaper credit was made available to the
Indian farmer, others have pointed to the Community Development
program, others have argued in favor of better transport, and still
others have placed their main confidence in co-operative farming
(which is merely another and a gentler term for "collectivization" of
farms). This last solution, in addition to fostering Community Development schemes, appears to be the pet theory of the Planning Commission, and I have heard several highly-placed officials of this
branch of the government argue heatedly and forcefully in its favor.

There is little doubt that several of these policies would contribute
to an improved farm output. If more capital was made available at
easier terms, more investment could take place in agriculture, and
if better transportation facilities were created, the losses from wast-
age and spoilage of farm products could be reduced. But it is doubtful whether these policies alone can achieve much, and it is certain
that if they were applied indiscriminately on a large scale they would
use up more resources than would be justified by the additional food
output procured. Nor have land reforms so far proven very valuable
as a means of increasing agricultural productivity, though they have
contributed perhaps to greater political stability in the countryside
and have thus indirectly helped to prevent a decline in agricultural
production. The Community Development scheme has, on the whole,

been disappointing, but chiefly because it was directed more toward the social elevation of rural dwellers in India rather than toward the improvement of agricultural output. There have been many evaluations of the program, but only in few instances have the opinions of farmers on how the programs affected them been collected. In a recent "attitude survey" carried out in a number of Development Blocks in Bihar, one of the most backward and poorest states of India, some interesting answers were obtained about the extent to which the Community Development scheme has affected farm productivity. To the question of whether they make use of improved seed, 79 per cent of the farmers answered in the negative; 95 per cent do not use "scientific implements," i.e., modern scientifically-tested implements; 66 per cent do not use artificial fertilizer; 87 per cent do not have their cattle artificially inseminated, and 63 per cent do not use veterinary aid for their cattle. Seventy-two per cent considered that employment opportunities in the countryside had not improved, and 70 per cent judged that there had been no improvement in crop production since the introduction of the Community Development Program.[6]

It may be argued that since the Community Development Program was designed chiefly to elevate the social position of the farmer--to make him more aware of health problems, to reduce illiteracy, and to make him a more politically-conscious member of his community-- it would be too much to expect the program to have achieved much toward increasing farm production. It also may be argued that many innovations were not introduced on the farms of Bihar because of the excessive poverty of many farmers there. But living standards in the Indian countryside are, on the whole, so poor that any program of improving health, education, or community consciousness makes sense only if the economic level of the cultivator is raised at the same time.

The average Indian has more land at his disposal than the average Chinese, but the average Chinese farmer produces twice as much food per acre as the average Indian farmer.[7] In part this may be due to better land in China than in India, but to a large extent it seems to be due to better farming methods. It may appear strange at first sight that a civilization as old as that of India, which for centuries, indeed, millennia, has had its main base in agriculture would not have developed more adequate methods of farming. But it should not be forgotten that the great population spurt, and with it the great pressure on land, came only after the turn of the present century and that before that time, with the exception of a few small portions of India, the present methods of tilling were sufficient for the subsistence, and more, of the farmers. Not enough time has elapsed in the fifty years since population pressure became severe, for farm methods to improve sufficiently to meet the new demands made on the land.

In China, farm output has been higher than in India for a long time. Apparently population pressure in China was consistently greater than in India and has led to the gradual adoption of more efficient techniques in agriculture. It is this greater productivity of Chinese agriculture which is regarded by many Indian officials as the main proof of the superiority of co-operative farming, and the argument for collectivization of farms in India is buttressed by citing the Chinese example. The second argument in favor of collectivization is that it would facilitate capital accumulation in agriculture. It is said that at present the individual farmer is too poor to be able to borrow and hence he cannot purchase improved implements or fertilizer, but that a co-operative village could do so.

In large part the argument in favor of collectivization of Indian farms rests on a fallacy. Certainly the example from China proves little or nothing, for Chinese agricultural productivity considerably exceeded that of India before the Communists collectivized farms in China. The argument concerning the improved creditworthiness of a collective farm as against that of a small cultivator has more validity, but it is doubtful whether it could be applied generally to all parts of India. In fact, it is my strong belief that the problem of improving agricultural productivity in India cannot be solved by applying any one general formula. Crops and soils, climate, and the patterns of landownership are so different in different parts of India that each area must be treated separately. In some cases the consolidation of farms, and in certain portions of India where dwarf farms predominate, co-operative farming, is perhaps the most effective policy. In other parts of India the main improvement would result from better farming methods, the use of more fertilizer and more irrigation, and in still others it would come through the changeover to new crops or the improvement of crop strains. Also, the Community Development Program should concentrate more on the improvement of farming techniques and the wider supply of agricultural extension services than on social policies. Perhaps the most important step that could be taken now would be to set up a careful research program in agricultural production and the possibilities of improving it in several parts of India.

It must be remembered that agricultural productivity in India is not merely a function of factor inputs but also of varying conditions of land tenure and general conditions of the social structure prevailing in a village. For example, some differences in agricultural output of different villages are doubtless dependent upon the particular form of caste relations prevailing in them or on traditions regulating the gradations in social status among the villagers. Moreover, since in many regions with poor or indifferent access to markets there exists still a considerable preference for subsistence rather than for cash-crop farming, the objective of farm families under these different conditions of market involvement presents another social variable affecting farm productivity. If the sample areas were carefully selected, much information could be gathered on what are the most suitable economic and non-economic policies for the various parts of India; and the Planning Commission could then put into operation a program which would be more likely to lead to positive results than have so far been shown by either the Community Development Program or by the dogmatic advocacy of co-operative farming.

There are several reasons why the increase in food output is so essential. To begin with, the increase in foodgrains production between 1949/50 and 1955/56 was only 11.3 per cent, an increase which has scarcely kept pace with the growth of population in the same period. Second, with increasing industrialization the demand for foodstuffs is increasing more than proportionately because of the Indian worker's high marginal propensity to consume. Third, Indian agriculture still operates with such a narrow margin apropos the minimum food requirements for the health and survival of its population, that inclement weather, an unfavorable monsoon, or some major disaster like an inundation leads to widespread famine in sizeable parts of the country. In these situations scarce foreign exchange must be sued for food imports, and this affects adversely imports of capital goods vitally needed for industrial development. The recent crisis of the Indian economy is to a large extent also a food crisis, and a glance at recent changes in the prices of food as against other consumer goods sheds ample light on this fact.

With the growth of population and increasing employment in non-agricultural pursuits, the demand for food is likely to rise greatly. I have stated earlier that--apart from some special commodities, such as tea, jute, or certain fruits and nuts--India does not appear to have a comparative advantage in agricultural production. But industrial output is not yet ample enough to permit India to play a role in Asia analogous to that of Britain in the nineteenth century: exchanging its industrial products against food and other agricultural raw materials. On the other hand, productivity in Indian agriculture is still so low that large improvements are possible without heavy capital outlays. Though it is improbable that India will become an exporter of food and other agricultural raw materials, it is not unreasonable to expect that India can supply even a larger population with food from domestic production at higher levels of consumption than at present.

IV. The Problem of Raising the Level of Savings

Next in importance to raising the domestic food supply is the increase in the level of savings. As shown earlier in this paper, the Planning Commission expects the level of savings roughly to double in the next twelve years from the present rate of rather less than 10 per cent of national income. Low as this rate is, there is no doubt

that it was attained in part because of forced savings induced by inflation. But inflation cannot be expected to raise savings to the level
anticipated by the authors of the Second Five-Year Plan. This can
only be achieved either by a program of higher taxation or by a change
in the savings habits of the people. It is concerning this aspect of the
program that doubts as to the realism of the expectations of India's
planners must be expressed. The level of taxation remained in 1954/5£
below 10 per cent of total net output, and government savings amounted
to only 1.17 billion rupees out of a total national income of 96.2 billion
rupees. It is difficult to see how in the prevailing economic and political climate the rate of taxation can be substantially increased. W.
Arthur Lewis considers this a minimum, if, in addition to routine
public services, the government intends to participate in the process
of capital formation.[8] Though economists and even some politicians
in India are agreed that a higher level of taxation is required, and
though in a three-volume report running to more than 1,300 pages a
Taxation Enquiry Commission manned by distinguished scholars and
public officials recommended increased taxes, the actual prospects
for substantially higher taxes in India are slim.

Nor can we expect that voluntary savings are likely to increase
substantially. It is generally found that within a society at any one
time the proportion of income saved is positively correlated with the
amount of income received. But one cannot conclude from this that
the proportion of income voluntarily saved will rise as income increases over time. In India, moreover, average and marginal propensities to consume on the part of large masses of the population
are so high, and savings institutions so badly developed, that in the
absence of forced saving of some kind a substantial increase in the
present rate of savings should not be expected.

This means that the problem of raising the level of savings becomes essentially a political problem, and its attainment, as well as
the form of its attainment, will depend upon political factors. But
even in countries whose politicians feel a greater degree of public
responsibility than do those of India, decisions which will be disliked
by the public are difficult to make. Hence it is not likely that Parlia-
ment will become the vehicle to induce a higher rate of forced savings
But the responsibility to achieve this rests with the government. It
may mean that in order to establish the rate of savings required for
the attainment of the development goals set out in the Second Five-
Year Plan, the government will have to take rather drastic measures.
This may expose it to the charge that it is less democratic than it
ought to be. But unless it can tackle the problem of increasing the
level of savings in a determined and forceful way, the attainment of
India's development goals may be seriously impaired.

V. The Problem of Employment

I turn finally to the problem of employment. There exists already
a considerable backlog of unemployment in India, and it is expected to
increase in the next few years. Though the primary aim of Indian
planning is economic development--the raising of total output--it is
inevitable that the development plans as well as all economic policy
should have a strong employment orientation. For any increase in unemployment would be regarded as a failure of the present government
to meet its task, tantamount to failure to provide for increases in output. Current debate centers around two opposed sets of proposals
about how to deal with the employment problem. One group recommends investment in those industries which will yield the greatest
surplus, and proposes the reinvestment of this surplus so as to create
capital at as fast a rate as possible. The faster capital grows, the
quicker will employment opportunities be created for the unemployed.
The other side recommends the subsidization of labor-intensive cottage and village industries to keep people working, even though the
value of the products they turn out may be less than their wages.

I fear that neither of these proposals is truly capable of effectively
attaining the growth-with-employment objectives of Indian economic
policy. The second proposal would sacrifice progress for make-work
schemes, it might significantly curtail the rate of capital formation,
and it might create vested interests in these inefficient cottage and
village industries which would place grave obstacles in the way of
economic development even after these industries have outlived their
purpose. The first proposal sounds much better in theory than when
applied to Indian reality. This can be shown by a simple example.
Let us assume that India will attain by the end of the Fourth Five-
Year Plan not the goals stipulated earlier in this paper but double
these goals. For example, instead of 20 million tons of steel, twice
that amount, or 40 million would be produced, and so on for coal, petroleum, and other commodities. Let us assume, moreover, that the
productivity of Indian labor in 1971 will be half that of the United States
labor at present. In other words, if Indian industry showed a composition similar to that of current United States industry, its output
would be approximately one-third of United States industry. In the
United States approximately 18 million persons are employed in industry. India's industrial employment, on the above assumptions,
would thus come to two-thirds of current American industrial employment, or 12 million persons. Since at present scarcely 3 million persons are employed in India's factory industry, this would mean a
quadrupling of the Indian industrial labor force in thirteen years.
Agriculture employs now around 120 million persons in India, and it
is doubtful whether it can absorb more workers. Hence agriculture
and factory industry together would provide employment for 132 million

persons. Since we estimated the Indian labor force by 1971 to be
around 230 million, close to 100 million workers would have to find
employment in the tertiary sector. It is difficult to see how that many
genuinely productive jobs could be found in service industries, even if
present patterns of widespread domestic and other menial services
and petty trading persist. This is the reason why so many Indian
policy-makers look to the handloom and the ambar charkha (hand
spinning-wheel) as a way out. But it must be understood that theirs
is a counsel of despair rather than an economic policy based on rational calculation for meeting the objectives of developmental planning
in India.

I cannot within the space of this paper argue extensively for some
alternative solution to the employment problem. In another place I
have indicated in some detail what appears to me as at least a partial
solution.[9] I shall only summarize my argument here and add a few
additional comments. Since I must be brief I may perhaps appear
dogmatic, but reference to my extended comments on this point would,
I hope, dispel this impression.

Concentration on large-scale industry is not likely to solve the unemployment problem within the next two Plan periods, and it may take
impossibly large amounts of capital to solve it by large-scale industrialization. It appears to me that the industrialization problem has
been posed too often in the form of extremes--modern capital-intensive industry of the most advanced countries versus the handloom--
and that the proper way of posing it is in terms of selecting a technology which corresponds more closely to the relative supplies (and
prices) of productive factors in India. This would call for the development of new technological solutions which, while labor intensive, use
productive methods of equipping a worker with enough capital so that
the net value added by him exceeds his wage. The study of various
Indian power-driven, small-scale industrial plants, employing up to
ten or twelve persons, reveals that such solutions are possible and
that many consumer goods and also tools and implements, especially
those of a rough and crude kind, which would find a demand primarily
in the Indian countryside, can be produced efficiently in small and
medium-sized plants. Moreover, these industries are flexible enough
that they can be established in small towns or large villages and, in
this way, substantial outlays in providing "social overhead" capital
could be avoided or postponed. It is not likely that these rural or
semirural industries would be developed by private enterprise, at
least not in the early stages, for private small-scale entrepreneurs
are too much attracted by the external economies offered in the large
cities. But if rural and small-town labor-intensive industries are
stimulated by government planning, they may provide substantial employment at wages at least commensurate with, and probably higher
than, agricultural earnings, and they would, moreover, scarcely

compete with urban large-scale industry, for they would chiefly supply commodities consumed by the village population. It is not expected that these intermediate industries would absorb the entire labor "surplus," but they might narrow the unemployment gap.

A second measure directed toward narrowing the unemployment gap is the provision of capital formation in the Indian countryside which can be carried out without the use of large-scale capital equipment. It is in this field rather than that of collectivized farming that India can take a leaf out of China's book. I have emphasized earlier the great need for the improvement of agricultural output in India. Though the chief means to attain this are the use of more labor, more fertilizer, and better seeds, as well as better farming methods, it cannot be denied that the supply of more capital for farming purposes would prove an added benefit toward this end. There is still considerable scope in India for better irrigation works, terracing to gain more land, the building, repair, and improvement of country roads, hedging and enclosing of fields against the inroads of roving cattle, and sundry other forms of capital formation. Now in China many of these improvements have been made and maintained over the past centuries with simple instruments of indigenous production, using materials found on the spot, and employing labor whose skills were easily acquired. The Community Development Program could earn great merit if its village-level workers could organize and sponsor such forms of capital formation.

It has sometimes been argued by some of my Indian friends that the establishment of rural industries and the organization of labor-intensive rural capital-formation projects would increase the demand for food. In more concrete terms this implies that unemployed rural persons eat less if they hang around the ancestral farm doing odd jobs here and there than if they are employed in occupations at which they produce a net addition to national income. This may be true, but it seems to me a strange argument for a country which is desperately trying to raise its level of output. It points, again, however, to the importance of the economic problem which I regard as the alpha and omega of Indian economic policy: the increase of productivity in agriculture and the raising of domestic food production. All efforts at industrialization, improvement of service industries, provision of more transport and power facilities, and other targets of developmental planning will ultimately be made nugatory if this crucial problem is not solved. I admit that easy and obvious solutions for it are not apparent and that much further study must be devoted to developing an intelligent policy to meet the challenge posed by the food problem. But if ways and means can be found to grow more food and other products on the Indian soil, the most important bottleneck in the path of economic development in India will have been broken.

NOTES

[1]Since it would be too tedious to cite references for all data on past and present economic magnitudes, I list here the sources from which they have been taken. This list is mainly illustrative; there exist numerous easily available statistical publications in which these data are published. My sources were: Government of India, Planning Commission, Second Five-Year Plan (New Delhi, 1956); Government of India, Central Statistical Organization, Estimates of National Income 1948–49 to 1955–56 (New Delhi, 1957); Government of India, Central Statistical Organization, Statistical Handbook of the Indian Union, 1951–1956 (New Delhi, 1957); Government of India, Ministry of Agriculture, Indian Agriculture in Brief (New Delhi, 1957); and Government of India, Planning Commission, Basic Statistics Relating to Indian Economy, 1950–51 to 1956–57 (New Delhi, 1957).

[2]See Ansley J. Coale and E. M. Hoover, Population and Economic Development in India (Princeton, Princeton University Press, 1958). A brief abstract of their results can be found in G. A. P. Carrothers and W. Alonso (eds.), Papers and Proceedings of the Regional Science Association, Vol. III (1957), pp. 219–222.

[3]See the unpublished paper by T. Chellaswami, "Population Projection for India, 1956–76."

[4]This figure appears in a privately circulated mimeographed monograph on the economically active Indian population, issued by the Indian Statistical Institute, Calcutta.

[5]See, e.g., Simon Kuznets, Secular Movements in Production and Prices (New York, 1930); Arthur F. Burns, Production Trends in the United States Since 1870 (New York, 1934); Walter G. Hoffmann, British Industry 1700–1950 (Oxford, 1955).

[6]See W. Arthur Lewis, "Consensus and Discussions on Economic Growth: Concluding Remarks to a Conference," Economic Development and Cultural Change, Vol. VI, No. 1 (October, 1957), p. 77.

[7]This viewpoint is expressed, for example, by Walter Galenson and Harvey Leibenstein, "Investment Criteria, Productivity and Economic Development," Quarterly Journal of Economics, Vol. LXIX, No. 3 (August, 1955), pp. 343–370.

[8]Loc. cit.

[9]See my paper "Economic Growth and Rural Industrialization," Economic Weekly, Vol. X, No. 10 (February 22, 1958), pp. 291–301.

Part IV

Commentaries

Goodrich Paper:	Ayres
	Polakoff
Kuznets Paper:	Coffee
	Nelson
Higgins Paper:	Danhof
	LaBarge
Singer Paper:	Cauley
	Chalk
Maynard Paper:	McDonald
	Thompson
Prebisch	No Commentary
Navarrete Paper:	Jones
	Lewis
Mayne Paper:	Blair
	Duncan
Bićanić Paper:	Copeland
	Spulber
Hoselitz Paper:	Eckstein
	Neale

ECONOMIC HISTORY AND ECONOMIC DEVELOPMENT

COMMENTS

Clarence E. Ayres

Professor Goodrich has made a number of points of great significance both for the theory of economic development and for the understanding of economic history. Whether because he is right, or because in our younger days both of us were exposed to the same formative influences, I agree with him in every particular. Certainly the study of economic history and the study of the current process of economic development would profit greatly by cross-fertilization. These two fields need more such bumblebees as Carter Goodrich. Obviously the economic history not only of the United States but of the entire Western world constitutes a case study of the process of the industrialization of a previously nonindustrial culture. Indeed, it is the prime case.

I agree, too, that technology fits awkwardly into the traditional conception of the economy. Or rather, it does not fit at all. Hence most economists have ignored it as something which, however important for other disciplines--anthropology perhaps--has no place in economic analysis. For the economics of stationary-states technology may be defined as constant. But that only means that the economics of stationary states is not very helpful for understanding economic development, either past or present. It is for the same reason that the rubrics of capital formation, having been devised to explain how change occurs in a stationary state, are not very pertinent to what Edwin Cannan called "the heritage of improvement." Whatever may be true of capital formation, Professor Goodrich is certainly right in insisting that the heritage of improvement must include the improvement of men and minds. No other "investment" is half so important.

In this connection also I would like to underscore the proposal that for the term "balanced" development we read "contagious and pervasive." How clearly such terms reveal their origins! Ledgers balance. It is technology that is contagious and pervasive; or if it is not, something is very wrong. In the case of the Indians of the Bolivian altiplano what is wrong is only too evident. These people are cut off--isolated, or insulated--from the contagion of twentieth-century technology and the scientific know-how which is inseparable from it not only by illiteracy but by the persistence in their daily lives of age-old culture

patterns to which the rhythm and tempo of the industrial way of life
are utterly foreign.

This brings me to the first of two variations, or developments,
which I would like to attach to the main theme of this stimulating
paper. Professor Goodrich has spoken of "break-throughs." That
term has recently come into general use to refer to any significant
technological advance. Such advances are frequently the result of a
strategic discovery or invention, strategic in the sense that it opens
up a whole new field into which other discoveries or inventions flow,
often with surprising rapidity. For example, the discovery of the
antibiotic properties of penicillium notatum has resulted in the development of a whole arsenal of antibiotics. But in the larger process
of economic development all the significant break-throughs are of
quite a different character. Thus in the case of the Bolivian Indians
it is obvious that what must be broken through, if the contagion of
economic development is to be effective, is a cultural barrier. The
whole institutional pattern of their tribal life stands in the way of
their assimilation of even the rudiments of industrial culture. It even
blocks their learning to read and write. What need has an altiplano
Indian to read and write? And what will learning the white man's
ways eventually lead to? One of our students from the Near East has
told me of the anguish with which his parents greeted his proposal,
as a schoolboy, to adopt Western dress. To them Western trousers
represented apostasy to all they held most sacred--indeed, to the
Prophet himself; and of course, they were right. It was in those
trousers that he came to Texas.

As Professor Goodrich has pointed out, what we need to learn from
the study of economic history is how economic development has come
about in the past; and I would like to suggest that one of the major
enigmas of our past is how early modern science and technology
managed to break through the superstition, the dogmatism and ob-
scurantism and institutional rigidities, of the Middle Ages. Not that
any other people can now follow the path we took five hundred years
or so ago! They now can see what industrialization means; and if
some of them are inspired by the promise of the industrial standard
of living, others are appalled by the cultural wreckage they see
strewn along our route. To the dervishes and mullahs of other lands,
industrialization obviously spells doom. Our path can be followed
only by those who wear trousers--and that goes, it begins to seem,
even for women.

In short, the biggest problem posed by the theory of the industrial
break-through is: Through what? And the answer that seems to follow directly from the asking of that question is: Through the jungle
of what Veblen called "imbecile institutions." If industrial development is a good thing, then the only possible comment on the fate of
dervishes and mullahs is Veblen's comment: "Good riddance!"

Prudence and a decent respect for the sentiments of other peoples may prompt us to draw a veil over this aspect of the process. But we must not delude ourselves.

In this connection I am reminded of another issue raised by Professor Goodrich's extraordinarily comprehensive paper, namely, that of the confusion which has befogged our efforts to understand the "condition of the working class," especially in the earlier part of the nineteenth century. In recent decades it has become the fashion to deny that the industrial revolution worked any great hardship on anybody; whereas a generation ago it was the fashion to hold the industrial revolution guilty of unimaginable crimes. But surely both dicta are in error. Industrial revolution does unquestionably displace persons in numbers commensurate with the magnitude of the revolution; and the distress of displaced persons is very real and very great, whether they are British orphans (one in every ten feeble-minded) or the Polish peasants described by Thomas and Znaniecky. But where does the responsibility for their distress lie: with the displacing agent, or with the social system of which they had previously been the victims? Granted that the victims of industrial revolution have been exploited: have they been exploited by the machines, by the technology itself; or are they the victims of imbecile institutions through which industrial revolution is in process of breaking? Granted again that as time passes, conditions improve. Does this validate those institutions, or does it validate the break-through?

These questions bring me to the second gloss I would like to add to Professor Goodrich's text. Early in his paper he referred to "the American ethos" of private enterprise and of the paradox that is posed by the contrast between our protestations and our actual performance. We live in a mixed economy, and have always done so. As Professor Goodrich's studies have so fully exhibited, our economic development has been conditioned from the very beginning and in very substantial degree by governmental subsidy and the participation of public agencies of every sort. Nevertheless our paeans of thanksgiving have been addressed almost exclusively to private enterprise, and they grow louder with every passing decade, even while our dependence upon public agencies grows steadily greater. Why is this?

The answer I would like to suggest at this time is not confined to our own case. I suspect that in every society in which visible economic development occurs it is the tutelary deities and their human representatives that get the credit. They do so because prevailing beliefs assign them the credit for everything. Such is the whole burden of tribal beliefs. Consider, for example, the Soviet Union. Very considerable technological progress and general economic development has been achieved in the four decades that have passed since the October revolution. Notwithstanding the de-emphasis of consumer goods, the Russian people are well aware of this. As goes without saying, they are proud of it. Inevitably, under the circumstances, they regard this achievement as proof positive of the truth of Marxist principles and the superiority of the Soviet system.

I believe that history affords many striking examples of this sort of cultural feedback. Anthropologists identify the vast technological revolution of modern times as the third such experience through which mankind has passed. Mutations, Ralph Linton called them. Although the first was perhaps the most important of all, since it set man's feet upon the path of culture, thereby separating him forever from the whole of animal creation, we can know it only by inference and conjecture. Even so, since the origins of ceremonialism seem to go back to the very beginnings of human culture, we may infer that the ceremonial adequacy of the shaman's incantations was established by cultural feedback from the demonstrable--and to simple minds no less extraordinary--efficiency of the primeval craftsman's tools. At all events it is well known that the second great cultural mutation, which turned upon the development of agriculture and of city civilizations, was in fact accompanied by a jungle growth of superstition, all of it apparently springing from the husbandman's preoccupation with the mysteries of procreation.

Is our own case altogether different? I don't mean to suggest that merchants and financiers are the necromancers of modern times. My point is rather that the process of cultural feedback is the same. Throughout modern times buying and selling, and especially financing, have seemed to be the key activities upon which the whole vast but shadowy process of economic development has turned. They have seemed so partly because they have been visible, and partly because under our institutional system buying and selling, and especially financing, have been the command posts at which authority has been exercised over the whole process; and as always, victories are attributed to generals. Thus it has become a matter of devout belief that economic development is brought about (since it is indeed commanded) by merchants and financiers; and the farther the development goes, the stronger this conviction becomes.

In short, I suggest that the American ethos of private enterprise is a myth, the growth of which has accompanied the pervasive and subtle process of technological revolution. It is more prevalent now than ever before because cultural feedback makes it so. But technological--including scientific--progress has a way of evaporating myths. Already it is increasingly difficult to think of A T & T, General Electric, U.S. Steel, or Jersey Standard as "private" enterprises, just as it is increasingly difficult to think of the Soviet Union as a "proletarian" paradise. Economic development may nourish myths, but it also outlives them.

ECONOMIC HISTORY AND ECONOMIC DEVELOPMENT

COMMENTS

Murray E. Polakoff

Professor Goodrich has written an interesting and suggestive paper on the relation of economic history to economic development. In stressing the fact that both disciplines are interested in long-run organic problems involving economic change, he is enabled thereby to demonstrate their basic affinity. By way of contrast with what Goodrich regards as the essentially short-term Newtonian character of economic analysis with its familiar "givens," both economic history and development are concerned with changes in forms of organization and patterns of behavior, variations in techniques and motives, and their relevance to the analysis of change.

The failure of economic history until recently to make more than a minimal contribution to the study of development is first of all due, in Goodrich's opinion, to the fact that the economic historian has not placed questions of growth in the forefront of his inquiries, being content at times with the collection of minutiae. Certainly the lack of concentration has had an inhibiting effect, though it should be noted that too much stress on the study of economic growth might unduly limit the field of economic history. As for the collection of minutiae, I am sure that Professor Goodrich would be the first to agree that such pursuits are not the exclusive province of the economic historian, and that more doctoral dissertations have been written by this formula than anyone here probably cares to remember. In a more serious vein, it may very well be the lack of analytical emphasis on the historian's part that has encouraged such devoted attention to chronology and the accumulation of "curiosa." Goodrich further observes that an important part of the literature of economic history has been concerned with the social costs of development rather than with its economic triumphs. Although he voices the hope that this "tradition of social criticism" will continue, he apparently feels that increasing emphasis should be put upon a more explicit examination of the growth process. While such a value commitment is on the face of it unobjectionable, one must always be clearly aware of the possible feed-back effects of such noneconomic variables on the process of growth. I for one would argue that the growing emergence of "other directed" and particularistic values in our own society is, in part, attributable to our rather exclusive preoccupation with material progress in the past. Such norms are bound to affect future growth rates in this country.

Having discussed some of the reasons why the economic historian has failed to aid the practitioner of economic development, Goodrich then goes on to show some of the potential contributions that can be made by the economic historian. The illustrations he employs to support his contention that closer attention by the economic historian to conscious developmental policy can aid in the common task is, in my opinion, one of the more interesting aspects of his paper. In emphasizing the importance of public efforts in providing the needed social overhead capital necessary for the early economic development of this country as well as its crucial role in the encouragement of manufactures and its land-grant policy, he corrects such misconceptions as may still exist about the laissez-faire nature of early American development. He even goes so far as to relate American money and banking policy to developmental policy, thus underscoring his contention that the economic historian's attention to the growth problem can lead to a quite different interpretation of early American financial history than has traditionally been given it. I would certainly agree with Goodrich that the agricultural and industrial development of the American West in the early and mid-nineteenth century was speeded up considerably by the practice of the "wildcat" banks in granting long-term credits rather than insisting upon the self-liquidating loans which could only arise from commercial transactions and which formed the main basis for credit along the Eastern seaboard. While such interior banks became in effect investment banks, unable to redeem their long-term assets in specie upon demand, and while, as a result, their note obligations steadily deteriorated in value, their refusal to be bound by the requirements of a "sound and stable" currency could only result in a quicker pushing westward of the American frontier.

Goodrich's observation that the economic historian can better his contribution to economic development by becoming more aware of, and proficient in, the concepts and manipulation of quantitative data needs no elaboration. Also calling for scant comment is his plea for including qualitative material in the study of growth problems on the grounds that such patterns of change as are being discovered raise questions to which general economic history can make its contribution through interpretation and understanding. Certainly no objection can be taken to a position which realizes clearly that in dealing with development we are dealing with a system of interdependent factors of which economic growth is just one, and that some of the more important of these interdependent factors cannot be quantified, at least in any conventional sense.

Finally, Professor Goodrich suggests that economic historians can maximize their contributions to the study of development by paying closer attention to the questions and concepts of developmental theory. To illustrate this, he discusses such major problems of development as technological progress, capital formation, and the doctrine of "balanced" growth. In commenting on balanced growth, with examples taken from earlier American development, Goodrich casts doubt on its value as an adequate explanation of the rapid rates of growth which prevailed in this country in the nineteenth century. While I am inclined, in many ways, to sympathize with his contention that excesses and imbalances more than orderly progression were characteristic of a system whose institutional arrangements and psychology left little room for the notion of a "moving equilibrium"--either as a postulated ideal or as a sound description of early American reality--I cannot help but confess to some uneasiness in my own assessment, owing to the very ambiguity and proliferation of the meanings of "balanced" growth as currently employed in the profession. Thus it was recently possible for an economist from Cambridge University lecturing in the Philippines to state: "The first major difficulty . . . was the fact that the Philippine economy, being neither agricultural nor industrial, was 'unbalanced.'" In the light of such a nonsense statement, it would appear perfectly justifiable for the economic historian in seeking clarification from his fellow economists to say along with Voltaire: "If you would discuss with me, define your terms!"

Whatever the meaning assigned to the term, however, it seems obvious from Professor Goodrich's remarks as well as from a survey of the literature that the matter of "balanced" growth vs. priorities is far more than just a verbal issue. To take a rather clear-cut example, the very rapid rates of growth of Soviet national income and industrial output over the past quarter-century certainly cannot be explained in terms of the doctrine of "balanced" growth. It is perfectly clear in this instance that the historical choice of Soviet planners has been in terms of the strategic importance of priorities. While the Soviets have borrowed heavily from the future in concentrating investments in heavy industry and education in relation to those in agriculture and light industry all these many years, there is little evidence but that until recently such imbalances have led to a slowing down of their growth rates. In fact, the evidence clearly points the other way. While all this is certainly not intended to disparage the concept of "balanced" growth and its importance in limiting the naive assessments of their economies' capabilities by many overenthusiastic planners in the underdeveloped countries, it is obvious that much work remains to be done before the concept can be employed with even a fair degree of assurance.

In discussing the matter of technical change, Professor Goodrich quite rightly points out that technology is an awkward subject for the "orthodox" theorist since it is usually treated as an exogenous factor in his theoretical models. Yet its importance in the growth process cannot be overestimated. Abramovits has estimated that in the United States from the decade 1869–78 to the decade 1944–53, between 80 and 95 per cent of the growth in productivity (per man hour) was associated with improved technical methods, whereas the remainder was associated with increases in capital per worker. While Goodrich makes no mention of the contributions of price theory to the explanation of technological change such as, Hicks's theory of "induced" inventions, there is little doubt but that in the main, technical change has not been successfully incorporated in such theoretical analysis. While Rostow's emphasis upon the propensities "to develop fundamental science" and "to apply science to economic ends," to which Goodrich alludes, is certainly a step in the right direction, so far as I know, Rostow does not analyze just how such propensities come to exist in the first place. Surely this is just the starting point for a sweeping comparative investigation of different social and economic structures, motivations, and norms which affect the shape of the propensities and, therefore, the differential rates of growth among various countries.

In conclusion, I would like briefly to pose a problem which Professor Goodrich refers to in his opening remarks and whose subtle overtones may be found throughout his paper, namely, the relationship between economic history and economic theory. Since the economic historian works within a broader framework than does the theorist, and since economic growth is not an autonomous phenomenon in the sense that it cannot be satisfactorily analyzed in purely economic terms, there is little doubt but that economic history has much to contribute to a comparative study of growth on the empirical and policy levels. Certainly Professor Goodrich has aptly demonstrated this in addition to indicating how it can also serve as a check on some of the concepts of developmental theory. At the same time, however, it must be remembered that developmental theory contains as an essential ingredient economic theory. In the light of Goodrich's opening statements concerning the relationship--or perhaps the lack of it--between economic analysis and economic history, a methodological question which remains unresolved throughout the paper is how on a comparable analytic level the broader orientation of the economic historian can be articulated with the methods and techniques of the economic theorist. Put somewhat differently, how can the institutional variables with which the historian deals be brought to the same cognate level of abstraction as the variables in which economic theory is interested and how can the two then be interrelated into a meaningful whole? Without necessarily assuming the role of devil's advocate, I would argue that because economic theorists in the past have not only worked but remained within the framework of technical economic analysis--Marx, Schumpeter and Veblen aside--and because economic historians, while close to the facts of institutional change, have tended to proceed without any theory on a comparable analytical level, the two fields of inquiry have heretofore failed to complement each other. And without going so far as to disinter the bones of the older <u>Methodenstreit,</u> I would suggest that unless greater cognizance is taken of this problem in the future, no amount of empirical work on the part of the economic historian will be completely successful in bridging the gap. How such a problem is to be tackled depends in large measure upon the interests and subsequent division of intellectual labor of all concerned, but certainly it appears necessary for all sides to make a conscious attempt toward its solution if a genuine start toward a truly <u>general</u> developmental theory is to emerge.

PRESENT UNDERDEVELOPED COUNTRIES AND PAST GROWTH PATTERNS

COMMENTS

J. Herschel Coffee

In the paper which Professor Kuznets has just presented, he set for himself the task of explaining and examining certain characteristics of underdeveloped countries, in pointing up differences between them and presently developed countries before their industrialization. In attempting this he did not seek to develop a general theory of economic growth. He was pointing up the proposition that because of different cultural and institutional patterns and antecedents of growth, the underdeveloped countries of today cannot be expected to follow the same growth patterns of the developed areas which had entirely different antecedents, and he suggested that errors could arise from trying to apply to them the same principles which have been observed in only a limited number of countries, especially if we merely attempt to extrapolate from growth patterns in industrial countries to the growth problems and policies of underdeveloped areas. He suggested that those differences, if viewed as obstacles to such extrapolation, might contribute to a more realistic appraisal of the magnitude and the recalcitrance of the problems of economic development of today's underdeveloped areas. Merely by emphasizing these points, he makes a contribution toward enlightened study of the processes and problems of economic development. A consideration always important to remember in economic research or theorizing is that economic theory is relevant to the particular institutional and technological setting which constitutes its background. It is redundant to comment that Professor Kuznets has proceeded to the task he assigned for himself in the capable and effective manner we have come to associate with him.

Proceeding from a definition of underdeveloped countries in terms of low per capita product, he has sketched an impressive series of significant characteristics of today's lowest income areas: low productivity, overpopulation, and low income tend toward great inequality in distribution of income, and to the social and political instability which exacerbates them. In each instance, he has found that these conditions were not present, at least in a comparable degree, in the pre-industrial phases of presently highly developed, high-income countries. From the premise of his definition of an underdeveloped country, there is certainly considerable evidence to support his conclusions, and as findings of fact they will likely be accepted without much serious reservation. He believes that some significance attaches to these differences, and that the aim of empirical research on economic development should be to establish and measure common and variant characteristics of the growth process to explain the interrelations of those characteristics and to integrate them into a theory of economic growth.

The most challenging considerations raised by his paper are, therefore, not its factual conclusions but rather what significance can be inferred from them. To raise this question is to suggest many others, for it involves issues of both definition and methodology. The ultimate purpose of scientific inquiry is to enable us to measure, predict, and control environment. Its immediate task is to solve general theories which are valid and useful tools for working toward those goals. Likewise, the object of economic inquiry is to measure, predict, and to help us direct the economic environment. This was the object of the early classical economists in their concern about the conditions underlying the wealth of nations. In the same way contemporary interest in the problems and processes of economic development is socially motivated toward yielding knowledge with which we can give direction to the processes of economic change. Whether or not one is specifically seeking to formulate a general theory of economic growth--and that has been a prominent theme throughout this Conference--both the validity and significance of his inquiry in relation to economic development should be tested by his contribution toward the formulation of a general theory of development by which we can measure and direct economic change. In the brief time available, I wish to comment on two matters suggested by Professor Kuznets' paper, matters which I believe are relevant to empirical research in this field and, at the same time, important to the development of a general theory of economic growth. The first prerequisite for meaningful study of economic development is to establish a correct and acceptable definition of the concept itself. Professor Viner recently observed that while the output of literature on economic development has reached massive proportions in recent years, it is extraordinarily lacking in explicit definition of basic terms which it implies, with the result that one discovers a wide range of different and often conflicting concepts being covered by a single label. He specifically cites as an example the concept of an "underdeveloped" country, noting numerous criteria of underdevelopment which have appeared in the literature.

Now, the importance of this point is: the characteristics of underdeveloped countries as we think of them will be related to what an underdeveloped country is defined to be, since the definition will reflect implicit notions about the factors that are important in economic growth. Because the concept of economic underdevelopment lacks precision at this time, one who proposed to study problems of economic development must, of necessity, define the concept as he proposes to use it. Professor Kuznets has done this, but the concept as he has defined it will likely be subjected to examination.

This factor, then, suggests the first reservation that might be raised to his findings. He begins his paper by defining an underdeveloped country as one in which per capita product is so low that material deprivation is widespread and reserve per capita accumulation is small. But the practical usefulness of this criterion is at once lessened because it necessitates an arbitrary decision about the level of per capita product to be required by the definition. Since he chose to set that level very low for this study, his conclusions are concurrently relevant to the lower-income society, and would, as he points out, be valid for them whatever the level of per capita product set. But if that level was raised enough to include, for instance, the countries of Latin America or the Mediterranean region, or even the U.S.S.R., would the same characteristics prevail? He suggests that many of them change. Does this imply that some apparently would not? It is evident that the concept of underdevelopment by this definition becomes relevant and makes it desirable to discover the general characteristics of underdevelopment.

Elsewhere in the paper this original definition is modified by the qualification that underdevelopment is to imply that the current low rates of performance are far short of the potential. Now the concept becomes even more indefinite, for by what criteria may the potential of an economy be discovered? And finally, when it is proposed to compare the characteristics of underdeveloped countries with those of developed countries before industrialization, does this imply that "underdevelopment" actually means "nonindustrialization"? In that case, at what level of industrialization does an economy become a developed one? It would appear that this concept of underdevelopment might yield different criteria of the characteristics of an underdeveloped country from those which were given in his paper relative to only lowest-income societies. And would not other questions about the characteristics of underdevelopment arise with yet other alternative definitions of the concept?

This comment is offered only to point up one inherent handicap that is imposed upon empirical investigation of underdevelopment until such time as the concept itself can be clarified. Without some consensus of what an underdeveloped country is, the significance and even the validity of generalizations relative to underdevelopment may be questioned. As Professor Kuznets has himself noted, the characteristics of underdevelopment are in large measure reflected in the notion of the factors that are important in economic growth, even though the ultimate purpose of inquiry is to discover, by empirical methods, what these very factors are.

Turning now to a second consideration, Professor Kuznets indicated that he proposed to consider the economic characteristics of under-developed countries in the light of past growth patterns of industrial-ized countries. Now this also raises some questions. In the first place, what patterns, if any, of past growth can we identify? And what are their characteristics? Do such patterns, when found, have suffi-cient general validity to be acceptable as patterns of economic devel-opment and to afford therefrom a general theory of growth relevant to present underdeveloped economies? By undertaking to compare those conditions characteristic of underdeveloped countries with those of presently developed economies at some earlier stage in their develop-ment, does one imply that there were certain conditions and factors present in that stage of the developed society which significantly por-tended their possibilities for development and which are or are not present in an underdeveloped country?

I believe this was the very tendency that Professor Kuznets warned against in stating the object of his paper. For to the extent that there are such factors, might it then be possible to extrapolate growth pros-pects from past experience? What we are asking here is, in effect, whether there is, or can be, any general theory of any economic growth in terms of which we can measure the significance of differ-ences in the economic characteristics or conditions of various eco-nomics, and in terms of which we can express their degree of progress toward economic development and the magnitude of problems of, and obstacles to, that development. Indeed, how can we learn from past growth and how can we proceed toward meaningful conclusions about the characteristics of underdeveloped countries in the light of past growth? These considerations are raised simply to point up the in-herent methodological difficulties encountered in trying to assess the significance of present economic differences, or in learning from ex-perience or experimentation in the areas of social dynamics. Pro-fessor Kuznets appreciates these difficulties, of course, as he re-vealed in his opening remarks. Among the major propositions of his paper, in fact, was his concluding comment that the aim of research about economic growth should be to develop a general theory of growth, and his plea for greater realization of how little is known. He has pioneered in the study of problems of economic development. This paper impresses me as a valuable attempt to clarify some con-cepts of growth and to use constructive approaches to their solution.

PRESENT UNDERDEVELOPED COUNTRIES AND
PAST GROWTH PATTERNS

COMMENTS

Eastin Nelson

The indebtedness of economic analysts and of economic historians to Professor Kuznets is so well known that to mention it is supererogatory except as a prelude to picking methodological flaws in the paper by an international authority in the field of growth economics. I think he has proved that a man who understands economic history can write a good paper turning on dubious, if not bad, data. On substantive conclusions drawn by Professor Kuznets, I am in hearty accord.

My first objection to this paper, although not my strongest, is that it has attempted to compare incomparables--money incomes in different economies. I do not wish to say that money-income comparisons from one economy to another are wholly misleading or useless. In spite of its limitations, the method has certain overall usefulness.

When such comparisons are made, as in one of Professor Kuznets' sources of data for determining what countries are underdeveloped--I refer here to United Nations Publications, Series E, No. 1, National Per Capital Income, 1949--I am disturbed. This publication expresses income estimates in the 1938 level of prices for the national economies compared, converting to United States dollars at the 1938 international exchange rate, and finally getting the figures to 1949 dollars by multiplying by the index of the cost of living for the United States. This, in spite of its many possibilities for compounding error in the calculation of income for any country, is better than an application of the crude purchasing power parity theory from which it is implicitly derived. It is certainly less objectionable to use 1938 exchange rates than it would be to use current exchange rates, because in 1938 the impact of the great demand for capital goods had been little felt in underdeveloped countries--and it is that demand which has driven the exchange rates in industrializing countries far below their purchasing power parity rates as compared with industrial suppliers.

The method still yields such palpable bloopers as classifying Venezuela, a country which did not have 2,500 miles of usable highways and railways in 1949, roughly on a par with Switzerland and Norway, with respect to per capita income. Venezuela, according to this document, had three and one-half times as much adjusted per capita income as Mexico--though Venezuela was a beachhead fragment of the United States economy, and Mexico had achieved national railway and highway systems and apparently had penetrated ten years into the developer's goal: "takeoff into sustained growth." Per capita income in Venezuela was half again as great as in Uruguay and Argentina, two countries generally recognized to have achieved European living standards.

One can argue very little with Mr. Kuznets about the fact that the Asian and African countries are underdeveloped, though one wonders about the validity of the income measure of development that puts Japan below most of the Latin American countries. With few exceptions, the Asian and African countries are underdeveloped both relatively and absolutely, judged by any criteria which may be applied.

The most severe shortcoming in Mr. Kuznets' acceptance of so low a standard as to exclude virtually all of Latin America from the category of underdevelopment is that he therewith excludes an important laboratory area as a source of methodology in building a theory of economic development. An important contribution of his paper is that the conditions of the highly developed countries of the world offer a very unsatisfactory base for the study of our twentieth-century problem areas, because pre-industrialization history was quite different, qualitatively, from economic reality in the presently underdeveloped world. My own view is that industrialization has been a much longer process than we who have been dazzled by the industrial revolution since 1760 are prepared to admit. This does not change the fact that the relatively well-explored modern history of the industrialized countries offers a very unsatisfactory base for the analysis of current problems of economic underdevelopment. However, the countries which are on the borderline of economic underdevelopment were for the most part underdeveloped countries with very similar institutional arrangements, and material poverty comparable to the worst of the neo-Mediterranean, Mohammedan, and South Asian countries--before the borderline economies began to edge into their takeoff some twenty-five to seventy-five years ago. The lessons to be gleaned from them will not be detected by so crude an instrument as per capita income with any international adjuster.

Mr. Kuznets' definition of underdevelopment as characterized by widespread privation and little or no economic reserve is also somewhat less than satisfactory--not that these conditions do not characterize underdevelopment, but they are not very sharp tools. Underdeveloped countries are also usually countries of low literacy levels, poor governmental services, high infant-mortality rates, low life expectancy, unstable political equilibrium, and similar unsatisfactory conditions.

I would prefer a definition like that of Daniel Creamer, who said that the universal characteristic of underdevelopment is a low ratio of reproducible capital. This is difficult to measure directly, though less difficult than measuring widespread privation or low economic reserve. The consumption of energy from commercial sources, with suitable deductions for climatic differences, is not a bad index of the ratio of capital to population, though taken alone it is still inadequate. A more refined measure should include the ratio of cultivated land to male agricultural workers with other measures of industrial consumption, such as steel and fibers for clothing, each weighted in a proper proportion to the others.

If such measures are applied, and we go high enough into the scale to include countries like Mexico and Turkey, for which the 1949 study referred to by Mr. Kuznets gave adjusted incomes of $121 and $122 per capita, respectively, then we can begin to discover classifications in the scale of underdevelopment and to work out a system by which change in underdeveloped nations can be identified in more precise degrees than the crude measure accepted by Mr. Kuznets makes possible. One of the first things which the application of even such a crude measure of economic development as the consumption of steel and energy from commercial sources would make apparent is that there is something inadequate about per capita income as a measure of comparable economic development as between countries as similar in recent institutional and developmental experience as these two neo-Mediterraneans. Mexico uses two and one-half to three times as much energy and three times as much steel as does Turkey, though the disparity in population was minor at any time between 1937 and 1950. The measure Professor Kuznets accepts indicates that per capita income was slightly higher in 1949 in Turkey than in Mexico. Disparities in the industrial consumption of fibers and in the production of refined sugar indicate that Mexico is, in point of fact, a country of two and one-half to three times as much reproducible capital as Turkey, excluding social capital.

A battery of crude quantity relatives gives a fair insight into comparable ratios of reproducible capital as between countries at levels comparable to those of Turkey and Mexico and at the same time furnishes a fairly sensitive instrument for detecting the rate and the range of economic change in each of the countries in terms of a given base. Such a battery need not be extensive and need not include any area where figures are not subject to offsetting checks of reliability. The two most obvious measures are the consumption of energy and steel. By way of illustration, quantity relatives for the consumption of electricity, clothing fibers, gasoline, and the production of refined sugar are closely related to ratios of reproducible capital in countries of the level of development suggested for laboratory inquiry for the evolution of a theory of economic development, and they are subject to no such wide uncertainties as per capita income reduced to dollar equivalents, ultimately based on dubious aggregate income estimates. Such a battery embraces elements which obviously move at differential rates at different levels of economic development. Consumption of steel and energy tends to move at rates very close to that of adjusted national income, while fiber consumption tends to lag. The consumption of gasoline and electricity, and to a lesser degree, that of refined sugar, tends to exaggerate the curve of total economic growth, that is, they are sensitive indicators of the rate of change.

These measures will be found to serve with differing degrees of accuracy at different levels of development. In general they would be only marginally useful in an economy made up of water buffaloes and rice paddies, or in very small countries of very slender resources. In the main they are very useful in countries of semicontinental scope or wide resource range. Upward of two dozen of such countries exist in the world, and they are facing up to problems of economic development in varying degrees of uncertainty as to policy, precisely because inadequate and conflicting data confuse the field.

It is within this group of countries that I find internationally adjusted per capita income figures seriously wanting as to comparability. The profile of half a dozen quantity relatives suggested here tends to divide larger underdeveloped countries into three main groups with respect to growth rate: (1) countries which have enjoyed twenty-five years or more of political independence, (2) countries which have achieved independence more recently, and (3) countries which have enjoyed some unusual natural-resource bonanza. Turkey and most of the Latin Americas fall into the first category; Egypt, India, Pakistan, and Indonesia into the second; and Venezuela and Iraq obviously fall into the third. The same measures are not equally desirable for any group. Venezuela exhibits as exaggerated a growth record in a battery of industrial consumption measures as she does in per capita adjusted income. Obviously we have no theoretical instrument applicable for all countries at all stages. A given level of energy consumption is not the same thing for Canada as for Colombia. It is by no means certain that a given rate of increase in energy consumption means the same thing in Sweden that it means in Egypt.

By differing with Professor Kuznets on the best measures for analyzing economic change statistically, I have not wished to obscure my admiration for the excellent quality of his theoretical approach. I should like to close by quoting what seems to me the most apt synthesis of method formulated in his paper:

> The aim of research on economic growth is to establish and measure the common and variant characteristics of the process; to "explain" the interrelations of the common and variant characteristics, that is, to integrate them into a theory of the growth of a country's economy viewed as a system of interdependent parts.

ELEMENTS IN A THEORY OF UNDERDEVELOPMENT

COMMENTS

Clarence H. Danhof

The current concern with the problems of
economic growth is, as Professor Higgins suggests, a revival of interest in problems which have long commanded attention. It remains
true, however, that work in the field entered a new phase about ten
years ago. The past decade has witnessed the appearance of a volu-
minous literature concerned with the problems of the less developed
countries. The role of the theorists over these past ten years has
been the proper one of aggregating the observations, assumptions, and
conclusions of the empiricists, of developing precise generalized and
therefore abstract concepts, and of placing those concepts in such
meaningful relationships as can be demonstrated to be logically necessary to the achievement of given objectives. Professor Higgins'
paper is a summary and synthesis of certain central elements of this
growing body of theory.

Since Professor Higgins presents no definition of "underdevelopment," let me suggest the concept of underdeveloped countries that
I am using in these comments. These are, of course, economies of
low per capita incomes, but they are also economies in which larger
incomes are assumed to be possible. It is useful to suggest, therefore, that the less developed countries are those which have failed to
adopt to any significant degree the advances in productive technology
and in economic organization which have characterized the Western
world in the last century and a half.

It may be useful to put the matter another way. Consumers in the
more developed countries have come to enjoy a flow of goods and
services in which food products, though perhaps absolutely greater,
have become a decreasing expenditure, and constitute now a comparatively small proportion of per capita incomes. In the less developed
countries, foodstuffs continue to constitute a very high proportion of
incomes, while the nonfood components have experienced some, but
relatively little, change. This point of view emphasizes the fact that
the rise in per capita incomes in Western economies has followed
from the effective incorporation within the economy of new and large
resource sectors that contribute nonfood types of products and services; these constitute a large and increasing proportion of total
production.

The failure to participate in these changes is marked in the less developed society. The necessary technology has been highly mobile and has been available for the asking, at least after it has substantially developed. It is true that the effective application of this technology requires at least some capital, and frequently large quantities of capital. It has been the experience of the more developed countries that the new technology has, to a large degree, stimulated and provided its own capital requirements. While capital is, of course, subject to the laws of scarcity, within those limits it also has been mobile to a substantial degree.

In Professor Higgins' paper, the two central topics are population and investment, the first constituting a force which intensifies the problem, the latter offering the opportunity for solution. The sectoral analysis supports the argument by detailing the sources of the problem. International trade is dismissed as offering no possibilities for increased per capita incomes. Investment projects must be large, and must be planned with a view to the problems posed by discontinuities.

It is mildly encouraging to see such concepts as changes in the labor force, changes in resources, and changes in technology given recognition among the symbols of a mathematical economic model. They are not, of course, working members of the model but rather necessary though embarrassing guests. Their presence, however, gives some hope that the mysteries of their measurement and of their relationships may somehow be uncovered.

One model tells us that increased income must come from increased investment, expressing a widely held view. The model further suggests that different sources of capital can be expected to have different effects, partly because of difference in magnitude, partly because Professor Higgins distrusts the appropriateness of the decisions that private investors can be expected to make and hence feels that governmental decisions based on a plan will be more effective. Though the reason for the preference is not clear, it may follow from the historical failure of private investment to achieve the desired objectives. The other model contributes a caution that a favorable output-capital ratio must be sought in investment application.

The sectoral analysis is significant, not because one sector is agriculture and the other something else, but because of the economic characteristics involved. One sector offers the possibilities of increasing the productivity of labor because of a favorable labor-resource ratio. The other sector is one of a persistently declining ratio of resources to labor and hence declining product and per capita income.

The sectoral analysis suggests, incidentally, that even countries currently maintaining a high level of per capita income drawn from a predominantly agricultural base face a dismal future. Technological

improvements in intensive land use are certainly possible. Even if
such improvements take place, population growth will inevitably reduce agricultural resources per capita, hence productivity and income
must decline. Economic development rests, then, upon an expansion
of the nonagricultural resource base.

The sectoral approach--which as here presented is a form of economic history--spotlights these central considerations. As a form of
historical interpretation, it is, however, open to a number of criticisms.

I wish to mention here only one impression I have. These analyses
imply that the economies suffering from what are now clearly unfavorable effects, possessed in the past a propensity to development--to
borrow and adopt--which was frustrated by the sequence of events
detailed. Certainly these economies suffer from opportunities passed
by and from an aggravation of problems. Is it useful, or correct, to
say more than that?

At this point Professor Higgins feels that he has gone far enough
to declare that "financing economic development is reduced to providing funds for public investment in a manner that does not bring
avoidable reduction in private investment or in the output-capital
rates and providing incentives to increased private investment and
more efficient use of the existing stock of capital."

We have moved quickly from analysis to conclusions and then to
policy recommendation. I feel that we have moved much too quickly.

It seems to me that policy recommendations can follow only if
many other facets are taken into consideration. Certainly the author
has given implicit consideration to factors other than those discussed.
To the degree that such considerations enter the argument implicitly,
the recommendations rest upon no distinctive theoretical basis.

Most of the important factors that must be a part of a satisfactory
theory relate in essential ways to the elements chosen for discussion.
It seems to me, for example, that the central part of the theory--in-
vestment--needs the support on the supply side of appropriate theories
of credit, of fiscal policy, and of income distribution, this last including special emphasis on the savings process. We need also something
I shall call a theory of aspirations to account for problems relating
to the labor force and also to the supply of and character of entrepreneurship. Such a theory of aspirations will also assist in relating the
economy to the total culture, desirable and necessary since the economic analysis involves sweeping changes in the cultural pattern.

There is a strong suspicion that meaningful policy recommendations must have a foundation also in a theory of administration.
Surely in assigning to government a big role in investment, certain
assumptions are made about the capacities of government. Are such
assumptions realistic? The historical record is not encouraging if
we are concerned with direct action by government to economic ends,

internally determined. The record is much more encouraging if we are talking about government lending its special powers to the objectives of private enterprise or, usually, groups of private enterprises. This latter relationship is what I think is meant by the "favorable business climate" in the United States. I do not wish to labor the point. But it does make a difference who makes the decisions and who carries them out. The matter is one which requires as careful analysis as any other part of developmental theory.

Professor Higgins has attempted a limited synthesis of the theory of underdevelopment. It constitutes an important and useful effort, even if we accept only the broadest conclusion: that economic development is tantamount to getting people out of agriculture. That conclusion is broad enough to apply even to the United States.

ELEMENTS IN A THEORY OF UNDERDEVELOPMENT

COMMENTS

Richard Allen LaBarge

Let us consider first the "planning approach" equations of Professor Higgins' paper, which are presented in Part I. Equations 1a and 1b read as follows:

$$\Delta O = a \cdot \Delta Q + a \cdot Q \qquad (1a)$$

$$= a \cdot I + \Delta a \cdot Q \qquad (1b)$$

These equations say: "The change in total output is equal to the net of two component flows. One flow is the change in output which results from changing the capital stock (in other words, making net new investment or disinvestment) at a given ratio of output to capital. The second flow is the change in output which results from altering the output-capital ratio with a given capital stock." The only change proposed in passing to equation 2 is to substitute the components of investment for total investment in equation 1b. However, there is an oversight in notation, for equation 2 reads:

$$\Delta O = \Delta a \cdot Q + a(\Delta I_i + \Delta I_a + \Delta I_g) \qquad (2)$$

This formulation makes changes in output with a fixed output-capital ratio dependent not on changes of capital stock as in equation 1b, but on changes in the <u>rate</u> of change in capital stock. Since the text of the paper indicates that Professor Higgins does not intend for first differences in output to be directly dependent on second differences in capital stock, we suggest dropping the deltas from the investment terms of equation 2, and rewriting:

$$\Delta O = \Delta a \cdot Q + a(I_i + I_a + I_g) \qquad (2')$$

or

$$\Delta O = \Delta a \cdot Q + a(\Delta Q_i + \Delta Q_a + \Delta Q_g) \qquad (2'')$$

Unfortunately, there is another discrepancy in the remaining equations so that we cannot immediately reformulate them on the basis of equation 2'. Consider equation 3:

$$I = I_g + I_a \ (\dot{K}, \dot{T}) \qquad (3)$$

This equation says: "We may now discard private induced investment as quantitatively insignificant. Therefore, total net new investment in a developing economy is composed of net new government investment, which is not subject to constraints from the profit motive, and net new autonomous investment from private sources, which is conditioned by profit expectations stemming from the rate of new resource discoveries and the rate of technological advance." This statement is inconsistent with equation 3a:

$$\Delta O = \Delta a \cdot Q + a(\Delta I_g + \Delta I_a) \ (\dot{K}, \dot{T}) \qquad (3a)$$

which says that both types of investment--government and private-- are functions of $\dot{K}$ and $\dot{T}$. Is net new government investment conditioned by these variables? The answer is "Yes" if government is run like a business, for it is assumed that all profitable undertakings have already been exploited, given existing resources and techniques. In this case the only way to open up new lines of profitable investment, either for government or for private development, is to discover new resources or new techniques which raise the marginal efficiency of capital. The answer is "No" if government is willing to invest in productive activity which utilizes existing resources and existing techniques without regard to the short-run profit motive. In this case the government assumes a longer time horizon than private businesses and says, in effect: "We grant that this type of investment will not pay for itself now or in the near future. But over a span of fifty years or more the investment we make today should provide the social capital for general economic growth which eventually will justify the outlay." Regardless of how governments do in fact behave, the latter attitude is the one recommended by most development theorists. Professor Higgins' views are no exception to this rule, and for that reason we suggest that equation 3a be rewritten to conform to equation 3 and to the modification noted earlier in equation 2':

$$\Delta O = \Delta a \cdot Q + a[I_g + I_a \ (\dot{K}, \dot{T})] \qquad (3a')$$

Fortunately, this reformulation does not alter the four policy goals which Professor Higgins deduces from the original version of equation 3a.

We may now turn to Part II of the paper, in particular to the mathematical presentation of the "Population Multiplier Principle." In equation 3 of this system, Professor Higgins writes:

$$\Delta N_i = I_i / j_i \qquad (3)$$

This equation indicates that changes in industrial employment depend directly on changes in the stock of industrial capital for any given capital-job ratio. Here we should add that the aggregate value of the capital-job ratio in industry is variable over time even if we grant the tendency (observed in Part III of the paper) toward rigid factor proportions throughout most of the industrial sector. If there are marked changes in the composition of the industrial sector, either through the introduction of new industries or through changes in the relative importance of existing industries, the aggregate capital-job ratio in industry is subject to change. In underdeveloped countries where new industrial projects are likely to be large relative to existing industry, this possibility is further enforced. We suspect that expansion in the industrial sector tends to be capital-deepening, in which case we should have to consider equation 3 subject to the constraint that $\Delta j_i / \Delta N_i /$. In other words, to employ more persons in the industrial sector would require a more-than-proportionate increase in net new industrial investment.

Some attention also should be given to the assumptions involved in the final equations 4a and 4b. Equation 4a reads:

$$\Delta N_a = K_i \left(I_i / j_i \right) - i \left(I_i / j_i \right) \qquad (4a)$$

This formulation simply says that changes in agricultural employment are equal to the difference between changes in the total labor force and changes in the labor force of the industrial sector. All new workers who do not enter the industrial labor force are able to find employment in the agricultural sector, a circumstance which suggests that there was no unemployment in the agricultural sector at the outset. Thus, equation 4a does not allow for the development of disguised unemployment when land becomes a relatively scarce factor. But consider equation 4b:

$$\Delta N_a = K(I_i / j_i) - (I_i / j_i) \qquad (4b)$$

In passing to this equation, Professor Higgins factors the term "i" out of the right-hand members in equation 4a and then sets "i" equal to one so that it drops out of equation 4b altogether. Now it is impossible to have any unemployment whatsoever, for the labor force in the industrial sector also remains fully employed. Of course, it is true, regardless of the state of economic development, that unemployed industrial workers tend to enter agricultural occupations if they remain unemployed long enough. But the desirability of abstracting entirely from employment cycles in the industrial sector of a developing economy is open to serious question. In order to free the model from these restraints we recommend dropping equation 4b altogether and rewriting equation 4a to provide for the possibility of disguised unemployment in the agricultural sector:

$$\Delta N_a = K_i(I_i/j_i) - i(I_i/j_i) - Va \qquad (4a')$$

In concluding his paper, Professor Higgins details nine "chief differences" between economic analysis of underdeveloped areas and economic analysis of advanced areas. We suggest that the differences cited are not so much differences which arise from the relative state of economic development in the areas studies as they are differences between development theory and other types of theory. For example, consider the first three of these supposed differences. (1) During the last twenty years economists have become increasingly aware of the presence of discontinuous functions in the advanced economies. Indeed, no small part of the debate on the usefulness of marginal analysis has centered on the rigidity of factor proportions which comes with extensive industrialization. Moreover, bulkiness in both input and output bundles appears to be at least as characteristic of advanced economies as of underdeveloped ones. (2) Intersectoral and interregional relations also lie at the core of all serious research on advanced economies. It was precisely because such relations were so vital that national income accounting, flow-of-funds accounting, and input-output tables were developed for the study of advanced economies. (3) The ever increasing disequilibration of growth rates postulated for underdeveloped countries is just the converse of what we would expect from applying Professor Solow's model. Variable factor proportions prevail in the lines of agricultural production which tend to predominate in the underdeveloped economies. Hence, these are the very economies which would be most likely to tend toward equilibrium growth rates. But regardless of the facts, the Solow model is sufficiently general to permit its application to both developed and underdeveloped economies. In like fashion the procedures recommended for studying underdeveloped economies in "differences" four through nine can easily be adopted with little or no change to the study of advanced economies. We do not imply that there are no differences in procedures for analyzing the economies of countries at different stages in the development process. We claim only that "traditional economies" is not so restricted as Professor Higgins would have us believe.

THE CONCEPT OF BALANCED GROWTH IN ECONOMIC DEVELOPMENT: THEORY AND PRACTICE

COMMENTS

Troy J. Cauley

Quite appropriately Professor Singer starts by undertaking to define the term "balanced growth." He gives three definitions, or more nearly three groups of definitions, of this term. He selects for his purposes the definition that balanced growth is the "balance between the size of markets, the volume of supply, and the demand for capital." Thus three items are involved. In terms of semantics, is there any possibility of "balance between" three items? Perhaps "equilibrium among" would be a better term. More seriously, these items are not mutually exclusive; instead, they overlap.

In any case, measurement of the three items is implied. The process of measurement includes three steps: (1) the identification of what is to be measured, (2) the selection of an appropriate unit of measurement, and (3) the application of the unit to what has been identified. If diverse items are to be measured, such as "size of markets," "volume of supply," and "demand for capital," they must first be reduced to a common denominator. This is simply another way of saying that the unit of measurement selected must be appropriate with respect to each of the diverse items. In so far as I have been able to discern, Professor Singer never identifies the three items involved in his analysis in anything like a precise manner, and most decidedly he does not reduce them to a common denominator. Which is to say that he never gives us any means of knowing whether "balance" or "equilibrium" prevails in any given situation or not.

As his analysis progresses, he makes important use of some other terms which he does not define. Among these are "output," "resources," "saving," "investment," and "pump-priming." These are not terms whose meanings are self-evident, nor is there sufficient unanimity of opinion among economists concerning the meaning of each of these terms to justify their use in an intricate analysis without explicit definition.

For example, when he says, "The output:labor ratio in agriculture appears in the statistics almost invariably as lower than the national average ratio," does he mean by "output" physical quantities of products, such as bushels of wheat or pounds of pork, or does he mean a sum of money values? Almost certainly he means a sum of money values, but by using this meaning of the term he has admitted all that motley array of factors such as varying degrees of competition, protective tariffs, government price supports, import quotas, and so on which influence the relative levels of market prices of agricultural products and of industrial products. And the significance of these factors varies enormously from one country to another.

Further, when he says that the basic reason why the typical underdeveloped country cannot achieve a "wave of investment" is a shortage of "resources," does he mean by "resources" an accumulation of monetary funds which has resulted from "saving" and is, therefore, ready for "investment," or does he mean diesel tractors, skilled workers, steel girders, highly trained engineers, and hybrid seed corn?

These various items are by no means equally difficult to come by. An accumulation of monetary funds can be achieved in a number of ways besides that of "saving" in the sense of people's refraining from spending the whole of their money incomes for consumer goods. Professor Singer apparently recognizes such a possibility when he uses the term "pump-priming." He never specifies, however, just what he means by "pump-priming." Does he apply the term to all bank loans whereby money in the form of demand deposits is created on the basis of prospective money income from business enterprises financed by such loans? If so, most of the banking transactions performed in this country every day constitute "pump-priming." Evidently he does not mean this, for he regards "pump-priming" as he uses the term as practically a certain means of bringing on inflation.

But to criticize Professor Singer for not defining all the terms he uses is, of course, quite unfair. We are all guilty of imprecision-- economists even more than most people, perhaps.

Professor Singer's basic thesis is that what has come to be called "the balanced-investment package" is not likely to be workable in the effort to achieve rapid economic development in a typical underdeveloped country. The fundamental reason for this, as he sees it, is that the balanced-investment package cannot be put into effect without a concurrent increase in agricultural production, and that the typical underdeveloped country does not have sufficient resources to launch "the package" and to expand agriculture simultaneously. In upholding this contention, he makes the rather positive statement: "Supply can create its own demand, or it can create its own finance--but it cannot conceivably do both." The sense in which he uses the terms "supply," "demand," and "finance" is not completely clear here, but if they are taken in their more or less standard meaning of total production, total purchases, and total funds for investment, respectively, does not "supply" consistently create, as a matter of fact, both its own "demand" and its own "finance"? If not, from what other source does either "demand" or "finance" come? For example, does not the steel industry, by paying wages to its workers, salaries to its managers, and dividends to its stockholders, contribute to the maintenance of the demand for steel products; and does it not at the same time retain enough of its net earnings to finance the expansion of its plants?

Since he does not believe that the balanced-investment package technique will work, Professor Singer suggests a number of less ambitious undertakings as being more feasible. He may well be right about the matter.

I am inclined to argue to the contrary, however. There are two basic ideas in the balanced-investment package approach to the problem of inducing economic development: (1) that the expansion should be integrated rather than disjointed, and (2) that saving in the sense of the accumulation of sums of money by private individuals is not a prerequisite of technological innovation. To the best of my judgment, nothing that Professor Singer has said damages the validity of either of these principles.

He concedes that the technique of the balanced-investment package will work satisfactorily in a "developed" country as contrasted with an "underdeveloped" one. I suggest that the difference between two such countries is one of degree only rather than of kind. What he really means is that the technique will work in any economy in which there are unemployed or underemployed human or physical resources. But he apparently defines an underdeveloped country as one in which there are no unemployed or underemployed resources, that is, as one in which the great bulk of the resources is fully employed in agriculture and the remainder in the relatively small nonagricultural segment of the economy.

I suggest that, instead, there is in the typical underdeveloped country which he describes a significantly large proportion of underemployment. The very fact that agricultural production is essentially a biological process and thus highly seasonal in its nature necessitates that most of the people engaged in it are idle during much of the year. There are apt to be considerable numbers of able-bodied people in such a society who are by institutional arrangement wholly exempt from working in agriculture and largely exempt from working at anything else except ceremonies of one sort or another. Much of the content even of farming is apt to be essentially ceremonial rather than technological in nature. This means that from a technological point of view there is chronic, in addition to seasonal, underemployment in agriculture. All of this means that workers in such a country can be transferred in relatively large numbers from agriculture to industry without reducing agricultural production.

In essentially the same way in which there is underemployment of labor in agriculture in such a country, there is apt to be underemployment of shopkeepers, tradesmen, notaries, governmental functionaries, and so on, in the villages and the towns.

It is true that in order to put these people to work in industry they must have machines, tools, buildings, raw materials, and so on with which to work. The "investment package" is designed to provide these. It may have to be a small package in some cases; but still its contents should be integrated rather than selected at random. Indeed, a part of its contents should consist of new tools and techniques for agriculture.

We have "cultural borrowing" nowadays as the great source of new tools and machines and the know how to operate them. Cultural borrowing is not, of course, new. It has been practiced in some degree for many centuries. What is new about it is that our vastly increased and improved facilities for transportation and communication among countries have enormously increased the scale on which it can be practiced. A further factor working in this direction is the great wealth of the technologically advanced countries, which makes it possible for them to extend huge aid to the technologically retarded countries without suffering hardship themselves.

In my judgment, the model of "low-level deadlock" which Professor Singer describes as prevailing in the typical underdeveloped country is not primarily a matter either of physical resources or of extent of markets. It is, instead, essentially a matter of institutions which constitute obstacles to technological progress. Institutions in this sense are "clusters of mores" which serve to distribute power, rank, prestige, and influence among the people. Therefore they define what is "right," "proper," "worthy of achievement," and what is not. To express the same basic idea in a slightly different way, we may say that an institution is an arrangement whereby somebody is designated as "the boss" without there being any reason for it in terms of technological effectiveness. Still another way of putting the same thing is to say that an institution is an arrangement whereby a certain way of doing things is designated as the "right" way regardless of the consequences in terms of physical output.

The point is that institutions in this sense prevail in all underdeveloped countries (we even have some of them in highly developed countries); and the first step in economic development should consist of the adjustment of these institutions. Institutions by their very nature are backward-looking and are strongly supported by the powerful emotional forces of the people. Therefore they stoutly resist change. In fact, to change the institutions of a people suddenly and completely would be to bring on social chaos. This means that gradual adjustment rather than sudden and complete change is the proper procedure.

In so far as Professor Singer deals with this problem of institutional adjustment at all, he does so indirectly under the heading of "development of the infrastructure" in which he mentions education and a few other items which might conceivably have a bearing upon institutional adjustment.

I urge that in efforts at inducing economic development institutional adjustment be given a great deal more attention than it has thus far received.

THE CONCEPT OF BALANCED GROWTH IN ECONOMIC DEVELOPMENT: THEORY AND PRACTICE

COMMENTS

Alfred F. Chalk

As Professor Singer has noted in his introductory remarks, the term "balanced growth" has been used in a number of different contexts in recent literature on economic development. The problem with which his paper is primarily concerned relates to the maintenance of a balance between the aggregate supply of, and demand for, goods and services in an economy that is in an early stage of economic development. If I understand his position correctly, the central thesis of his remarks is that the concept of balanced growth, whatever its merits from a purely theoretical point of view, offers little promise as an operational slogan for a stagnant economy which, in the words of Nurkse, is in a state of "underdevelopment equilibrium."[1]

Leaving aside the theoretical issues for the moment, let us turn briefly to the so-called "practical" problem of breaking the economic deadlock of low-level equilibrium in a stagnant economy. Nurkse and others have suggested that the answer may lie in attacking the problem on a broad front by means of a wave of investments in new industries, thus taking advantage of complementarities on both the supply and the demand sides. In brief, supply would create its own demand, and the perennial problem of markets in underdeveloped nations would ostensibly be resolved. I agree with Singer, however, that such a wide range of more or less simultaneous investments in industry would probably require more resources than any truly underdeveloped country could reasonably be expected to obtain. The problem of capital requirements would, of course, be magnified if additional investments in agriculture were necessary.

In discussing the subject of the availability of capital, however, I think mention might have been made of a theoretical point emphasized by such authors as Rosenstein-Rodan and Nurkse. In numerous densely populated countries, a substantial amount of "disguised" or "concealed" unemployment exists in rural areas, that is to say, the marginal productivity of labor is zero over a wide range. Under such

---

[1] Ragnar Nurkse, Problems of Capital Formation in Underdeveloped Countries (New York, Oxford University Press, 1953), p. 10.

conditions, it has been suggested that the disguised unemployed are an important potential source of saving and capital formation. This is based on the assumption that the unemployed in agriculture could be shifted to industrial employment without increasing the total food requirements. The following excerpt from Nurkse illustrates this thesis quite clearly:

. . . the use of disguised unemployment for the accumulation of capital could be financed from within the system itself. There is no question of asking the peasants who remain on the land to eat less than before, only of preventing them from eating more. What is wanted is that they go on feeding their dependents who leave the farms to go to work on capital projects and who, in effect, continue to be dependent for their subsistence on the "productive" peasants remaining on the farms. All that happens is a re-allocation of labor in favour of capital construction.[2]

As Nurkse admits, this analysis is based upon a static view of the population problem. Moreover, its implementation as a developmental policy would probably require that the government play an extremely authoritarian role. Indeed, one wonders whether any type of political organization other than a police state could force those remaining on the farm to refrain from increasing their consumption of food, not to mention the problem of preventing those who leave the rural areas from increasing their food consumption.

Such problems as these raise serious doubts about the operational value of Nurkse's so-called "hidden source of saving" as a means of financing an across-the-board type of investment program. Although substantial gains might be derived from such utilization of the disguised unemployed, the question at hand is whether this potential source of capital formation, plus that available from outside the system, would be sufficient to finance the kind of investment program on a broad front visualized by the analysis. I am inclined to doubt that it would suffice for that purpose. And finally, it should be borne in mind that Nurkse's analysis is generally applicable only to underdeveloped countries with a high labor:land ratio, and as a consequence, it does not purport to offer a theoretical solution to the problem of financing a "wave" of investment in many underdeveloped nations which do not have significant amounts of disguised unemployment, for example, many of the countries in Latin America. Be all this as it may, these remarks are obviously intended to buttress Professor Singer's position concerning the basic problem of resource requirements for a balanced-growth policy in a stagnant economy.

The concluding section of Singer's paper, which deals with what he calls the various "roads" to economic growth, reveals a kind of eclecticism which probably reflects, at least in part, the breadth of his experience with a great variety of developmental problems. Perhaps

---

[2]Ibid., p. 38.

the essential point he makes is that, regardless of how underdeveloped an economy may be, one almost invariably confronts an existing condition of imbalance which in turn dictates, to a greater or lesser extent, imbalance in the allocation of resources. Expressed another way, the end result of the very nature of economic change is such as to require the use of investment priorities, emphasis upon "growing points," the breaking of bottlenecks, or some variant of these as a means of achieving a greater degree of balanced economic growth.

Within this general context, however, I should like to suggest that the kind of investment program adopted in any given country will be profoundly affected by the meaning which the planners ascribe to the term "economic development." As Kindleberger has observed, for example, one may view development either as a process or as a condition.[3] Thus if one is dealing with a stagnant economy and the objective is to create a self-sustaining process of economic growth, priorities should probably be given to such economic and social overhead investments as education, transport, and communication. The reason, of course, is that investments of this type have the effect of changing people and institutions, and by this process the problem of sustaining economic growth may ultimately resolve itself through the instrumentality of a well-organized market economy.

If, on the other hand, one views economic development as a kind of state of being, or condition, then priorities would likely be given to heavy industry. The appropriateness of such investments in capital-intensive projects has been widely discussed in the current literature on economic growth. Suffice to say, the experience of Poland and Yugoslavia illustrates the serious character of the maladjustments that may result from such a policy. Symbolic of this problem are the reports from Yugoslavia concerning widespread disguised unemployment in industry.[4] It is nevertheless true that capital formation may spread more rapidly in this manner "provided the lack of proportionality between output and consumer demand can be repressed in some fashion."[5]

Although the subject of priorities is not entirely appropriate in the light of Professor Singer's chosen topic, I will nevertheless close by suggesting that if one is dealing with a stagnant economy characterized by great institutional rigidities, a low literacy rate, and similar "blocs" to economic growth, the appropriate policy would be to give a high priority to overhead investments of the kind referred to above. This suggestion is based, of course, on the assumption that the planning goal is to establish a largely self-sustaining, cumulative process of economic development, in which case the problem of "balanced growth" might be reduced to its proper proportions.

---

[3]Charles Kindleberger, Economic Development (New York, McGraw-Hill Book Company, 1958), pp. 163–165.
[4]Ibid., p. 165.
[5]Ibid.

INFLATION IN ECONOMIC DEVELOPMENT

COMMENTS

Stephen L. McDonald

Professor Maynard's thesis is premised upon the proposition that the deliberate economic development of the poorer countries involves the necessity to force saving. He shows that whether inflation is an efficacious method of forcing saving, and whether saving can be forced without inflation, cannot be decided on a priori grounds. Accordingly, he asks a pair of related but different questions: What sort, or pattern, of growth is almost certainly associated with inflation? Can this pattern of development be avoided?

The argument proceeds to the effect that since the income elasticity of demand for food tends to be relatively high in the poorer countries, a particular danger resides in concentration upon industrial development to the neglect of agriculture. The consequence of this approach to development is a rise in food prices. Food being the principal wage good, labor then attempts to raise wages, and the basis for a wage-price spiral is laid. The tendency is intensified by militant unionism and the absence of money illusion, by high rates of population growth under conditions of improving real wages, loose monetary-fiscal practices, and the transfer of agricultural enterprise and effort from the fields to the black market. Professor Maynard is distrustful of the adequacy of fiscal measures to cope with this problem and is doubtful that in the earlier stages of development sufficient export trade in manufactures can be created to buy the required additional food products abroad. He thus concludes that the sole dependable solution to the problem of development without inflation is a pattern in growth of output which assures that the domestic supply of food will rise proportionately to the demand for food.

I think Professor Maynard poses the correct sort of questions and places emphasis on a fundamental problem in growth, namely, that of the relative composition of increments to output and demand. I find it impossible to differ with him in a fundamental way. My comments will be directed first at suggesting some qualifications to the argument, some of which are at least implicit in Professor Maynard's paper, and then at stating a somewhat more optimistic view of the possibilities of controlling inflation in rapidly developing countries.

Assuming that planning authorities are fully conscious of the problem of matching incremental output and demand for food, it is clear that the need for, and feasibility of, deliberately stimulating the agricultural sector will differ from country to country and, within the same country, from stage to stage in the development process. One thinks, for instance, of the situation in which a country is a major producer and exporter of foods, with international terms of trade deteriorating. Considerable emphasis could be given to nonagricultural development without doing more than halting the fall in food prices, while the resultant stabilization of the terms of trade would protect the ability to import capital goods and avoid governmental deficits. Then there is the case in which the principal limitation to improvements in agricultural technology and output is surplus farm labor, excessively small units, and depressed farm wages, due to high rural reproduction rates and restricted employment alternatives. Labor must be induced to migrate from the land to urban residences and occupations in order to render more productive agricultural techniques economically feasible and attractive. In this situation also, emphasis upon industrial development would yield the most rapid rate of growth and yet be consonant with stable food prices. There are many other possible situations one could hypothesize, including the exact opposite to those specified, in which cases Professor Maynard's argument would operate with a vengeance, but these are sufficient to illustrate the matter of variety among the underdeveloped countries.

As a developing country progresses into successively higher planes of per capita real income, the problem of matching incremental output and demand for food tends to diminish. The income elasticity of demand for food at the farm declines, the rate of population growth may fall, reliance upon external sources of capital goods is reduced, and the possibility of developing an export trade in manufactures in order to buy foreign-produced foods is progressively enhanced. In connection with the last point, however, it should be noted that a late-developing country probably has more restricted opportunities to become an exporter of manufactured goods than a country which passed into the advanced stages of growth when a larger area of the world was characterized by relatively primitive and self-sufficient pastoral and agricultural economies. But in any case, it is apparent that Professor Maynard's thesis applies most severely to those countries with the lowest per capita incomes and to those most likely to remain in this condition in consequence of population tendencies.

In growth models of the Harrod-Domar type, the feasible rate of growth in output is seen to be directly proportional to the marginal propensity to save and indirectly proportional to the marginal ratio of required capital to output. The size of the latter ratio, often called the capital-depth ratio, is a function in part of the composition of increments to output, since the specific ratio varies from industry to industry. Accordingly, the more relative emphasis given in development to industries with relatively high capital-depth ratios, the lower is the resultant rate of growth in total output. The more relative emphasis given to low-capital-depth industries, the higher is the aggregate rate of growth.[1]

Combining these facts with Professor Maynard's thesis, we see the possibility of some serious dilemmas in attempting economic development without inflation. In some situations, particularly when new lands must be opened, settled, and connected with transportation facilities, the marginal capital-depth ratio in agriculture is very high (and the gestation period long). Consequently, an effort to avert inflation by carefully promoting an increment to food output suitable to the income elasticity of demand for food may entail a discouragingly low rate of growth, given the problem of adequate "take-off" momentum, and thus enhance the attractiveness of alternative approaches.

Since there are so many possible circumstances in which the problem posed by Professor Maynard is not acute, or in which the prescribed cure may be especially limiting to the rate of growth, we are perhaps justified in looking once again at the alternatives. First, consider the possibility of restraining the excess demand for food through fiscal measures. Professor Maynard's mathematical illustration on this score leads to the conclusion that fiscal restriction of the growth in demand for food will lead to an excess supply of non-food consumer goods, <u>given</u> the before-tax propensity to save and income elasticities. The illustration leaves me dissatisfied on two points. In the first place, the postulated constant proportions between food spending, non-food spending and saving, despite the imposition of additional income tax, suggests to me a proportional or slightly progressive rate structure. Clearly, a <u>regressive</u> rate structure is called for, both to restrain incremental demand for food and to maximize the after-tax propensity to save. This would minimize the excess supply of non-food consumer goods; but that subject leads us to the second point. Professor Maynard's example leaves unanswered the question of governmental disposition of incremental tax receipts. If they are spent in the proper proportions by the government, the excess supply of non-food goods can be absorbed and the rate of capital formation maintained. The more regressive the tax rate structure, the smaller is the excess supply of non-food goods and the larger is the proportion of increments to output that can be channeled through government into capital formation; in short, the greater is the amount of saving that can be forced without inflation.

I do not mean to suggest that regressive taxation is necessarily desirable in underdeveloped countries. Indeed, a progressive rate

---

[1]Similar, but not identical, observations can be made with reference to the related concept of capital gestation period. Since elaboration of this point would add little to the present argument, it is left with this passing note.

structure may be indicated in countries with great extremes in income and in which private saving tends to flow into real estate investment and hoardable valuables. Rather, the point is that fiscal policy may be a much more flexible and potent instrument than Professor Maynard suggests, particularly when combined with development plans which call for greater increments to capital goods output than could be justified by the marginal propensity to save. This does not necessarily imply more socialization of investment than is common to capitalist countries, for one of the more fundamental needs in the early stages of development is public capital in the form of roads, schools, utilities, and other community facilities.

There is another alternative which Professor Maynard does not mention, possibly because he intends to restrict his attention to purely domestic-policy actions. That alternative is the deliberate creation of conditions under which international investment is encouraged to supplement domestic saving, voluntary and forced, in the underdeveloped countries. After all, it was not merely North America's food-producing capacities that permitted its growth without secular inflation in the nineteenth century. Substantial credit for that goes to European capital, too. While the circumstances pertaining to this instance are not likely to be repeated, it does seem possible to give more relative emphasis to international investment than is now common without significantly interfering with national self-determination in the developing countries. If so, the chief burden rests with the developing countries to devise attractions and safeguards suitable to their individual circumstances. A successful program would have the advantages of reducing the need to force domestic saving and risk inflation in the process, allowing domestic investment to be concentrated in agriculture and public capital, and introducing from without methods, skills, attitudes, and experiences most likely to break down institutional rigidities and foster the growth of a native entrepreneurial class. Moreover, it would be consonant with the short-run trading interests of the wealthier industrial powers, a consideration not to be overlooked.

In conclusion, I find myself somewhat more optimistic than Professor Maynard about the possibilities of economic development without inflation. His thesis may not apply with particular force to some given situations. In others, where it clearly does, perhaps there are adequate means of meeting its challenge without unduly limiting the rate of growth. For the very poorest countries in the early stages of development, external capital seems essential and may be highly efficacious in producing a satisfactory rate of growth without inflation. For those countries in intermediate stages of development, where income taxation through withholding has become feasible, appropriate fiscal policy and planning may be sufficient.

INFLATION IN ECONOMIC DEVELOPMENT

COMMENTS

Carey C. Thompson

My reading of Professor Maynard's paper provides me with a great deal to admire and very little to condemn. He has given us no impression of wishing to inveigh against the evils of inflation per se in connection with economic development. He is, rather, concerned with an effort to answer a more fundamental question as to the type of economic development which is most likely to be characterized by extreme inflationary pressure. As a result of his consideration of this question, through both a simple analytical model and certain empirical evidence, he comes to the conclusion that "schemes of development . . . are more likely to achieve their aim with the minimum of inflation if due priority is given to agricultural development and to industries complementary rather than competitive to it." This conclusion reached by Professor Maynard underscores one of Professor Higgins' recommendations for policy in connection with the need for emphasis on increased productivity in the rural sector of the underdeveloped economies. My own judgment leads me to wholehearted agreement with this point. I feel that it is as correct as almost any generalization concerning the underdeveloped economies can be.

With this endorsement made, I may be permitted to record the fact that certain statements in Professor Maynard's paper have left me a bit disturbed. When I read that "the problem of underdeveloped countries is to force saving," I wonder if Professor Maynard is not ascribing to the saving process, at least by implication, a causal role in economic development which in fact it does not possess. I would not deny that saving plays a certain permissive role in growth. The amount and the uses of saving are surely matters with which policy-makers must be concerned, but the Maynard statement suggests a primacy and a dynamism in saving which I would question that it deserves.

Further, the Maynard judgment that "during the over-all process of growth the yield of investment should be in accordance with the distribution of consumer demand" also proved somewhat puzzling to me. I am here not sure of his meaning for the term "yield of investment," but I do not see any reasonable interpretation of the term

which would free me of the feeling that there is in the statement a
valuation that assigns to the "free market" an efficacy in the growth
process that in fact it may not have. I would, for my own part, dis-
claim any tendency of animus toward free markets, but they appear to
be types of economic arrangements that do not invariably permit
easier attainment of such a goal as development. Indeed, as Myrdal
has so forcefully contended, they may often serve to force the underdeveloped economy in the wrong direction. It seems to me that, taking
into account some of the Myrdal warnings, we might well be especially
alert to note our own predilections in behalf of certain economic institutions, such as free markets, which may serve the advanced economies quite well for certain purposes but which might serve the less
developed areas poorly indeed. At some later stage, to be sure, an
institution such as consumer sovereignty may come into its own in the
underdeveloped regions and there perform with substantial efficiency
the role that orthodox economics has traditionally ascribed to it, but
I doubt that it can do so, or even make a heavy contribution in this
direction, until a better support for such functioning can be provided.
I am not, of course, attempting to argue or suggest that Professor
Maynard is an all-out advocate of laissez faire, since he is obviously
nothing of the sort. But it does occur to me that in comments such as
those I have mentioned, and perhaps in his characterization of price
control as "an administrative subterfuge," there may appear certain
predilections that merit a notation. I admit, of course, that the points
I have raised may arise from my own hypersensitivity to some of the
issues involved, and I may have read into Professor Maynard's words
some implications that do not exist.

I am pleased to note that Professor Maynard is not to be included
among those who regard inflation as an evil to be avoided at whatever
cost. Some analysts and policy-makers among us appear to have
come to regard the avoidance of inflation, both in the advanced and in
the underdeveloped economies, as a problem to be given the highest
priority. Such a view, I would maintain, can have most unfortunate
consequences. It seems that, especially in the less advanced areas,
the necessarily strenuous pressure on extremely limited resources
implies that a successful development program will involve such
proximity to inflationary circumstances that constant adherence to
stable price levels simply cannot be maintained. I would suggest that
a policy of somewhat greater tolerance for unsuccessful efforts to
combat these inflationary pressures would be appropriate for Western
analysts and advisors. With our considerable advantages over the
underdeveloped areas, we have been less than completely successful
in our own efforts to avoid inflation during periods of substantial
growth, and there are forceful arguments to suggest that, in our own
case, the rise of price levels has played at least a permissive role in

this growth. A recent study of Korea's monetary and fiscal systems suggests that we "might be more useful if [we] accepted inflation as inevitable, at least for the present, and attempted to make the inflationary . . . system . . . work as well as possible."[1] Such a view has much to recommend it, in my judgment, especially as an alternative to the view that the minimization or elimination of inflation should be the Number One policy concern within the underdeveloped areas.

---

[1]C. D. Campbell and Gordon Tullock, "Some Little Understood Aspects of Korean Monetary and Fiscal Systems," American Economic Review, Vol. XLVII (June, 1957), p. 349.

MEXICO'S ECONOMIC GROWTH:
PROSPECTS AND PROBLEMS

COMMENTS

Robert Cuba Jones

Dr. Navarrete is optimistic about his country's future because recent economic trends in Mexico, on the basis of practically all available knowledge, seem to warrant such a view. But it is also true that the well-directed enthusiasm of Mexico's able leaders in almost all realms of life is one of the most favorable elements in the situation. Dr. Navarrete's excellent presentation merits applause, and I can only indicate a few factors which have not been mentioned because of the limitations of time, and expand a little on some which have necessarily been mentioned in a rather cursory manner.

Mexico today is a very active participant in the world economy; nevertheless, more might have been said about the disadvantages as well as the advantages of having a wealthy and powerful nation as a neighbor. The United States is not only a readily available market as well as a source of supply for Mexico but it also has a tremendous cultural and political impact upon that country. This has some economic significance. For example, as Dr. Navarrete stated, opposition in the United States, as well as in other countries, to the Mexican Government's expropriation of the oil industry was apparently just strong enough to unify the country's determination to prove itself, and the showing it has made has pretty well convinced the world that Mexico can and will meet its obligations. On the other hand, part of Mexico's difficulty with consumer pressure to attain a higher level of living than the country's economic structure would immediately seem to permit, has been to a measurable degree brought about through the induced desire to follow the example of the northern neighbor. Such pressure is not a deterrent to development usually, even when extreme, except that perhaps this influence is too much felt through the media of American movies and American commercial advertising. Material well-being, I would say, is today as important to Mexicans, at least in the urban centers, as it is to the people of the United States with this difference in the national ethos that Mexico is not in general engaged in a struggle for economic development as an instrument for power.

   The international and the internal migration of workers, both of
which are serious problems to Mexico, are also due to the quickened
yet frustrated aspirations of the rural population, to the mechanization
of agriculture with its consequent release of manpower, and to the
precarious character of much of Mexico's agriculture. There is a
large movement from rural to urban areas within Mexico as well as
across the international boundary. Many in the latter group, I am
convinced, return to Mexico after an experience in semi-industrialized
American agriculture to fill the rapidly-increasing ranks of factory
labor in Mexican cities. Little has been done as yet about the decentralization of industry, although two sizeable manufacturing centers
have been set up in new areas which recruit labor from the surround-
ing older villages. It is costing rural Mexico a great deal to produce
this labor, whether it goes abroad or not, and there is considerable
evidence that city-centered industry has been favored in comparison
with rural development. There is also a problem relating to the diversion of investment funds to urban real-estate speculation. Available statistical data show that only 18 per cent of the national income
goes to farmers, though they constitute about half of the total labor
force. Real income is slightly larger, but farm income in Mexico
needs to be much greater if the rush to the cities is to be slowed,
even if one does not adhere to the idea that a balanced economy is a
healthier one. Two important studies of Mexico's agriculture have
recently been made: one by Luis Yáñez Pérez, director of the Mexican Institute for Economic Investigations, assisted by Edmundo Mayo
Parras; and the other by Armando González Santos, who did his research under the direction of Dr. Navarrete in the Department of
Economic Studies of the Nacional Financiera. The latter study particularly reveals that there exist in Mexico two major types of agri-
culture--one considerably mechanized and modern and the other quite
outmoded--and that there is very little interrelationship between
them. Nevertheless, the Economic Commission for Latin America
sponsored a recent study which declared that Mexico has made the
greatest effort of any Latin-American country to improve the techniques and methods of production in agriculture.
   Dr. Navarrete has indicated that Mexico's imports must necessarily decrease if the present rate of development is maintained unless new sources of capital funds are developed or discovered. He
mentions the tourist trade as one source which could be easily en-
larged. To my mind it is very reasonable to expect such an increase
if proper measures are taken in other countries and in Mexico to
stimulate, guide, and protect those interested in travel. Much more,
however, needs to be done on both sides if travel in Mexico is to be
made a more satisfying experience.
   Whether one begins the study of the economic development of
Mexico with the Revolution of 1910, with the reformation of 1857, or

with the initiation of the active independence movement a half-century earlier, it is evident that there have been tremendous upheavals in Mexican history that represent enormous concentrations of effort by large numbers of people to bring about improvement in conditions. As the celebrated artist José Clemente Orozco and others have so clearly shown, there have been extremely wasteful and destructive aspects to these movements. It was, for example, nearly twenty years after the upheaval of 1910 before Mexico was able to settle down to united concentration on national betterment. More attention needs to be given as to how such popular efforts were stimulated and guided so that other attempts at development can be directed along more constructive lines.

I would like to conclude my remarks with a statement regarding Mexico's population problem. Although Mexico's high birth rate is a constant threat to her levels of living, the country is not presently overpopulated in relation to her readily utilizable resources, although that point might be reached in the not too distant future if present population trends continue. There is need for more numerous studies and more continuous research in this field, and such studies as are being made should be carefully co-ordinated and utilized. Manpower resources need to be better known and more effectively employed. There is a real crisis in technical education. The government should not be expected to solve all of the problems alone nor bear all of the costs. The critical situation of the middle class, with rising costs of living and increasingly heavy obligations of leadership, must be alleviated, and new traditions, techniques, and methods of management, more in keeping with Mexico's democratic profession, should be cultivated.

Mexicans can rightfully be proud of their country's growth, but, as Dr. Navarrete has indicated, there is still much to be done. Mexico's present high international status and its dependence, in part along with other nations, on world conditions not only permits but should also practically compel its leaders to share their problems with those of other countries so that they can be jointly worked out. Such sharing should have characterized relations with the United States long ago.

MEXICO'S ECONOMIC GROWTH:
PROSPECTS AND PROBLEMS

COMMENTS

George King Lewis

      Dr. Navarrete's excellent paper, summarizing Mexico's economic growth over the last two decades, leaves me with two rather definite conclusions: (1) that Mexico has succeeded in maintaining a phenomenal rate of growth in real output since 1939, and (2) that this process of development defies any explanation that is limited to the prevailing frontiers of quantitative economic analysis. My conclusions are inversely related to the emphasis given by Dr. Navarrete to quantitative, as opposed to institutional or qualitative, factors in economic analysis. It seems to me that Mexico's experience in transforming the institutional dimension of political economy is at this time somewhat more important to an understanding of the processes of economic development than is an interpretation of statistical relationships which, being fixed in the context of a given conceptual framework, can at best reflect only such questions as are inherent in the model to begin with.

      Regarding Mexico's rapid economic growth, I think the figures speak for themselves--so I shall direct the rest of my commentary to the implication in my second conclusion that without an open-ended inquiry into the socio-psychological dimension of the change which is Mexico's economic development--not the figures--without this behavioral foundation, I repeat, quantitative relationships in Mexico's growth cannot be singled out and measured without creating controversy at best and confusion at worst. I should like to accept Dr. Navarrete's invitation to use his paper as a point of departure--a point from which to consider issues for further research respecting the dynamics of the Mexican economy.

      My feeling that there is great need for a reverse emphasis in research on the institutional foundations of Mexico's development stems from two characteristics of the interesting paper delivered by Navarrete. First, there is the casual way in which he passes over such an important fact as is embodied in the statement that "a hard-working type of new local managers for the railroad and oil industries . . . began to develop" (and I might add that but for his modesty he would certainly have singled out for special mention the administration of

Nacional Financiera). But back to his mentioning the emergence of an entrepreneurial type in the management of public enterprise: perhaps Dr. Navarrete is being too diplomatic in allowing this "sleeper" to lie undeveloped. In view of much that North American economists have written of entrepreneurship in public institutions, I can well understand his reluctance to develop a point that might challenge the foundations of so many economic models which rest their case on the acceptance of the rationale of the profit motive. Whatever the reason, this statement of an important fact upon which much of Mexico's success may turn is submerged by Navarrete in deference to his extended interpretation of Mexico's development in terms of a more or less related group of statistical concepts derived from a model for which credit is usually given, I believe, to Harrod and Domar.

This brings me to the other characteristic of Dr. Navarrete's paper to which I attribute my feeling of a need for a differently directed emphasis--the fact that so much of his statistical interpretation rests on the matter-of-fact acceptance of the Harrod-Domar approach to economic development. Now, I would be the first to concede that this model has beautiful symmetry, built around the concepts of the capital-output ratio and the consumption function, but the fact remains that this particular model is by no means accepted as a valid referent for policy decisions. So far as I know, there is no substantial empirical foundation which supports its use. In a way, this may be fortunate, considering the policy problems that would follow if the thesis were "true." I agree with Leland B. Yeager's statement that "the Harrod-Domar analysis almost has the reader visualizing the economic system as a nervous tightrope walker."[1] The system gets into trouble unless it sticks to a precisely determined path of "balanced" economic growth, the rate of which is governed by a moving equilibrium position of the savings-income and investment-income ratios. Carter Goodrich has made only too clear the short-run limitations to equilibrium analysis, and it does not seem to me that the "other things that remain equal for the purposes of short-run economic analysis" become any more dynamic when moving an "equilibrium" through time than when limited to a movement about an equilibrium point at a given time.

What seems to me to be far more investigable than the "ideal" of an equilibrium rate of growth, implicit in the Harrod-Domar thesis, is Dr. Navarrete's identification of an emerging entrepreneurship in the social personalities of the managers of those public "business" concerns known as "decentralized autonomous public corporations." I believe that the verification of this fact, and an investigation of the conditions out of which these professional entrepreneurs have evolved

---

[1]L. B. Yeager, "Some Questions about Growth Economics," American Economic Review, Vol. XLIV, No. 1 (March, 1954), pp. 53-63.

(which would reveal their motivation) would be of an importance as basic to an understanding of economic growth in the twentieth century as the identification of the profit motive has been in the development of theory in the nineteenth.

It is my contention, then, that an inversion of emphasis which would shift analysis more in the direction of Mexico's institutional trans- formation would lead to a better understanding of the structure of Mexico's evolving system of political economy and, in turn, provide a better foundation from which to derive suitable concepts for quanti- tative analysis. I believe that such an investigation would reveal the pattern of an important institutional innovation in political types--a system which is developing a democratic process based on functional representation, one which is coming to rest on the foundation of an explicit social-function theory of property, one in which the value- orientation of judicial bodies looks deliberately to the future--to the aspirations of the nation as a whole, as expressed through the political authority--and which recognizes social power relationships as a basic fact in economic behavior (a fact that is probably here to stay). In short, I believe that the investigation would reveal a system which is moving away from the ideological extremes of both capitalism and communism and in which economic justice is coming to be identified with social justice. I call this system of political economy "executive government." The economic agents of the future are, I believe, clearly indicated within this framework: (1) the decentralized public corpora- tion, and (2) the labor union, so far as the basic capital-forming ac- tivities are concerned.

In conclusion, I am suggesting that a closer investigation of execu- tive government, its policy of economic intervention, its concept of value which springs from the social-function theory of property, the potential power positions of the public corporation and the labor union, and the psychology of entrepreneurship apparently emerging in the public administrator--that an examination of all these factors would reveal more clearly the strategic physical relationships and motives which are necessary to isolate variables for quantitative analysis. This type of research should help resolve such controversial ques- tions as the future role of private enterprise under executive govern- ment. It should point up the dangers of a matter-of-fact application of concepts invented by economists of the developed nations to the conditions of poor countries, such relational concepts as (1) forced saving through inflationary financing, (2) balanced growth through a relationship of the coefficients of the propensity to save and the capi- tal-output ratio, and (3) the differentiation of the productivity of labor and the productivity of capital.

Finally, I would like to make clear that I recognize that Dr. Navar- rete is much more aware of these institutional dynamics than I am-- and much closer to them--and in no sense should my remarks be taken as critical shots aimed in his direction. Rather take them as an appeal for economists to accept Mexico's success as evidence that they, not we, are finding answers to problems which we can at best know only vicariously; take them as an appeal to encourage Mexican economists to translate their experience into new concepts of their own upon which we can then, co-operatively, construct new tools of analysis.

PROGRESS, PLANNING, AND POLICY IN PUERTO RICO

COMMENTS

Calvin Patton Blair

Mr. Mayne has given us a fine review of the impressive achievements in Puerto Rico, properly prefaced with a word of warning about the special circumstances under which the Puerto Rican economy operates, and appropriately concluded with a summary of lessons which the Island's experience offers to other lands aspiring to rapid economic growth. By way of discussion, I would like to relate the special circumstances in his preface to the lessons of the conclusion, and to raise some questions about Puerto Rican policy and its applicability to other underdeveloped countries.

This tiny island dominion, whose per capita real product has grown at one of the fastest rates to be found outside the Communist world, is, despite the legalistic decisions of United Nations debate, a de facto political and economic appendage of the United States. While that fact may wound the Latin-half of Puerto Rican pride, it is tacitly acknowledged in Commonwealth policy. It is clear from Mr. Mayne's synopsis that Puerto Rico, since the earlier days of its agrarian reform and socialized industry, has shifted away from economic-development planning relevant to a country with national autonomy and the responsibilities and costs which it entails, to a policy based squarely upon the exploitation of the peculiar position of the Commonwealth, with its differential incentives vis-à-vis the mainland and its extra special "escape valve" of outmigration, which shifts much of the economic-development adjustment burden onto the United States, especially to New York City.

The fiscal arrangements granted in Commonwealth status allow Puerto Rico to make tax concessions which are legally impossible in any of the forty-eight states and politically impossible for most other underdeveloped countries. The use of a common currency, the absence of United States import duties, and the shelter of United States law make investment of mainland capital attractive in a fashion that can hardly be duplicated elsewhere; while Island culture has absorbed enough of "the American way of life" to make political leaders cultivate its inflow with--to steal a phrase from Gordon K. Lewis--"a judicious tenderness for its prejudices." Moreover, dual citizenship and the sharing of culture mean that Puerto Rico can accept a large volume of direct investments from the United States without quite the sentiment of foreign domination that would prevail in independent countries. It seems likely that much of the mainland capital now on the Island was not "generated" but rather "transferred" through the use of incentives; we really have no way of knowing how much was "called forth" anew and how much simply located there instead of elsewhere.

I do not wish to leave the impression that Puerto Rico has become simply a crude champion of private enterprise; as Mr. Mayne's paper makes clear, public welfare, too, is accorded considerable tenderness. The Puerto Ricans in their wonderful ebullience took the New Deal to heart; their enthusiasm for planning and their unabashed recognition of government's duty to "create income for those . . . left behind in the development of the economy" might arouse the envy of many of us who are interested in facilitating adjustments to economic change. But again, the absence of defense expenditures and the receiving of federal government financing for such things as highways leaves Puerto Rico free to use for health, education, and other welfare projects a larger part of its revenues than could be used were it an autonomous political unit; the migration of as many as 50,000 persons annually greatly reduces the welfare burden.

Migration also makes it possible for the government sector to devote to public capital formation a share of its revenues which otherwise might go to unproductive transfer payments. To the extent that public-works projects could be substituted for unproductive relief payments, and public capital formation thus be derived from job-creating expenditures, this effect of migration would be nullified.

But migration to the mainland affords Puerto Rico another luxury that is denied the majority of underdeveloped countries: the chance to pursue rapid economic growth without the full impact of an unwelcome choice between productivity, low cost, and high output on the one hand and the creation of jobs, "giving people something to do," on the other. When Mr. Mayne acknowledges the fact that rapid growth and the wiping out of unemployment are not identical objectives and later urges that the goals of the development program should not be set in terms of jobs or reduced unemployment, he is speaking in part from a peculiarly Puerto Rican position. One of the characteristic tragedies of economic development is the loss by many individuals of their traditional claim on the social product, a claim which derived out of prior economic organization and which was sanctioned by community mores and sentiment. One such claim with almost universal validity and respectability is the holding of a job. It might be demonstrated that a number of people are doing something which could well be done by half as many, that the marginal productivity of half the workers is thus zero, and that their transfer to something else would not reduce the real income available per capita; but it is quite another

thing to expect the half who remain employed to be willing to see the
unemployed get half the real income; and, indeed, they might even object if the half be transferred to tax-financed public projects with real
social value but no immediately identifiable individual income benefits
to those not transferred to public works. In underdeveloped countries
whose old low-wage sectors "disgorge unemployment in an almost
never-ending stream" and which do not have the New York labor
market to absorb many of them, the providing of jobs becomes more
pressing than it is for Puerto Rico (though it is by no means insignificant there, as unemployment statistics demonstrate all too well).
Since "spreading of employment" is not a very intelligent public policy,
the alternative for most underdeveloped countries is likely to be a
greater emphasis on public works or socialized industries than Puerto
Rico has chosen.

   Thus Puerto Rican policy is hardly a model for other underdeveloped countries; and, of course, it has not been suggested by our
speaker that it is. In particular, the tax-exemption incentive for industrial development depends at least in part for its success on the
existence of higher taxes from which capital can flee; obviously all
countries cannot have lower taxes than everybody else. Serious
voices in the Commonwealth have questioned whether current policy
is even very good for the Island itself, but that is a matter which I do.
not propose to treat here.

   What Puerto Rico can offer for the enlightenment of other underdeveloped countries is the example of its enthusiasm and the very
valuable record of its experience in many specific development problems. In addition to administrative technique and planning apparatus,
one should point out the general high quality of its public administrators, whose zeal, competence, and honesty merit them a place as
models to whom all countries, developed and underdeveloped, might
well look.

   Many of Puerto Rico's lessons are valuable in pointing up the ob-
stinate character of certain problems. Despite a fabulous rate of
growth in per capita product, 13 per cent of the labor force is unemployed, and 30 per cent of the employed work fewer than thirty-five
hours per week. A government with no special historical distaste for
welfare programs has failed to provide education and technical training enough to meet its own development designs; and little is being
done to alter the unfavorable demographic impact produced by the
outmigration of the skilled, the young, and the healthy. In the past
decade, the crude death rate has been reduced from twelve per thousand to seven, and the crude birth rate from forty to thirty-five, leaving an unchanged crude rate of natural increase. The high birth rate,
in particular, sounds a word of warning for development planning.
Puerto Rico has a combination of factors favoring a sharp decline in
birth rates: even among uneducated rural women, knowledge of

birth-control techniques is widespread; an expressed desire for small families (if we are to believe the results of carefully conducted interviews) is nearly universal, government clinics dispense free contraceptives, and even religious opposition to birth control seems slight; yet the rate stays up. Whether the fact indicates that Puerto Rican enthusiasm extends into all fields, or whether it is indicative of a Latin rebellion against monotonous routine, is a question which I leave to your conjecture; but it so clearly indicates the difficulty of controlling one strategic variable in economic development.

I should like to conclude this discussion with something of a jest at our profession. Puerto Rico offers to developmental economists an important lesson in the relation of knowledge to accomplishment. If knowing were enough, there would hardly be a problem left unsolved in the Commonwealth. It has been studied by economists, cultural anthropologists, political scientists, population experts, family sociologists, public-opinion specialists, public-health specialists, military strategists, social workers, and group dynamicists. The Island has a population density of 670 persons per square mile; at least 600 of those must be visiting social scientists! Puerto Rico surely must qualify for the title of "the world's most overstudied underdeveloped country."

PROGRESS, PLANNING, AND POLICY IN PUERTO RICO

COMMENTS

Julian S. Duncan

Puerto Rico cannot be taken as a typical case of a densely populated, underdeveloped area. It has a special position, as Mr. Mayne points out, because of its position as a part of the United States. When the population level is described as "stationary," what is meant is that the net migration to the United States mainland is approximately equal to the excess of births over deaths in Puerto Rico. The advantages of free access to the rich United States domestic market cannot be duplicated in other countries. But all this does not mean that other underdeveloped areas will not profit by a careful study of how Puerto Rico has used its unique position to accelerate its pace of economic growth.

Latin America, for example, can speed its rate of economic growth by economic integration. The six Central American countries of Costa Rica, El Salvador, Guatemala, Honduras, Nicaragua, and Panama are comparable in size to Puerto Rico. Despite presently unresolved differences between El Salvador, Guatemala, and Honduras, on the one hand, and Costa Rica, Nicaragua, and Panama, on the other, prospects for ultimate economic integration are not unpromising. Steps have also been taken toward a freer exchange of goods between the larger republics of Latin America. It would be still better, as Governor Nelson Rockefeller has proposed, if the entire hemisphere became a tariff-free area. To integrate or not to integrate is a decision for the Latin-American countries, but certainly the economist is entitled to point out the very significant gain that would come from large tariff-free areas. With each passing month the pace of economic integration in the area of the European Common Market quickens, and with it the amount of United States business investment there grows.

Furthermore, it is within the power of Latin-American and other underdeveloped countries also to devise incentives to attract private foreign capital. One of the most significant sentences in Mr. Mayne's able report is that capital did not flow into the Commonwealth merely by passing legislation and making regulations exempting mainland capital from income taxes, personal and corporate: "It can be demonstrated that the exploitation of this relationship so as to generate capital flows on a large scale has required specific organization and a concerted drive on the part of the Puerto Rican government." Obviously the magnitude of this capital flow into Latin America could be substantially increased, as the recent levels of investment in the European Common Market area show, if economic integration on a significant scale should take place.

There is increasing agreement among students of economic development that population growth is one of the most important variables. Coale and Hoover's study of the effects of population growth in India and Mexico, and Higgins' Economic Development are two recent examples of this concurrence. The initiation of policies aimed at family limitation, as has been done in Roman Catholic Puerto Rico, could be duplicated in other countries. The family-limitation legislation of Puerto Rico admittedly has not accomplished all that its advocates hoped for, but at least it is on the statute books awaiting the time when some combination of circumstances will markedly increase the degree to which it is utilized. Not without significance is the fact, underlined by Mr. Mayne, of continuing large-scale unemployment on the Island.

Table 1 compares the rate of growth of the population of Puerto Rico with that of El Salvador for the period 1940 to 1957. There has been a decline in the birth rate in Puerto Rico since 1944-47. It is no exaggeration to say that all Latin America is watching what is going on in Puerto Rico. If the large doses of capital for development, more education, the trend toward urbanization, plus a family-limitation program on the statute books bring a continued fall in the birth rate, other countries in Latin America now feeling the pressure of a

Table 1

Crude Birth Rates, Crude Death Rates, and Annual Increase
in Population by Percentage: El Salvador and
Puerto Rico, 1940–1957

Year	El Salvador			Puerto Rico		
	Crude birth rates	Crude death rates	% annual population increase	Crude birth rates	Crude death rates	% annual population increase
1940	42.2	17.7	2.45	38.5	18.4	2.01
1941	40.0	16.8	2.32	39.5	18.4	2.11
1942	38.6	20.7	1.79	39.7	16.3	2.34
1943	38.1	20.4	1.77	38.4	14.4	2.80
1944	37.9	17.7	2.02	40.5	14.6	2.59
1945	38.1	16.2	2.19	41.9	13.9	2.80
1946	36.1	15.5	2.06	42.1	13.1	2.90
1947	41.2	15.0	2.62	42.7	11.9	3.08
1948	44.6	16.9	2.77	40.2	12.0	2.82
1949	46.2	15.4	3.08	39.0	10.6	2.84
1950	48.5	14.7	3.38	39.0	9.9	2.91
1951	48.8	15.1	3.37	37.6	10.0	2.76
1952	48.7	16.3	3.24	36.1	9.2	2.69
1953	47.9	14.7	3.32	36.1	9.2	2.76
1954	48.1	15.1	3.31	34.9	7.5	2.74
1955	47.9	14.2	3.37	34.4	7.2	2.72
1956	47.0	12.4	3.46	34.5	7.3	2.72
1957	48.9	14.0	3.49	32.6	7.0	2.56

Source: United Nations, Demographic Yearbooks.

Table 2

Crude Birth Rates, Crude Death Rates, and Annual Increase
in Population by Percentage: Spain, 1932–1957

Year	Crude birth rates	Crude death rates	Annual increase in population by percentage
1932	28.3	16.5	1.2
1933	27.9	16.5	1.1
1934	26.4	16.1	1.1
1935	25.9	15.8	1.0
1936	24.9	16.8	0.8
1937	22.7	19.0	0.4
1938	20.1	19.3	0.08
1939	16.6	18.5	loss
1940	24.5	16.6	0.8
1941	19.7	18.8	0.09
1942	20.2	14.8	0.5
1943	22.9	13.3	0.5
1944	22.5	13.1	0.4
1945	23.0	12.2	1.1
1946	21.4	12.9	0.9
1947	21.3	12.0	0.9
1948	23.1	10.9	1.2
1949	21.4	11.4	1.0
1950	20.2	10.9	0.9
1951	20.1	11.6	0.9
1952	20.8	9.7	1.1
1953	20.6	9.7	1.1
1954	20.0	9.1	1.1
1955	20.6	9.4	1.1
1956	20.7	9.9	1.1
1957	21.9	10.0	1.2

Source: United Nations, Demographic Yearbooks.

rapidly growing population on relatively limited resources may be led
to consider limitation policies.

Perhaps it may not be too much to ask that the able publicists for
Puerto Rico show an awareness of the problems created for New York
City by the migration to it of large numbers of whites and Negroes
from the South and Puerto Ricans. This influx has prompted Judge

Samuel Simon Leibowitz to suggest that New York discourage newcomers until it can begin to absorb the immigrants it has received during the past two decades.

In this connection the declining fertility rate in Roman Catholic Spain deserves more attention than it has so far received. Table 2 shows the crude birth rates, crude death rates, and percentage of annual increase in population of Spain between 1932 and 1957. Your reviewer very much hopes that some research organization will sponsor a study of the decline in the birth rate in Spain: from 28 per thousand per year in 1932 to 21 in 1957. The answers would be significant for Latin America.

The Commonwealth of Puerto Rico, as Mr. Mayne points out, is taking steps to avoid a "backwash effect" from the concentration of industries in and around San Juan. Extra financial incentives are provided to manufacturing industries willing to locate outside the San Juan area. Fortunately, there was early realization that the initial effort of setting up government-owned factories was not enough to get the industrialization drive off the ground. Nine years ago the massive effort to attract mainland private capital to the Island began. The opportunity to migrate to the United States tends to diminish Puerto Rico's danger of falling into a "low-equilibrium trap." The magnitude of the effort Puerto Rico has made and is making indicates awareness that a "minimum effort" is necessary.

Unfortunately, Mayne presents no estimate of the changes in Puerto Rico's per capita income since the big push for industrialization was launched in 1951. We are told that there has been a 5.4 per cent rise per annum in gross product and that by 1957 the percentage of gross product invested in fixed assets had grown to 21 per cent. His data, however, provide no basis for estimating what percentage of gross product is saved. Unemployment is high, remaining at 13 per cent of the labor force. The government of Puerto Rico has shown political courage in resisting pressures to subsidize the less efficient parts of the economy. The classic pattern of decrease in agricultural and increase in industrial employment has resulted from the Island's developmental policies. The endeavor now in agricultural policy is what theory says it ought to be, namely, augmenting output per acre. The land reform of the 1940's augmented the number of medium-sized farms; however, as on the mainland, it is the large operators of farm land who are more prosperous.

Your reviewer knows of no democratic regime, with the possible exception of Frondezi's government in Argentina, that has made more hard choices and has more correctly followed generally-accepted policies for economic development. Ten years is too short a period, however, to say that Puerto Rico has successfully made the "take-off into sustained growth." Much will depend on her ability to continue to offer the tax incentives now available. Much depends, also, on whether the policies of the United States are such as to bring about a higher growth rate on the mainland than post-1952.

ECONOMIC GROWTH, DEVELOPMENT, AND
PLANNING IN SOCIALIST COUNTRIES

COMMENTS

Morris A. Copeland

Professor Bićanić emphasizes the quantita-
tive aspect of all three of the basic concepts he employs in his very
interesting and penetrating analysis. Nonetheless there appears to be
a qualitative aspect that is of fundamental importance for at least two
of them: economic growth and economic development. Economic
growth, as he conceives it, is something more than a mere increase
in physical volume of national product. He makes this clear when he
draws an analogy to ontological maturation that permits him to distinguish "more advanced" countries from "less developed" ones.
Presumably a "more advanced" country differs from a "less developed" one in institutional structure as well as in absolute or per capita
size of national product. And I assume that he means by "more advanced" what is often called more industrialized.

Professor Bićanić distinguishes between economic growth and
economic development on the basis of planning. Development is
planned growth. And apparently what is planned is not only the increase in national product but also the accompanying institutional
changes. Development, he says, is growth "from one level to another,
higher level of equilibrium (or quasi-equilibrium)." I take it this
means from a less to a more "advanced" stage of development. Apparently, too, the change from the one stage to the other may extend
over a number of years, or several of his specific planning periods.
"One developmental scheme," he tells us, "can consist of several
planning periods."

A brief mention of a terminological usage that differs from Professor Bićanić's seems in order, with a brief comment on both. This
other usage would make the term "economic growth" refer solely to
quantitative change in national product and would employ the term
"economic development" to designate the process of institutional
evolution called industrialization, regardless of how it comes about.
I prefer this usage partly because it is easy to overstate the extent
to which longer-term institutional developments have really been
planned. This usage seems preferable also because it makes it easier
"to avoid" suggesting that different countries can all be arranged on

a single scale of higher and lower degrees of development. Certainly any such arrangement vastly oversimplifies the real world. Moreover, I doubt that it is wise to use terms like "higher" and "lower" and "more advanced" to characterize whole economic systems. Indeed, I question the wisdom of using the adjective "underdeveloped." Such terms do have value connotations, and the comparisons they involve are likely to be controversial. And it may be added that when a (North) American uses the adjective "underdeveloped" in dispensing international aid, the response may be one of resentment.

I want, therefore, to propose using the qualitative concept, the state of the industrial arts, rather than any statistical measure like per capita income as the main criterion of economic development. And I would urge that ratings of institutional progress be confined to an area where they can be made objectively. I would suggest employing such ratings only in connection with differences in technology and degrees of industrialization, only in expressions such as a "less industrialized country," a "more advanced technology." Even here the idea of a single scale does not exactly fit. There is a considerable technological diversity among countries that are relatively unindustrialized. However, I think the idea works well enough for the technologically more advanced economies to make it a useful approximation.

And I want to say a word about Professor Bićanić's third basic concept, economic planning. For him this means a particular form of plan, a plan for a specific period, such as five years, and one that emphasizes specific quantitative production targets. Still there is a qualitative aspect to such plans too. Thus he notes that in the case of the five-year plans of the U.S.S.R., and of others that conform to a somewhat similar pattern, the production targets have been fixed with a view to promoting institutional change in a particular direction. "Stalin's basic law of socialism," he says, "has first a negative developmental decision: Continuous expansion of socialist production excludes all production which is outside the socialist sector. . . . the growth of the capitalist forms is restrained or prohibited."

Much the most interesting part of Professor Bićanić's paper is, for me, his analysis of the experience with planning and planned development in socialist (or, as most of us would say, Communist) countries. One very significant finding is that what is planned has changed. I think it is fair to say he means that the direction of institutional change aimed at has changed. In fact I find myself wondering whether the growth of all capitalist forms is now discouraged in the U.S.S.R. Professor Bićanić refers to the need to introduce economic incentives. He does not say pecuniary incentives but I assume that these are mainly what he means. And I submit that to say with Dr. Oscar Lange that economic incentives "make people automatically react in the way desired by the planner"[1] sounds just a little like what has been said

---

[1] See the quotation in Professor Bićanić's paper.

of free enterprise. If we take the planner's aim to be the common welfare, it sounds something like the proposition that "each man seeking his own greatest good so acts as to contribute to the common welfare."

I have just finished reading the galley proof of the paper Professor T. S. Khachaturov, Corresponding Member, Academy of Sciences of the U.S.S.R., would have presented before the American Economic Association last December had he been able to attend the Philadelphia meeting as planned. His paper is concerned with the considerations that determine capital-investment decisions in the U.S.S.R. What particularly impresses me is the extent to which the considerations he proposes resemble the considerations here. I will mention only one point. Khachaturov has quite a bit to say about the pay-out period. This period is a way of relating the expected value product attributable to a given capital addition or betterment during its active life to the cost of the addition or betterment. The reciprocal of the pay-out period is the expected rate of return on the investment. And Khachaturov makes comparative rates of return a major criterion in investment decisions. Indeed, he insists that the marginal rather than the average period--or may I say the marginal efficiency of capital?-- should govern the extent of investment.

Let me conclude my comment with two broad questions that it seems to me a theory of economic development should clearly deal with: (1) Professor Bićanić quotes Lange as saying that the introduction of economic incentives into a Communist type of economic system is "a planned and guided development by the conscious will of the organized society." But is such a development really the result of planning? Or is it, as Professor Bićanić proposes, a result of total economic growth? Is it not a necessary accompaniment of the adoption of a somewhat more detailed division of labor and a more advanced technology? Does not the industrialization of a country mean also its pecuniarization? At all events the growth of pecuniary institutions seems to have accompanied the process of industrialization both under communism and under capitalism.

(2) My second question is broader still. Technological improvements have proven to be an extraordinarily contagious type of culture trait. And modern technology seems now to be in process of spreading over most of the world. Indeed, nearly all the less industrialized countries today want to get more industrialized. Quite a number of them, too, would like to do this and still keep most of their social institutions largely intact. Can they industrialize without a concomitant growth of pecuniary institutions? And while a wide diversity of social institutions can surely be counted on to survive such changes, one may well ask: Can any country go through the process of industrialization and pecuniarization without having its social institutions undergo substantial changes?

ECONOMIC GROWTH, DEVELOPMENT, AND PLANNING IN SOCIALIST COUNTRIES

COMMENTS

Nicolas Spulber

The very stimulating paper of Professor Bićanić poses a host of problems which can hardly be examined in the limited space assigned for discussion. Therefore I shall focus on only one problem, namely, the shift from "administrative" planning to "decentralized" planning, in which economic incentives are called upon to play a much broader role. The characteristics of this new planning, however, are emerging only slowly and are far from having aquired a stable form.

Authoritarian centralized planning, or "administrative" planning, has been identified with the Soviet planning of the Stalin era. Its basic features are systematic emphasis on large capital accumulation and correspondingly on depressed consumption levels within an economy bent on self-sufficiency; a skewed pattern of allocation of investments, with the methodic stressing of industry and of the machine-tool branch; a combination of certain economic incentives with a wide use of para-economic measures; and extreme centralization in planning and management. This system of directing and managing the economy, which has come to be known as the Soviet "model" of industrialization, was readily applied after the Second World War by all the East European countries. It is this complex of methods and measures with its underlying assumptions which is now questioned and re-examined, not only in Yugoslavia--which broke with the Soviet bloc in 1948--but also in Poland and, in a limited way, even in the Soviet Union itself.

Professor Bićanić notes that this re-examination has been prompted by the fact that the four main underlying assumptions of the "model"--unlimited demand for producer goods, unlimited demand for consumer goods, unlimited efficiency of administrative incentives, and congruence between planning and performance--have been invalidated by a set of reasons which are indicated only partially in his paper. I should like to stress that, to my mind, the re-examination of the model has a substantially different scope and nature in the Soviet Union from what it has in the East European countries. Consider, in turn, the two basic groups around which this re-examination is centered: (1) the size and pattern of investment, and (2) the management of economy and the question of incentives.

To my knowledge, the problem of the size of investments has not been questioned directly in the U.S.S.R. In principle, accumulation has been kept there methodically at around 25 per cent of the value of the net material product. Since, however, prices of producer goods are arbitrarily low, while consumer-goods prices are burdened by heavy turnover taxes, the actual shares in physical terms diverge sharply from the apparent shares in value terms. The large accumulations in real terms exacted by countries of limited size and resources, such as Poland and Hungary, overstrained sharply their economies and led, after only one long-term "all-around" plan, to serious dislocations. While the Soviet Union, during the short-lived period of the new course, toyed with the idea of increasing the share of consumption and of diminishing the share of accumulation in the national product, this idea has become a perennial preoccupation in some East European countries where the pressures against the forced pace of the first long-term plan ended with the upheavals of 1956 in Poland and Hungary.

Furthermore, only the East European countries suffer acutely from the "narrowness" of the so-called "second" world market (the intra-bloc market), where the fact that each one has been attempting to plan along parallel lines has led to competition for the sale of the same surpluses of machinery and metallurgical products and for the purchase of the same industrial raw materials. While the Soviet Union can displace the plans of the smaller units of this market, the small countries have no recourse other than to discard the most autarchic features of their previous planning model, shift the pattern of their investments from steel and machine tools to plastics, and perhaps electronics, and attempt, moreover, to increase their trade with the non-bloc countries. While the East European countries are sensing sharply the limits of the demands for steel and machinery, the Soviet Union can continue to stress these very lines of production. Not only can it displace the weaker links in the market at its periphery, but it can also more easily increase its sphere of operation outside this market. Thus, the Soviet Union can still seemingly operate under the assumption of "unlimited" demand for producer goods.

It is quite true that the competing needs of an increasingly diversified economy pose for the Soviet Union itself, urgently, the problem of achieving sound accounting in the husbandry of its resources and, hence, the question of reconsidering its highly arbitrary pricing system. This is the reason for the newly-revived Soviet discussions on the question of prices of producer goods. While these discussions are apparently focused on a point of doctrine--namely, on the question of determining whether the producer goods are or are not "commodities" under socialism--the deeper problem under consideration is whether these goods should continue to be priced arbitrarily or be priced in agreement with their "cost of production." The revision of prices will in all likelihood pose also, in an open way, the question of the actual shares of accumulation and consumption in the national product. But, let me underline that the need for revising the pricing system is even more compelling in Eastern Europe, where the problems of division of labor and of plan co-ordination in the area, have become very urgent.

The question of management and incentives in the Soviet Union has, also, a quite different scope from what it has in Eastern Europe. In the Soviet Union, the reorganization of management is confined, in a rigid sense, to limits familiar to the big Western corporations. The Soviets are essentially preoccupied with the decentralization of the operational managerial functions, which are henceforth transferred to the newly created regional bodies (Sovnarkhozy), while planning continues to remain centralized. In this reorganization, the enterprises will find themselves under even closer scrutiny than before: the scrutiny of the Sovnarkhozy replacing that of the Ministry.

On the other hand, decentralization schemes are, in Poland for instance, of a quite different caliber. In the newly-devised Polish "model," the central planning board is to: (1) plan the output of a limited number of key commodities, and (2) fix the prices of a larger set of commodities. In turn, the (state-owned) enterprises should attempt to minimize cost and maximize output at the established prices. The price-fixing role of the central planning board would differentiate the Polish model from the Yugoslav experiment (from 1951 to the present) in which most prices are established through the market. The question of incentives also takes different aspects in Eastern Europe. There, new incentives for managers will be tied to profits achieved and not to the fulfillment of the gross indexes of output; the "interestedness" of workers will be increased through their eventual participation in profits; the "interestedness" of peasants will be spurred through the liquidation of compulsory deliveries and through price differentials, and so on. The wider scope taken by the problem of incentives in Eastern Europe is, of course, directly tied to the wider scope of the changes in planning concepts.

Perhaps the broader interest of this debate is to reveal that once the initial "big push" of industrialization is given, such dislocations occur in the smaller, poorly endowed countries that it then becomes unavoidable for them to attempt to return to some more rational ways of allocating resources than the decisions of a planner who follows some pre-established "industrialization model." In a direct way, the example of the East European countries shows that each country cannot reproduce in miniature the Soviet economic development. Indirectly, the experience seems to suggest that it is also somewhat questionable to believe that all that matters for an underdeveloped country is to draw (and apply) any developmental scheme--in order to achieve a "general sense of moving"--and leave for later the problem of solving the bottlenecks created by this scheme. Actually, the problems thus created might lead to unpredictable and often uncontrollable dislocations.

THE PROSPECTS OF INDIAN ECONOMIC GROWTH

COMMENTS

Alexander Eckstein

As a commentator on Professor Hoselitz' most interesting and stimulating paper, I am placed in an awkward position. I find myself in broad agreement with both his analysis and conclusions and have very few, if any, bones to pick. Therefore I will confine my comments largely to amending, emphasizing, and elaborating some of the issues that he raises. I would like to focus on the basic problems raised by Professor Hoselitz--namely, the agricultural problem and the problem of saving and resource mobilization.

So far as the agricultural problem is concerned, it is interesting to note how an economy such as that of India is almost completely dependent upon the quantity of its harvest. Economic progress under planning proceeded rapidly as long as favorable weather conditions produced a succession of bountiful harvests. Under these circumstances, food imports could be reduced, foreign-exchange resources were released for imports of capital goods, and generally the pressure on the balance of payments was relaxed. However, this process was reversed after 1954/55 with the apparent end of a favorable monsoon cycle. As a result, strong inflationary pressures began to mount in the Indian economy, and food imports had to be stepped up to the point that foreign-exchange resources were being used up at a much more rapid rate than contemplated in the Second Plan. This, in turn, necessarily forced a reduction of investment and production targets.[1]

At the same time, food shortages in domestic markets were reflected in the rising prices of farm products and in shifts in rural-urban terms of trade. Such shifts--to the extent that they led to an actual redistribution of income in favor of agriculture--entailed a reduction in saving and taxable capacity: in saving, because this involves shifts from income-receiving units with a comparatively high marginal propensity to save to units with relatively lower propensities; and in taxable capacity, because in India the urban sector is much more effectively taxed than the rural sector.

Harvest fluctuations as a prime factor conditioning or limiting the pace and rhythm of development are, of course, not peculiar to India;

---

[1] See New York Times, May 5, 1958.

they characterize all underdeveloped economies in which agriculture looms large. As in the case of India, shortfalls in the harvest tend to exert a pressure on the balance of payments and bring about a shift in the internal terms of trade, leading to a redistribution of income, reduction in savings and taxable capacity, and last but not least a cutback in investment. Thus, even in Communist China, fluctuations in the annual rates of economic growth are closely correlated with the changing level of agricultural production. It is not surprising, therefore, that China faced a minor economic crisis in 1957 very similar in character and origin to that in India.

Of course, to the extent that economic planning involves agricultural expansion based on bringing new land under cultivation and/or intensifying the use of land already under the plow, these fluctuations may be expected to revolve around a rising trend in output. In the long run, with improved farm organization, better methods of soil conservation and crop rotation, and greater diversification, the amplitude of fluctuations may be reduced. However, in the short run--as the Indian experience well illustrates--a succession of unfavorable harvests can seriously undermine the best-laid economic plans unless such contingencies are explicitly allowed for in advance and government fiscal and monetary policies are rapidly adjusted to deal with them.

In this syndrome the aspects and implications of the tax system are perhaps of greatest importance in assessing Indian development prospects. The Second Five-Year Plan assigns to the public sector the major share of responsibility for saving and investment. At the same time, it leaves the tax system, with its quite narrow revenue base, more or less intact. In general terms, the Indian tax system is based on indirect taxes, income taxes, and land taxes. Land taxes have become eroded over the years under the impact of fixed land assessments on the one hand and inflation in land values and in the prices of farm products on the other. As a result, the land tax absorbs less than 1 per cent of total agricultural product in India. At the same time, indirect taxes reach only that portion of farm output which enters marketing channels. Income taxes, though steeply progressive, are necessarily paid by only a small number of households in an underdeveloped, low-income economy.

Therefore, unless the tax system is reformed so as to tap more effectively the largest sector of the economy, i.e., agriculture, it is most unlikely that the rate of public saving can be raised significantly. This fact, possibly more than any other, accounts for the large gap between available finance and investment targets in the Second Five-Year Plan.

Of course, one might argue that low levels of agricultural taxation coupled with a redistribution of income in favor of agriculture are likely to lead to increases in rural savings and investment. To the extent that some of these investments take a non-monetized form, they may not appear in the national income and investment accounts. Yet, they may contribute to raising unit yields, farm productivity, and farm output. The evidence on this is quite uncertain thus far, and in any case such a process is bound to work itself out rather slowly.

For all of these reasons combined, it is conceivable that the Indians might learn something from the Chinese in that an agricultural tax in kind, perhaps not as heavy as China's, but still one that, let us say, would tax up to 5 per cent of farm product--as compared to the present 1 per cent or less--might make a very decisive difference in affecting the internal terms of trade between agriculture and industry and in affecting the balance-of-payment position of the country as well. Such a tax in kind would place at the disposal of the government consider-able reserves of buffer stocks which could be used as a means of sta-bilizing food prices and of counteracting shortages whenever and wherever they developed. Admittedly, such a system of taxation would have to be administered wisely and cautiously in order not to undercut farmer incentives for expanding agricultural production.

So far as the actual prospects for raising agricultural production are concerned, I would tend to be more optimistic than Professor Hoselitz. If we compare the unit yields of principal grains in Japan, China, and India, we find that productivity per acre in India is about one-third that of Japan and about one-half that of China. These dif-ferences can be largely accounted for by the much more intensive use of chemical fertilizer in Japan and of night soil in China, coupled with a proportionately much larger irrigated area in these two countries as compared to India. This suggests that the scope for improvement of yields is still quite considerable in India. Irrigation may be quite costly, as Professor Hoselitz points out; yet there should be consider-able opportunities for utilizing underemployed labor in agriculture to expand irrigation facilities, although admittedly certain complemen-tary fixed capital inputs are needed. Perhaps a great deal could be done, however, with mass labor-intensive projects somewhat on the Chinese model.

And I would tend to place greater emphasis upon the importance of land reform, both for economic and institutional reasons, than Pro-fessor Hoselitz does. It seems to me that land reform must be viewed broadly as a means of breaking up and restructuring the whole tradi-tional framework in agriculture, including not only tenure and property arrangements but also agricultural marketing and farm credit. Tradi-tional tenure arrangements in agrarian societies such as those of India necessarily tend to be closely associated with very marked market imperfections, inefficient marketing arrangements, and high rates of interest. They also place a great premium upon land speculation, thereby tying up considerable capital resources which could otherwise be channeled into productive investment. Hence land reform may be an essential precondition not only for raising farmer incentives and therefore agricultural productivity in the long run--though it may bring about a curtailment in farm output in the short run--but also for possibly facilitating the whole process of mobilizing savings. At the same time, to the extent that land reform undercuts the incentive for continuing land speculation and investment in land, it tends to encourage the former landholders to put the funds obtained as compensation for their lands into productive investments outside of agriculture. If this general line of reasoning holds at all in the case of India, then the slow progress of land reform may be one of the factors retarding the rate of agricultural expansion and resource mobilization in recent years.

I completely agree with Professor Hoselitz' conclusions concerning the effects of collectivization upon agricultural output. One might add that the primary purpose of collectivization in China, just as in the Soviet Union previously, is not to increase agricultural productivity but to raise the rate of extraction out of agriculture. For understandable and obvious reasons, however, the rationale in Communist Chinese writings for the collectivization program usually runs in terms of raising productivity. Unfortunately, the Indian delegations who have gone to China and who have so greatly influenced Indian thinking on the subject seem to have accepted much of the official Communist Chinese line at its face value. So far as the actual record is concerned, it may be worth while to note that the Chinese have on the whole been much more successful in collecting the crop than in raising farm output. It is, of course, much easier to disseminate agricultural information and administer a program of farm extension in a collectivized agriculture than in a small peasant-family–operated system of landholding; from this standpoint, then, the opportunities for spreading innovating influences are undoubtedly greater under a collectivized system. At the same time, however, the inducement and incentives to adopt these new practices, or actually to introduce them, may be much less in a collective than on a private farm. For this reason I would tend very much to agree with Professor Hoselitz' position that one should not expect too much from collectivization as a means of raising farm productivity.

Finally, let me say just a few words about the employment problem. It seems to me that in the long run this is the most intractable and most difficult of the problems that India faces. It is interesting to note in this connection that Japan, after eighty to ninety years of industrialization, still faces a very serious problem of unemployment and underemployment, with from 40 per cent to 45 per cent of the labor force still engaged in agriculture and with an agricultural labor force which in absolute size is today just about the same as it was at the time of the Meiji restoration. Therefore, in effect, the extremely rapid rate of industrialization in Japan has been barely sufficient to absorb the growth in population and in labor force. In a sense, two other highly industrialized countries--Italy and the Soviet Union--face roughly a similar situation. In both of them 40 per cent or more of the population and labor force is tied down in agriculture. Of course, in the case of Italy, this may be a special problem of southern Italy, which perhaps is not as intractable in the long run as the problem faced by India and China. It may very well be that in countries with a high degree of population pressure in relation to arable-land resources and with comparatively high rates of population growth, even rapid industrialization will not be equal to the task of absorbing all the actual or latent unemployment and underemployment in agriculture. Looked at this way, it may very well be that even fifty years from now, when China and India may be quite highly industrialized, they would still be facing a very critical unemployment and underemployment problem. Therefore, what I am suggesting in effect, is that the success of the Indian Five-Year Plan, or that the progress of industrialization, or the adequacy of economic growth under conditions such as those of India and China cannot be measured by how effectively the employment and unemployment problem is resolved. Under these conditions, possibly all that one can expect is precisely what the Indians are trying to do--that is, not to aggravate the unemployment problem and at least to absorb the new entrants into the labor force.

THE PROSPECTS OF INDIAN ECONOMIC GROWTH

COMMENTS

Walter C. Neale

One cannot help but agree with Professor Hoselitz' analysis of the critical need for agricultural development if India is to fulfill her intentions. I am, however, more optimistic than Professor Hoselitz, and this on two counts.

First, it is not impossible that India will develop sufficient lines of export to pay for a continuing importation of foodstuffs. There is no need for India to match Britain or Japan in this respect, but only to move in that direction. As Professor Hoselitz has pointed out, India has all the requisites for a large iron and steel industry and the heavy industries which can be built thereon. It can also become a large producer of cement and medicinal chemicals, and already has a highly-developed textile industry. Beyond these it has the coal and hydro-electric power on which to base fabricating industries, and may be expected to develop power from atomic energy.

One can do more than state the areas in which India does and will have a comparative advantage, for the outlines of bilateral and tri-lateral trade can be seen emerging in Asia and Africa. The mainland Southeast Asian nations are exporters of food and do not appear--at least within the next two decades--to be able to develop broad indus-trial bases. Bilateral trade of Indian manufactures for Burmese and Thai rice and Burmese timber is probable. Trade of Indian textiles and manufactures for East African produce (and for Persian Gulf oil) also fits the bilateral pattern.

There are already close relationships between Japan and India. No doubt the Indian industrial pattern foreseen here will compete with the Japanese pattern, but as has happened in Western Europe, there should be meshing of particular products within the broader categories. One envisages Indian exports of iron ore, jute products, pig iron, coal, and rare minerals in exchange for Japanese currency which India can use to buy food imports from Southeast Asia and East Africa. (Where this will leave the British is not our problem here, but it may become our problem later.)

If it is impossible for this pattern to mature in 1958 or 1959, so is it impossible for India to develop her agriculture that rapidly. Power will become available as fast as irrigation, and the gestation period of industry is no longer than that of agriculture.

The second cause for optimism is the intelligence and capacity of the Indian peasant. Professor Hoselitz has mentioned the failure of the Community Development Program to pay rapid dividends in in-creased farm output. The expectations common among Delhi officials were unwarranted. Although remarkable increases in productivity can be achieved on individual plots, farm output as a whole--even for a single village--does not increase rapidly. The Community Develop-ment projects are "extension work on the grand scale," and extension work is a slow process. What took the county agent years to accom-plish in the United States is likely to take the Indian Block Develop-ment Officer even longer. Widespread adoption of new techniques and new crops requires time, and not because the peasant is stupid or foolish. Years of experience have taught the peasant a system of farming which is not highly productive and is not commercially profit-able, but it is a system which does provide a high degree of security against total crop failure, and in which all the parts are closely meshed. He does not want a change that will increase the gains if it also increases the risks. Furthermore, changes will destroy the highly-integrated character of farm operations and social relation-ships[1] and must therefore promise big gains if they are to be accept-able.

---

[1]See McKim Marriott, "Technological Change in Overdeveloped Rural Areas," Economic Development and Cultural Change, Vol. I (December, 1952), p. 261.

Rational resistance to change implies a capacity for rational acceptance. Time and proof are the things needed. There are many evidences of the adaptability of the peasant: around every town, some villages shift to market gardening and dairying. Potato cultivation is new, as is the cultivation of groundnuts. The introduction of sugar cane has been rapid wherever there is a mill. Above all, the use of nitrogenous fertilizers has spread. Ten years ago the Sindri fertilizer plant was planned to produce 350,000 tons a year--India's anticipated needs. All is being sold and plans are afoot to triple capacity. Experience proved fertilizer's usefulness and the peasantry will now pay for fertilizer.

I think we underrate the intelligence and adaptability of the peasant; and underrate the importance he attaches to knowing he will get a minimum crop. When he is presented with opportunities--roads, urban markets, means of processing, new ideas--he does not adopt them wholesale, to be sure, but he does adapt them and use them.

On both grounds then--that a new pattern of comparative advantage and of trade will develop, and that the Indian peasantry will respond to opportunity--I am inclined to optimism. When one looks at the long history of poverty in India, optimism seems unwarranted, but I am assuming that the government will press on with the building of industry, roads, irrigation works, and extension services. If it does, why doubt that the Burmese will trade, that the Japanese will trade, and that the peasant will respond?

It is also doubtful whether Professor Hoselitz' fears about the capacity of small-scale industries to expand and his faith in government efforts are justified.

Small--very small--industrial establishments have been springing up in the Punjab for a decade, many of them in small cities and small towns. Ludhiana, with 150,000 people, is an explosion of small-scale industry. Towns of less than 25,000 are developing engineering industries.

What are these establishments like? They consist of two and four workers in a room opened to the street. They consist of one and two or three looms in a back room. They are situated in the owner's house or in a small building never designed as a factory. The machinery is limited; many of the operations are manually performed.

What do they make? Underwear, sandals, suitcases, utensils, metal boxes, bicycles, power saws, jigs and drills, pump parts. Let me describe some operations. Bicycle wheel rims, hubs, and spokes are turned out mechanically, but the wheel is assembled with hands and feet. The worker holds the rim and spokes with his toes and bends the spokes into the hub with his hands, assembling wheels with remarkable speed. In a box factory a worker sits with metal sheets, hinges, rivets, handles, hasps, and a hammer. In less than five minutes he produces a suitcase, a trunk, or a strong box.

The products are by no means crude. My Herculas bicycle did not differ in looks from its British Hercules model, although the steel was soft. Only close inspection showed that the label on a sewing machine did not say "Singer."

These industrial establishments are often unknown to the planners. Who is to tell them? Why would anyone want to attract the attention of the tax collector? They certainly exist, but seemingly Delhi does not realize it.

While many of the operations are manual, many utilize power. In the Punjab the power is usually electricity, sometimes a diesel engine. Wherever electricity is supplied, one-, two-, and ten-man establishments arise. To appreciate how fully the local entrepreneurs utilize the opportunity, one need only watch a light bulb during an evening. After dinner there are 40 watts coming from a 75-watt bulb. At ten o'clock one is reading under 60 watts. At midnight the nearby establishments close, and the bulb is up to par.

Industry does not develop only in towns and where there is electricity. I have seen a small village in Bombay State where there is a hand-weaving co-operative making woolen blankets. In the same village a group has bought a diesel engine to power a flour-milling and oil-pressing establishment, while masons quarry building stones with hammer and chisel. This village was not part of a Community Development project. Its business acumen was its own.

In another Bombay village it is reported that villagers, finding their earnings from spinning on an ambar charkha -- India's version of the spinning wheel--too small, turned to producing ambar charkhas to sell to the government.

These industries cannot grow independently of government action, but the government action required is not specific. Communications with markets, providing power, and maintaining demand--these are the needed government activities. Humanity in India, as elsewhere, has the wit to put them to work.

The government of India is not suited to engaging in rural and small-town industries, even to the extent of supplying credit. It is unsuited because of its civil-service traditions and because of its social structure.

For a century the civil service has given orders, and the Indian official still gives orders. If he does not really expect compliance, he expects respect and the forms of compliance. A great difficulty arises because the official says to himself "I can do this better than anyone else around." Experience will not teach him that he is wrong because he is right. The trouble is that he cannot do everything and must leave much to others. When there is disagreement, the official is apt to attribute opposition to foolishness, ignorance, or willfulness. This attitude is true of organized banking, and the supervision and management of co-operative societies as well. Although present policy is opposed to this attitude, it is still the common one.

This civil-service tradition is reinforced by the stratification of Indian society. There are social barriers between high and low castes; between Hindus and non-Hindus; between the educated and the uneducated. These barriers become walls when communal dislikes or resentments occur.

It is very difficult to visualize a meeting of minds between one of India's small businessmen, untutored if not illiterate, skillful but not, suave, intelligent but not sophisticated, and one of her State Bank executives. America knows no differences so great. The business-man probably distrusts the banker. The banker certainly distrusts, and also lacks respect for, the businessman. What the borrower wants is venture capital while the banker follows the British tradition of lending only for self-liquidating working capital. And of course the borrower cannot produce enough assets as security, or enough wealthy friends to stand surety. If he could, he and his friends would already have borrowed elsewhere and set up business.

It is, therefore, likely that a government program of public improvements will do more to stimulate small-town and village industries than will efforts to stimulate them directly.

INDEX

agrarian reform: in Bolivia, 5–6; in Mexico, 128; in Puerto Rico, 1940 policy for, 154

agricultural production: in Argentina: necessary increase in, 106; and decrease in, 109; and beef cattle in, 110; and projection of, to 1967, 110; in Puerto Rico, 147; in India: increase in, 193; and methods to increase, 200; and comparison of, with China, 201; and varied solutions for, necessary, 202; and importance of, 203

agriculture: in Argentina: 104–105; and farm population of, 104–105; and production in, 105; and closing frontiers in, 109; in Puerto Rico: land-man relationship in, 142; and ownership of land in, 146; and co-operative associations for, 147; in U.S.S.R., real and official, 184–185; in India: usable land in, 192–193; and land supply in, 193

allocation of resources, U.S.S.R., economic proportions of: 182

Andean Highlands Commission: 8

anti-inflation taxes and growth: 94

Argentina: grain-price guarantee in, x; agriculture in, 104–105; farm population, 104–105; agricultural production, 105; industrial production, 105; service trades, population engaged in, 105; industrial employment, necessary increase in, 106; imports necessary for, 108; national income, reduced in 1950's, 108; closing frontiers in, 109; decrease in agricultural production, 109; price policy, agriculture, 109; terms of trade, fluctuation in, 109; agricultural machinery, 110; beef cattle in, 110; import substitution, 111–113; projection of, in 1962, 111; importance of, 112–113; petroleum production and reserves, 113–114; import substitution of pulp and paper, 114; import substitution of iron and steel, 114; transportation, 117–118; energy, industrial, 118; capital investment, 119; capital investment, foreign, 119–120, 122; and maldistribution of, 122; economic development, 122–123; industrialization, 154

Ataturk, étatisme of: x

Australia, state enterprise of: 13

balanced growth: 6, 235, 239; in nontechnical, emotional usage, 71; concept of, 71–73; in general technical usage, 71–72; between sectors, 72; and "big push," 72, 77; and demonstration effects, 72; excessive demand, upset by, 72; and external balance with, 72; and infrastructure, 72; and "investment package," 72; limited by aggregate resources, 72; and markets and supplies, 72; and specific technical usage, 72–73; upset by "bottlenecks," 72; upset by unfavorable "mix," 72; and "waves of investors," 72; structural change and the marketing problem, 73–75; doubtful applicability of, 75–81; and complementarities, 76; and external economies, 76; and "balanced diet," 77; and changes in institutional framework, 77; need for additional agricultural investment in, 77; vs. priorities, 217

balanced-growth doctrine: orthodoxy of, 77; twofold implications of, 77; pump-priming argument not vindicated by, 78; suited to sustained growth in developed countries, 78; premature, not wrong, 79; limitations of, summarized, 79–81; doubtful operational value of, 80; as one of several paths to development, 84; merits of, 84–85; operational critique of, 240

balanced-investment package: 82, 236, 238

banks: American experience in, 14; "wildcat," 216. See also Central Bank; Golembe, Carter, H.; Nacional Financiera; Second Bank of U.S.

beachhead economy, limited: x

Bihar (India), community survey in: 201

birth rates, crude, in underdeveloped countries: 20–21

Bolivia: land reform in, 5; tin

INDEX OF NAMES